10/2/89

Treatises of
Fistula in Ano

AND OF FISTULÆ IN OTHER PARTS OF THE BODY
AND OF APOSTEMES MAKING FISTULÆ, AND OF
AND TENASMON, AND OF CLYSTERS HÆMORRHOID
ALSO OF CERTAIN OINTMENTS, POWDERS AND OILS

EARLY ENGLISH TEXT SOCIETY

Original Series. No. 139

1910

(Reprinted 1968)

PRICE 35*s*.

Sloane MS. 2002, leaf 24, back.

PLATE I. A Fourteenth-Century Master Surgeon operating for Fistula in Ano.

Treatises of Fistula in Ano

Haemorrhoids, and Clysters

BY

JOHN ARDERNE

FROM AN EARLY FIFTEENTH-CENTURY MANUSCRIPT TRANSLATION

EDITED BY

D'ARCY POWER

Published for

THE EARLY ENGLISH TEXT SOCIETY

by the

OXFORD UNIVERSITY PRESS

LONDON NEW YORK TORONTO

FIRST PUBLISHED 1910
REPRINTED 1968

Original Series, No. 139

ORIGINALLY PRINTED BY
RICHARD CLAY & SONS LTD., LONDON AND BUNGAY
AND NOW REPRINTED LITHOGRAPHICALLY IN GREAT BRITAIN
AT THE UNIVERSITY PRESS, OXFORD
BY VIVIAN RIDLER, PRINTER TO THE UNIVERSITY

To

Joseph Frank Payne,

M.D. Oxon., F.R.C.P. Lond.,

These Treatises

of Arderne

are Dedicated

as an Acknowledgment of his

Zeal in the Cause of

The History of English Medicine.

LIST OF ILLUSTRATIONS

FOREWORDS

The history of mediæval medicine, says Prof. E. Nicaise,[1] has been divided into four great epochs. The first, lasting from the fifth to the eleventh century, was remarkable for the Arabian school of medicine. The second period embraced the eleventh and twelfth centuries, and witnessed the rise of the schola Salernitana : it was the time of the Crusades and of that intermingling of the East and West from which sprang the marvellous work of the twelfth and thirteenth centuries. The work of the third period was all too short, and was brought to a sudden close by the Black Death which ravaged the world in 1348–9. It is properly described as the beginning of the modern era, the pre-Renaissance. A mere list of the Universities established will give some idea of the intellectual activity of the time. Montpellier (1137); Paris (1176); Oxford (1200); Cambridge (1209); Padua (1222); Naples (1224); Salamanca (1230); Toulouse (1230); Orléans (1231); Valladolid (1250); Seville (1254); Coimbra-Lisbon (1290); Lerida (1300); Avignon (1303); Rome (1303); Grenoble (1332); Angers (1337); Pisa (1343); Prague (1347); Florence (1349); Perpignan (1349); Huesca (1359); Cracovia (1364); Pavia (1365); Orange (1365); Vienna (1365); Erfurt (1379); Heidelberg (1385); Cologne (1388); Buda (1389).[2] The fourth period was retrograde. Wars abroad and economic troubles at home seemed to have crushed the spirit of the few survivors from the previous generation.

John Arderne belongs to the thirteenth century in spirit and in thought, although the accident of birth placed him in the next generation. He was well educated, and he reflects the current ideas of his time just as every well-educated surgeon at the present day is an epitome of his surroundings. Nothing is known of his history except for the autobiographical details given in the various manuscripts of his works and a small body of floating tradition which has been handed down through the centuries.

[1] "La grande chirurgie de Guy de Chauliac." Paris, 1890, pp. x–xv.

[2] The dates appended to the Universities are merely intended to show when each was known to be actually in existence—a few were created, the majority developed from small beginnings.

Biographical Facts.

There seems to be little doubt that he was a member of the family of Arderne, or Arden, who claimed descent from Saxon times. The best known representative of the family was Turchill or Turketil, styled de Warwic in Domesday, and De Eardene in the Register of Abingdon Abbey, "being one of the first here in England that, in imitation of the Normans, assumed a surname.[1] The Ardernes were Lords of Watford in Northamptonshire from 1140, and spread thence to Cheshire and Staffordshire. In the Aldford, Cheshire, branch the name of John was borne hereditarily by John de Arderne (fl. 1220); Sir John de Arderne (1266–1308?); Sir John de Arderne (1307–1349); and John de Arderne (fl. 1332).[2] It was possibly the last-named John Arderne[3] who received a grant of land in Connaught from Edward the Black Prince (Appendix, p. 105), and who is mentioned in John of Gaunt's Register[4] as having been appointed Seneschal of the manor of Passenham in Northamptonshire on October 7th, 1374. The name of John Arderne, or John de Arderne, therefore, was well known in London,[5] in the midlands and in the counties of Cheshire and Lancaster during the fourteenth century, but there is no evidence forthcoming at present to show to which branch of the family the surgeon belonged.

The date of Arderne's birth is fixed by his own statement that he was seventy in the first year of the reign of Richard II. Edward III died at Sheen on June 21, 1377, and was immediately succeeded by Richard II. Arderne, therefore, was born in 1307.[6] It is clear too that he practised abroad, for he says that he tried a remedy "in foreign

[1] Dugdale, 675.

[2] "Parentalia," Genealogical Memoirs, compiled by George Ormerod, D.C.L. F.R.S., privately printed 1851.

[3] Perhaps it was this John Arderne who is mentioned in Rymer's "Fœdera" (vol. ii, part 2, p. 119, col. 2). He was commanded to attend the King in war to Guienne in the year 1324.

[4] I, 337, leaf 64, back. I am indebted to the kindness of Mr. Sydney Armitage-Smith for this reference.

[5] In London John Arderne was a Fishmonger in 1361, and Richard Arderne was a prominent Skinner in 1376. John Arderne, esquire, was living in the parish of St. Mary Aldermariachurch in 1425. (Dr. Reginald Sharpe's "Calendar of Wills—Court of Husting." London, part 2, pp. 63 and 439.)

[6] Sloane MS. 75, leaf 146. De Curâ Oculi. "Et sciant presentes et futuri quoad Ego Magister Johannes de Ardern, cirurgorum minimus, hunc libellum propriâ manu meâ exaravi apud London; anno, videlicet regis Ricardi 2di primo et etatis me lxx. ("And be it known to present and future generations that I, Master John of Ardern, the least of the surgeons, scribbled this book with my own hand in London in the year, viz. the first year of the reign of King Richard the Second and in the seventieth year of my age.")

parts upon one King and two Bishops."[1] I have no doubt in my own mind that the king was John of Gaunt, "Roy de Castell et de Leon, Duc de Lancastre," who was always addressed as "Monseigneur d'Espaigne."[2] In 1376 John of Gaunt was the best hated man in England, says Mr. Sydney Armitage-Smith in his valuable study of his life. It was undesirable, therefore, John Arderne would think, to draw too close attention to the fact that he had once been attached to his person, for the book was written in this very year 1376. The precaution was wise in view of the events which happened when a London mob burnt the Duke's palace at the Savoy in 1381 and killed his physician, merely because he was a trusted and valued friend.[3] Mr. Sydney Armitage-Smith[4] says that the name of the physician was William de Appleton, and that he was retained by the Duke of Lancaster at 40 marcs per annum for life. An interesting example of the caution which was habitual to Ardern in this matter is to be found in two of the manuscripts in the British Museum. The one[5] tells of a certain noble knight in the service of the Duke of Lancaster at Algeçiras, in Spain, who had a sudden attack of facial paralysis, which so twisted his mouth that it was drawn back nearly to his ear and prevented him from speaking. The manuscript continues, "I, the aforesaid John Ardern, made a cure of him." The second manuscript[6] gives an account of the same case, but, instead of giving any name to the leech who cured him, it merely says "for whom the King of Spain's doctor made a cure in this way."[7] The latter MS. is a magnificently written copy on vellum, with such carefully executed illustrations that it is usually exhibited in the British Museum as an example of fourteenth-century work. It was possibly a presentation copy to John of Gaunt himself; the first one is a poorly written paper manuscript, such as would have an ordinary

[1] MS. bought at the Towneley Sale. It is now in the Surgeon General's Library at Washington, U.S.A. The extract on leaf 54 is, "Hoc probavi in uno rege et duobus episcopis in transmarinis partibus." It is quoted in the "Johns Hopkins Bulletin," vol. v, 1894, pp. 21 and 67, but I am indebted to the courtesy of Lieut.-Col. Walter D. McCaw, Librarian S. G. O., for a complete transcription of the passage.

[2] "John of Gaunt," by Sydney Armitage-Smith, p. 258.

[3] Johannes de ordine Minorum in armis bellicis strenuus, in physica peritissimus, domino Johanni duci Lancastriae familiarissimus."—Knighton's Chronicle-Rolls Series, ii, 133.

[4] *Op. cit.* p. 248, note. [5] Sloane MS. 3548. [6] Sloane 29301.

[7] "Quidam miles nobilis Ducis Lancastriae apud Agezir in Hispania passus est subito torturam oris ita quod os ejus distractum fuit fere retro aurem nec loqui poterat. Ego Predictus Joh. Ardern talem feci sibi curam" (MS. 3548). "Cui medicus regis hyspaniae talem curam fecit," says MS. 29301.

circulation. It was copied at a much later date, for the scribe, by mistake, has written Henrici de Arderne, and it belonged to Robert May.

Haeser[1] says that perhaps Arderne was educated at Montpellier and practised in France as a military surgeon on the English side during the earlier and most brilliant years of the One Hundred Years' War. E. H., who translated his "Latin practises and consailes concerning the helping of all diseases,"[2] in the early part of the seventeenth century, is responsible for the statement that he practised at Antwerp, and he certainly knew a few words of Flemish, for, in speaking of the Nightshade, he says that in Flanders it is called "Naghtstach" (p. 32).

Dr. Milward[3] believed that he was present at the battle of Creçy, but this I take leave to doubt. He practised, or at any rate he treated patients, in Wiltshire,[4] and from 1349 until 1370 he lived at Newark in Nottinghamshire.[5] He came to London in 1370, but I have found no record of where he lived. It was the year of his grand climacteric, in an age when men lived a much shorter time than now, yet he practised with vigour and success for five or six years. By this time he had secured a competence and he set himself to write. In 1376 he issued his treatise on the cure of Fistula in ano which is here printed, "written," as he says, "with my own hand, in the year when the strong and warlike Lord" (Edward the Black Prince) "was taken to God."[6] It is possible that the treatise on Clysters[7] was already written; it is certain that the treatise "De cura oculorum" was written in 1377,[8] but we know nothing more than this about John Arderne. There is nothing to show that he was living in the reign of Henry IV, who came to the throne in 1399. The reference to Henry IV (p. 74), "With this medicine was kyng Henry of ynglond cured of the going out of the lure," is a side-note written in a different hand in some of the MSS. and has only crept into the English text in

[1] "Lehrbuch d. geschichte der Med.," ed. 3, Jena, 1875, i, 784.

[2] Sloane MS. 2271.

[3] A circular invitatory letter . . . concerning . . . British Physical and Chirurgical Authors, by Edward Milward, M.D., Lond. 1740, p. 23.

[4] "Hoc probavi in vicecomite Wilteshure," says the MS. in the Surgeon-General's Library at Washington, U.S.A., quoted in the "Johns Hopkins Hospital Bulletin," vol. v, 1894, pp. 21 and 67, and I am again indebted to Lieut.-Col. McCaw for verifying the reference.

[5] Teste all the MSS.

[6] "Et eodem anno quo Dominus strenuus et bellicosus Princeps migravit ad Dominum, scripsi libellum istum manu propria, viz. Millesimo ccclxxvi. . . . quem Deus absolvat, quia fuit flos Miliciæ Mundi sine pare."

[7] See postea, p. 74 *et seqq.*

[8] P. x, note 6, of these Forewords.

process of time. The Hunterian copy of the Commentary in English on "Aegidii Corboliensis tractatus metricus de Urinis," which mentions the leech of "our Lord King the most illustrious prince Henry the Fourth, on whose soul may God have Mercy, Amen," was clearly written after 20 March, 1413, and the scribe has forgotten Arderne's right name, for he says that it is written by Master John Arderon.[1]

It seems to me that the easiest way to correlate the various facts recorded about John Arderne is to assume that he was attached at first to Henry Plantagenet, the first Duke of Lancaster, and afterwards to John of Gaunt, who married his younger daughter Blanche as his first wife—the White Lady of Chaucer's "Book of the Duchess." Henry, as Earl of Derby, was at Antwerp in 1338, and John Arderne is said to have practised there. Henry, in company with the Earl of Salisbury, fought against the Moors at the siege of Algeçiras in 1343, when much use was made of Greek fire, and gunpowder is said to have been employed for the first time. John Arderne had been to Algeçiras because he treated a knight there who was suffering from a trivial complaint from which he would have recovered during the long journey, if he had visited Arderne in England. Arderne was interested both in Greek fire and in gunpowder, for he gives a receipt for making Ignis Græcus and for an artificial fire to burn ships. Henry of Lancaster was Lieutenant and Captain of Aquitaine in 1345, and was granted the town of Bergerac with the right of coinage in 1347. John Arderne nowhere says specifically that he served with the Earl of Derby, Duke of Lancaster, but he betrays an intimate knowledge of this campaign, for he gives the names of the towns in the order in which they were reached by the invading army and not in their geographical succession; his knowledge is even remarkable, for he gives the towns in the order in which they were reached by a single column of the army, and he was writing more than thirty years after the events.[2]

[1] "Ego Magister Johannes Arderonn hoc opusculum composui de judiciis urinarum per colores et contenta secundum indicium Egidii et Ypocratis, Walterii, Gilis, Gilberti, Gordoni, Johannis de Sancto Amando, Ysaac, Auicenne, theophili, Galyeni, Galterii et tholomei in medicinam et medicum domini regis illustrissimi principis henrici quarti cujus anime propicietur deus. Amen." The MS. is in the Hunterian Library at Glasgow, No. 328, U. 7, 22 (cf. Notes, 59/32).

[2] "The forsaid sir Adam (p. 1, line 12 *et seqq.*) forsooth suffering from fistula in ano asked counsel of all the leeches and surgeons that he could find in Gascony, at Bordeaux, at Bergerac, Toulouse, Narbonne and Poitiers." Arderne seems to have had a soft place in his heart for Narbonne. He calls one of his favourite plaisters Emplastron de Nerbon, and says, "Istud emplastron dicitur Norbon quia quamvis sit nigrum tamen bonum." ("This emplastre is called Noirbon, for although it be black nevertheless it is good." P. 91, l. 31.)

The campaign ended and the Duke of Lancaster returned to London, 13th January, 1347–8, and died of the plague at Leicester in 1361. John Arderne may then have attached himself to John of Gaunt, the son-in-law of the Duke, who called himself King of Castile and Leon from his marriage with Constance, daughter of Don Pedro I of Castile, in September 1371, until his own daughter Katherine married Enrique III in 1388, and became Queen of Castile and Leon in 1390. If Arderne was really surgeon to the King of Castile it must have been after the year 1370, and this perhaps gives the reason why John Arderne left Newark after he had practised there for so many years. Mr. Armitage-Smith tells me, however, that there is no record of such an appointment in the Duke's roll which he has lately published.

Arderne as a Surgeon.

John Arderne is a good example of a type of surgeon who has happily never been absent from England. He is the earliest example that we know at present, but he was followed in direct succession by Thomas Morstede, who was present at Agincourt in 1415, and was buried in St. Olave, Upwell, in the Jewry, in 1450; by Richard Ferris, who wrote nothing, but was revered as their master by many succeeding generations of surgeons in London. He died, an old man, in 1566, and had seen much service in the wars of Henry VIII. William Clowes (1540-1604), my great predecessor at St. Bartholomew's Hospital, learnt much of him. Clowes handed on the tradition to John Woodall (1556–1643), and Woodall to Richard Wiseman (1622–1676), the surgeon of the Commonwealth. Wiseman was succeeded by Samuel Sharp (1700 (?)–1778) of Guy's Hospital, and by Percivall Pott (1714–1788) at St. Bartholomew's. The distinguishing mark of each was the possession of the qualities which make an English gentleman as well as a fine surgeon. They were all men of good education, wide experience, and sound judgment. John Arderne possessed these qualities in abundance. He preferred personal experience to the teaching of the schools. He would rather learn by experiment than by authority, and with characteristic frankness he related his failures as well as his successes (p. 83). He was not in advance of his time, for he believed, like every one else, in Astrology (p. 16). He kept his methods as secret as he could by giving fancy names to his ointments and plaisters (p. 89), and by writing his charm in Greek letters "ne a laicis perspicietur" (p. 103).

John Arderne wrote on Fistula, on diseases of the Eye, on Clysters, on Bleeding; on Plants and their Uses, and he also published a common-place book containing various receipts and notes of cases arranged without any method. There exists also his Commentary on Giles de Corbeil's metrical treatise "de Urinis" (p. xiii, note 1), and he is the author of a "Scala Sanitatis contra plagas." By some means he had access to a large medical library, for he quotes the very words of the manuscripts to which he refers in his treatise on Hæmorrhoids (p. 55, line 3), and it is evident that they were lying before him as he wrote. It is clear from the number of manuscripts which still remain in the various libraries (Bibliography, pp. xxxiv and xxxv) that Arderne's works were read and valued by his contemporaries and immediate successors. They were written originally in Latin, and, as he is careful to explain, with his own hand, but English translations were soon produced. The Latin is of the colloquial type like that in which the "Epistolae Obscurorum Virorum" was written in the early years of the sixteenth century, neither better nor worse, and when Arderne was at fault for a Latin word he never scrupled to use its English or French equivalent. His handwriting was as crabbed as his style, if, as there is some reason for believing, the Sloane MS., No. 75, is a holograph in so far as it deals with diseases of the eyes. The treatise on Fistula in Ano is certainly the most interesting and practical of Arderne's works. John Read published an abstract of a part of this treatise in the reign of Queen Elizabeth, but it has never been printed in full until now, and for this purpose an early fifteenth-century translation has been selected.

The Treatment of Fistula in Ano.

Arderne's attention was no doubt called to the subject of Fistula by the actual cases which came to him for relief. The hardship of the Hundred Years' War must have produced many cases of ischio-rectal abscess which ended in fistula. Wet, cold, long hours in the saddle weighted down by the heavy armour of the time, would readily lead to this condition in the knightly class; whilst the sedentary habits and gross feeding causing chronic constipation would account for it in the religious and civic population. Tubercle, too, was rife in the fourteenth century, but it would be interesting to learn whether the Black Death left an aftermath of boils and abscesses. The work is full of detail, and shows the author to be original, thoughtful, observant, and a master of his art both in theory and practice. He says, very rightly, that the treatment of fistula in ano had fallen into disrepute because it was a troublesome condition which brought very little credit to surgeons, whilst it required long and patient treatment for which the majority of the sufferers were not prepared to pay. An examination of the writings of the immediate predecessors and contemporaries of John Arderne shows that these statements are literally correct. To go back no farther than Albucasis, who died in 1013,[1] it was taught that complete fistulæ were incurable, and that all operations and the application of ointments was but labour in vain. Some believed that a cure could be obtained occasionally, and Albucasis advised, therefore, that a small copper or iron probe should be introduced into the bowel through the fistula which should then be laid open in its whole extent until the probe fell out. But if the bleeding were so severe as to stop the operation, or the surgeon was afraid of the hæmorrhage, the actual cautery might be used. In other cases, Albucasis taught, a probe armed with a ligature of five strands might be passed from the external orifice of the fistula through its track into the rectum. The end of the probe was then caught by the finger and drawn out through the anus bringing with it one end of the ligature. The two ends of the ligature, the one hanging out of the fistula and the other from the anus, were then tied tightly together, care being taken to include as much tissue as possible. The knot was tightened on the second or third day, and as often afterwards as was necessary. The fistula was thus cured by the ligature cutting its way out, the track behind it healing by granulation.

William de Salicet (fl. 1245), who taught surgery at Bologna, and was considered the most skilful surgeon of his age, had so great a dread of fistula that he wrote:[2] "When the fistula is complete it is assuredly so difficult to cure that it is better and more honourable for the surgeon to give up the case at once. But if he decide to undertake it the orifice should be dilated with a sponge tent and the whole track burnt with the actual cautery. If this fails the fistula may be laid open into the bowel by a seton of silk, horsehair or cow's hair pulled to and fro daily like a saw until it cuts its way out; but," he adds, as a warning, "I have seen bad results from this method of cure."

Lanfrank, the most distinguished pupil of William de Salicet, who

[1] "Methodus Medendi certa, clara et brevis," Lib. ii, cap. 810. Basil, 1541, p. 132.

[2] "Chirurgie de Guillaume de Salicet." Paul Pifteau. Toulouse, 1898, p. 139.

died in 1306, the year before John Arderne was born, contents himself with saying that fistulæ are incurable, and he utters a lamentable cry against those who would attempt to operate even if it were only by applying a corrosive.[1]

Henri de Mondeville (1260(?)–1320(?)) merely enlarged the orifice of the fistula with a tent, and utterly condemns the teaching of the school of Salernum, as represented by Roger and Roland, who would operate and afterwards apply a painful corrosive,[2]—and de Mondeville was in Paris what Arderne was in London, a first-rate surgeon.

Guy de Chauliac (d. 1368), prince of the mediæval writers of surgical text-books, published his "Great Surgery" thirteen years before Arderne wrote his treatise on Fistula. After the manner of text-books various operations are described for the cure of fistula, each with insufficient details, and the reader is left in doubt as to which, if any, is to be employed.[3]

Arderne's Operation for Fistula.

John Arderne's operation is clearly a modification of the method recommended by Albucasis, and, like a good surgeon, he preferred a clean incision to fretting the fistula through with a ligature tied tightly. He recommends that the patient should be secured in the lithotomy position. A probe—called appropriately enough, sequere me—is passed through the fistula until it is felt in the rectum. The eye of the probe is then threaded with a ligature of four strands—the frænum Cæsaris—which is drawn through the fistula as the probe is pulled out of the rectum until one end hangs out of the anus and the other from the opening of the fistula. These two ends are knotted together and the whole ligature is tightened by means of a peg—the wrayste—fixed into the widest part of a gorget—the tendiculum—in the same way that a violin peg tightens the strings passing round it. The use of the ligature is partly to control the bleeding and partly to maintain a correct line while the fistula is being divided. The gorget or tendiculum is pushed well up into the fistula and a grooved director with a curved end—the acus rostrata, or snowted needle—is passed along it until the end projects into the rectum where the probe had

[1] Lanfrank's "Science of Cirurgie," Early English Text Society, No. 102, pp. 292–3.

[2] "Chirurgie de Maître Henri de Mondeville." E. Nicaise. Paris, 1893, p. 465.

[3] "La Grande Chirurgie de Guy de Chauliac, composée en l'an 1363." E. Nicaise. Paris, 1890, p. 134.

been previously inserted. A shield—the cochlearia, or spoon—with a depression in its centre is then passed through the anus until the grooved director engages in the depressed notch. The object of this shield is partly to prevent the surgeon cutting down upon his own finger and partly to protect the opposite wall of the rectum should the patient struggle or make a sudden movement at the moment the fistula is divided. A scalpel—the razor or lance—is passed along the groove in the acus rostrata, and the fistula is cleanly divided along its whole length by drawing the knife, the acus rostrata, and the spoon out of the rectum with a single movement, the ligature or frænum Cæsaris coming away at the same time. Each branch of the fistula may be laid open in turn if the patient can bear it, or any farther operation can be postponed, as Arderne had found by experience that when the main track was laid open the other channels often healed of themselves.

The operation was a good one, except that his instruments were needlessly cumbersome, and would cure a fistula equally well at the present day, but the great advance which Arderne made was in avoiding the corrosive and irritating after-treatment used by every one else. It is difficult now to put ourselves in his position and to realize what an amount of originality it meant for a surgeon in the fourteenth century to leave a wound alone and not to try and kill it with the actual cautery or with caustics. Such a method was contrary to all teaching, and would seem to be undertaken with the very greatest risk. Yet John Arderne only applied a little oil of roses with the white or yolk of an egg, and he washed the wound with tepid water and a sponge. He never changed the dressings oftener than he could help (p. 87), but he was careful to see that they were not soiled, whilst his experience with simple enemata led him to prefer a clyster of salt and water to the powerful purgatives in ordinary use. Some of his patients recovered, therefore, and he was not slow to advertise the fact; but the weight of authority was against him, and in spite of his success, surgeons preferred to mundify their wounds and use incarnatives for nearly five hundred years after his death.

The Master Surgeons.

The position which Arderne occupied was perfectly well recognized both in England and France, and was identical with that which we occupy at the present time as consulting and operating surgeons. In France such surgeons were known in Arderne's time as surgeons of the long robe, to distinguish them from the barbers practising surgery, who were surgeons of the short robe. In England the prefix of Master indicated the difference, and John Arderne is careful therefore always to style himself Magister Johannes de Arderne, Magister being his title as Master of Surgery, which distinguished him, on the one hand, from the Doctor of Physic who was his superior, and, on the other, from the Barber and the Apothecary who ranked below him. The Master Surgeons formed a small guild in London from very early times, and records of persons entrusted with its supervision are known as early as 1369.[1] Arderne calls himself "cirurgorum minimus" (p. x, note 6), and he was probably admitted a member of this guild when he came to London in 1370, in which case Master John Dunheued, Master John Hyndstoke and Master Nicholas Kildesby would be three of his colleagues. The guild never contained many members, but what it lacked in numbers it made up in influence, and, in spite of many struggles with the more numerous Guild of Barbers, it was able to hold its own for many years. The Guild of Surgeons united for a short time with the Physicians about 1423, and finally became merged into the United Company of Barbers and Surgeons in 1540. But it is unnecessary to trace the growth and development of the Guild of Surgeons, and those who are interested in it will find a fuller account in "The Medical Magazine" for 1899. The present treatise contains slight references to the struggle which was going on between the Surgeons and the Barbers at the time it was written. There is the case, for instance (p. 100), of the rich fishmonger who had a lacerated wound of the arm which was made worse by the incompetent treatment of a barber who had stuffed it with corrosive dressings. Arderne tore off the dressings and replaced them by a soothing fomentation which allowed the patient to have a good night's rest.

But the human interest of the treatises here published is concentrated in Arderne's description of the qualities required in a good surgeon (p. 4). It sets forth his ideal of the morals and etiquette of the highest class of surgeons—the Masters of Surgery—during the thirteenth and fourteenth centuries, and shows that it was at least as high as it is amongst the best men of the present day. Pity, charity, continence in all things, the patient first but the fee not unimportant, because then as now the labourer was worthy of his hire, were the distinguishing characteristics of the educated surgeon.

Henri de Mondeville gives similar rules in somewhat greater detail.

[1] South's "Craft of Surgery," p. 17. Messrs. Cassell & Co., London, 1886.

I quote partly from Prof. E. Nicaise's splendid edition of his works,[1] and partly from the contemporary translation into French, published by Dr. A. Bos:[2] "A Surgeon ought to be fairly bold. He ought not to quarrel before the laity, and although he should operate wisely and prudently, he should never undertake any dangerous operation unless he is sure that it is the only way to avoid a greater danger. His limbs, and especially his hands, should be well-shaped with long, delicate and supple fingers which must not be tremulous. He ought to promise a cure to every patient, but he should tell the parents or the friends if there is any danger. He should refuse as far as possible all difficult cases, and he should never mix himself up with desperate ones. He may give advice to the poor for the love of God only, but the wealthy should be made to pay well. He should neither praise himself nor blame others, and he should not hate any of his colleagues. He ought to sympathise with his patients in their distress and fall in with their lawful requests so far as they do not interfere with the treatment. Patients, on the other hand, should obey their surgeons implicitly in everything appertaining to their cure. The surgeon's assistants must be loyal to their surgeon and friendly to his patients. They should not tell the patient what the surgeon said unless the news is pleasant, and they should always appear cheerful. They must agree amongst themselves as well as with the patients, and they must not be always grumbling, because this inspires fear and doubt in the patient."

De Mondeville then shows how an honest surgeon may be replaced and damaged by one who is less conscientious, for he says: "A rich man has the beginning of an inflammation. He calls in an upright surgeon, who says after examining him, 'Seigneur, there is no need for any operation here, because nature will relieve herself, etc.; but if the inflammation gets worse, send for me.' It then happens that the patient calls in another man who is a quack, and he is told, 'Seigneur, you have a great deal of inflammation, I can feel it inside, and if you are not treated at once you will certainly regret it.' This surgeon then sets to work and makes an inflammation, which he afterwards cures, so that the whole proceeding redounds to his credit and profit, for he discovered an inflammation which did not exist, whilst the first surgeon is damaged both in his reputation and his pocket because he did not find out what was not there."

[1] "Chirurgie de Maître Henri de Mondeville, composée de 1306 à 1320," par Ed. Nicaise. Paris, 1893, pp. 91 *et seqq.*

[2] "Soc. des Anciens Textes Français." Paris, 1897, tome i, p. 140.

"Then again, one of these second-rate surgeons will come to a sick man who is wealthy, and will say to him, with the voice of an archangel—taking care that no witnesses are present—'Seigneur, you must remember that you are the one who is ill and in pain. It is not your son or your nephew. It is you who are kept awake by the pain whilst your friends and servants sleep. Others won't take care of you if you don't take care of yourself. You are rich enough to get advice and to buy health and whatever else you want if you choose to do so. Riches are not more than health, nor is poverty worse than sickness. Have you not made the greater part of your money yourself and for yourself, so that if you are not a miser you can apply it to relieve your wants? Would to God that those who look after you so badly had your complaint. But all this is between ourselves, and what I tell you is only out of pity for you and for your good.' Then, in the absence of the patient, he speaks to the relatives and says, 'Seigneurs, this man has the greatest confidence in you, and, truly, if you lose him, you will lose an excellent friend. It is not to your credit either to let him go without advice, for if he died without advice you would be blamed everlastingly, even if it made him as poor as Job. He is really in great danger, and it is a serious case, but nature sometimes does better than we have any right to expect. He is sure to die if no one treats him, but if he is properly treated it is just possible that he will escape and not die. If he dies it won't be the result of the treatment, because he is nearly dead already, his only chance is to have a consultation, etc. I am speaking to you as a friend and not as a doctor.'

"But it is quite another matter when this same surgeon has to treat a poor man, for he says, 'I am really sorry for you, and I would gladly help you for the love of God only. But I am very busy just now with a lot of difficult cases, and, besides, the season is not a very favourable one for an operation. You can't afford to buy what is necessary for your case, such as drugs and dressings, so I would put it off until the summer. You will then be able to get the herbs and whatever else is wanted and so save expense. The summer, too, is the best time for the poor.' When the same pauper comes back in the summer the surgeon says to him, 'I am very sorry that I put you off in the winter and told you to wait until the summer, because the winter is really the best time. Summer is too hot and there is a fear of stirring up the disease. I should advise you to wait until the hot weather is over.' And this goes on everlastingly, for this kind of surgeon never finds time to operate upon a pauper."

De Mondeville classifies his patients according to their ability to pay fees. "The first class are paupers who must be treated for nothing; the second class are a little better off, and may send presents of fowls and ducks; they pay in kind. The third class are friends and relations who pay no fixed fee, but send victuals or presents in token of gratitude, but no money. Our assistants ought to suggest the presents to this class, saying behind our backs, and as if we knew nothing about it, when anything is said about money, 'No, indeed, the Master would not like it, and you would do much better to make him a little present, though I am sure that he does not expect anything.' Indeed, a sharp assistant sometimes makes more by such suggestions than the Master does by his operation, and it is just like doubling the fee on account of the horse when the Master makes his visits on horseback. Then there is a class embracing those who are notoriously bad payers, such as our nobility and their households, government officials, judges, baillies and lawyers, whom we are obliged to treat because we dare not offend them. In fact, the longer we treat these people the more we lose. It is best to cure them as quickly as possible, and to give them the best medicines. Lastly, there is a class who pay in full and in advance, and they should be prevented from getting ill at all, because we are paid a salary to keep them in health."

The difficulty of obtaining payment for operations in the fourteenth century must have been very great, for De Mondeville still further emphasizes it and says, "The chief object of the patient, and the one idea which dominates all his actions, is to get cured, and when once he is cured he forgets his own obligation and omits to pay; the object of the surgeon, on the other hand, is to obtain his money, and he should never be satisfied with a promise or a pledge, but he should either have the money in advance or take a bond for it. As the poet says, 'Sæpe fides data fallit, plegius plaidit, vadium valet—The promise is often broken, the security is worthless, the bond alone holds good.'" De Mondeville also thinks that it is better on the whole for the surgeon to be paid for what he does rather than by a retaining fee, because a salary is apt to make him so hopeful that he will think the blind can certainly see and the lame can walk or even run. The surgeon too must beware of those who will make infamous proposals to him, because from time immemorial it has been an article of faith with the common people that every surgeon is a thief, a murderer or a swindler. He should also be careful to estimate the strength of a patient before he operates. If a patient dies of the operation and not of mere weakness the surgeon is held excused so long as the friends think the wound looks healthy, but if the wound looks badly the surgeon is credited with the death even though the patient has simply died of weakness. The surgeon must not put too much faith in appearances. The rich have a nasty habit of coming to him in old clothes, or, if they are properly dressed as befits their station they invent all kinds of excuses for beating down his fees. They say Charity is a flower when they find a man who helps the poor, and think that a surgeon ought to assist the unfortunate, but they never consider that a like rule is binding upon them. "I often say to such folk," De Mondeville adds, "Well, then, pay me for yourself and for three paupers and I will cure them as well as you. But they never make any answer, and I have never yet found any one in any position, whether he was a cleric or a layman, who was rich enough, or rather honest enough, to pay what he had promised until he was made to do so." Lesser surgeons must have fared very badly if this was the experience of the surgeon to the King of France.

De Mondeville returns to the question of fees in another part of his book (Nicaise, *op. cit.* p. 199). "The surgeon ought to consider three things when a patient comes to see him and arrange about the fee for an operation. First, his own position; secondly, the condition of the patient; thirdly, the state of the disease. As regards himself the surgeon should think whether he is celebrated or at least better known than his colleagues, whether he is the only surgeon in the country, whether he is rich and not obliged to practise, whether he has enough cases to fill up his time, and whether he is on the point of undertaking more important cases. On the second point, viz. the condition of the patient. He either knows or he does not know him; if he knows him he is aware whether he is rich or poor, whether, for example, he is the nephew of a bishop or of an abbé. But if he does not know him he ought to make careful inquiries, or rather he ought to get his assistants to make them, because sometimes, indeed often, it happens that the rich come to the leech dressed like paupers. If the surgeon suspects this he should say to his patient, 'Seigneur, I have examined your case but I must think it over, and I should like to see you again when I have done so, because he who judges in haste repents at leisure,' and in the interval the surgeon should make inquiries. As to the third point, the surgeon should think of the disease whether it is serious, if it is difficult to cure, and if long attendance will be required, whether few people know how to treat it, if it is chronic, and if it presents any unusual characters.

"When the surgeon has considered all the points under these three headings he ought to charge the patient boldly a very large fee, though he may moderate it according to circumstances. To a rich man he should say, 'The fee a surgeon ought to receive is a hundred pounds for this operation,' and if the patient is staggered by the sum he would continue, 'but I did not say that I was going to charge you that amount,' and thus little by little he lowers his fee. But he should always have a minimum for each operation and never go below it. In such cases it is more graceful for him to say, 'I am ready to do this operation as you and your friends wish, but I would rather do it for nothing to please you than for so small a fee.' And the surgeon should pretend that he has no living (prebende) nor capital except his profession, and that everything is as dear as possible, especially drugs, and ointment; that the fee is as nothing compared with his services; and the wages of all other artisans, masons, for example, have doubled of late. I repeat that the surgeon ought to charge the rich as much as possible and to get all he can out of them, provided that he does all he can to cure the poor. You then, Surgeons, if you operate conscientiously upon the rich for a sufficient fee and upon the poor for charity, you ought not to fear the ravages of fire, nor of rain nor of wind; you need not take orders or make pilgrimages nor undertake any work of that kind, because by your science you can save your souls alive, live without poverty and die in your houses. Live in peace and joy and rejoice because your recompense is so great in heaven, as necessarily follows from the words of the Saviour, spoken in the psalm by the mouth of His prophet, 'Beatus qui intelligit super egeneum et pauperem. . .' For this reason surgeons enjoy such immunities and are free from all personal service and from all common burdens, such as the repair of walls, moats and roads, from the night watch in towns, and from all kinds of things. The Surgeons are classed as Surgeon-major and as Surgeons of the palace or Examiners, who are generally called Archiatres by the common people."

William of Salicet, another surgeon, experienced in war and of the same high standard as Arderne and De Mondeville, had written in 1275 ("Chirurgie de Guillaume de Salicet Achevée en 1275, Traduction et Commentaire, par Paul Pifteau." Toulouse, 1898, p. 3) in somewhat similar terms. He says a surgeon should grant the wishes of his patient so long as they do not interfere with the operation. He ought also to comfort his patient as far as possible by kind actions and by soothing words. He should hold out hope even in the most desperate cases, because the patient's courage reacts to these words and promises, and they may have a more powerful influence on his recovery than any of the surgeon's remedies. But the matter should be discussed with the friends whenever there is danger, partly to save them the shock of an unexpected death, and partly to protect the surgeon from any suspicion of having caused it. Neither a surgeon nor a physician should talk to the women of the house with closed doors, whether she be mistress or servant. He should never speak improperly to her, nor make eyes at her, especially in the presence of the patient. Such actions may cause a patient to lose confidence in his surgeon, and thus the operation may prove unsuccessful because the patient has lost the good opinion he had of the operator. A wise surgeon too will do well to refrain from stealing anything whilst he is in attendance; he will not stir up strife amongst the patient's friends or quarrel with the people of the house; he will be careful, too, not to employ notoriously bad characters as his assistants, for all these things may spoil a good operation and thus detract from the dignity of medicine. Above all things, he must refrain from becoming too familiar with the laity. They are always ready to speak ill of doctors, and too great familiarity merely means that one cannot demand the proper fees for an operation with any assurance and safety. It is well known that a large fee increases the authority of the doctor as well as the confidence the patient puts in him, even though the doctor is very ignorant, because it is thought that a large fee secures better attention. The surgeon ought to observe the rules of those with whom he is living or amongst whom he finds himself. He should visit the poor because it is a good thing to have a reputation for Charity, partly because it increases his estimation in the eyes of the people, and partly because it enables the Divine Power to extend its influence over his spirit. The surgeon ought not to allow himself to be swayed by the entreaties of the patient, because if he yields the patient will lose faith in the operator, and the operator may himself become timid and hesitating. The assistants ought to be amiable and helpful to the patient, and they should never repeat to him what the surgeon has said unless it is pleasant and encouraging. Leeches should be especially careful not to discuss matters with the patient or in his presence, and above all things, they must avoid whispering or talking together in corners, for such actions rouse all kinds of suspicion in the mind of the patient and his friends.

Lanfrank, who was in Paris in 1295, and is looked upon as the founder of French surgery, says in the English version transcribed in

1380 (Early English Text Society, No. 102, 1894, p. 8): "Needful it is that a surgeon be of a complexion well proportioned. . . He must have hands well shaped, long small fingers, and his body not quaking. Also he must be of subtle wit, for all things that (be)longeth to surgery may not with letters be written. . . Be he no glutton, nor not envious nor a niggard; be he true; humble and pleasingly bear himself to his patients; speak he no ribaldry in the sick man's house; give he no counsel but if he be asked; nor speak he with no woman in folly in the man's house; nor chide he not with the sick man nor none of his household, but courteously speak to the sick man, and in all manner of sickness promise him health although you despair of him, but nevertheless tell his friends the truth. Love no hard cures and undertake no desperate cases. Help poor men as far as possible and ask good reward of the rich. Praise he not himself with his own mouth, nor blame he over sharply other leeches. Love he all leeches and clerics, and, as far as possible, make he no leech his enemy. So clothe he himself with virtue that he may obtain a good name and a fair reputation. This is the ethical teaching."

It is clear from these extracts that Arderne had read Lanfrank's rules for a surgeon, and that he amplified them from his own experience, which corresponded very much with that of the French surgeons who were his contemporaries. But Arderne's teaching of the duties of a surgeon compares very favourably with that of William Salicet or Henri de Mondeville. He had a higher moral tone, or, at any rate, he based his warnings on morality rather than upon self-interest, and there is nowhere any reference to a surgeon as a common thief. His fees are high, but, as a contemporary writer explains, this is to make up for the long periods when he had nothing to do, and it is clear that it was extremely difficult to obtain money from patients.

Every surgeon was taught never to treat cases which appeared incurable or were unlikely to run a straightforward course. This was due to ignorance, to the weakness of the law, and to the arbitrary treatment to which individuals might be exposed. Throughout the Middle Ages, and long afterwards, there was no science of toxicology and very little knowledge of morbid anatomy. Persons who died suddenly, therefore, were usually thought to have been killed by poison, and the histories of the present day are full of accounts of the deaths of great men who are said to have been poisoned, when it is clear to every medical reader that they died a natural death from some acute disease. A perforated gastric ulcer, a perforated duodenal ulcer, an acute gangrenous inflammation of the vermiform appendix would present all the characters of poisoning to the lay mind. Failure after an operation was liable to be followed by the most undesirable consequences to the leech. King John of Bohemia, from whose body Edward the Black Prince took an ostrich feather for his crest, sewed up his French leech in a sack and threw him into the Oder because he had not cured his cataract as he had promised.

Arderne must have led an interesting and adventurous life, and his treatises contain many sidelights on contemporary events. He appears to be the only contemporary authority for the story of the means by which Edward the Black Prince obtained the ostrich feather which has since become the cognisance of the heir apparent to the English throne. The passage runs as follows, "We are not able to cure rhagades unless the remedy can be put through the anus either as a clyster or by means of a suppository, since remedies applied outside are either useless or do very little good. We ought, therefore, to work with stimulating applications until the wound is clean, and afterwards with applications which both heal and dry, as has been said already in the chapter on internal piles, to wit, where Nastar is painted—and Nastar is a kind of clyster or enema known as a glister-pipe.—The feather of the Prince of Wales is also shown there, viz. on the preceding page. And note that Edward the eldest son of Edward King of England bore a similar feather above his crest, and he obtained the feather from the King of Bohemia, whom he killed at Cressy in France. And so he took the feather which is called an 'ostrich feather,' which that most noble Lord King had used hitherto to bear above his crest. And in that year when our Lord the strenuous and warlike Prince departed to God, I wrote this little book of mine with my own hand, viz. in the year one thousand three hundred and seventy-six. And our Lord Edward the Prince died on the sixth June on Trinity Sunday at Westminster during the great Parliament, and may God assoil him, for he was the very flower of chivalry, without peer in the world."[1]

[1] "Rhagades curare non possumus nisi medicinis infra anum inferamus aut in clystere aut modo suppositorii quia medicinæ exterius appositæ parum vel nihil prosunt, unde primo oportet cum corrosivis operare ad mundificationem et postea cum consolidantibus et desiccantibus ut prædictum est capitulo de hæmorrhoid. infra anum latentibus ubi nastare depingitur et penna Principis Walliæ, viz. folio præcedente. Et nota quod talem pennam albam portabat Edwardus primogenitus filius Edwardi Regis Angliæ, super crestam suam. Et illam pennam conquisivit de rege Boëmo, quem interfecit apud Cresse in Francia. Et sic assumpsit sibi illam pennam quæ dicitur 'Ostrich fether,' quam prius Dominus Rex nobillissimus portebat super crestam suam et eodem anno quo

This passage is omitted from the English translation which is here printed (Sloane 6), as well as from the later and different English translation (Sloane 76), which are often merely abstracts of what Arderne wrote. But it is present in the Latin texts (Sloane MSS. 56, leaf 74; 335, leaf 68; 2002, leaf 333; 176, back; 29301, leaf 42, col. 157; in MS. 1153, leaf 41, in Trin. Coll. Camb.; and in the MS. No. 339 in the Hunterian Library at Glasgow, leaf 77).

It was from the last MS., which was then called Sloane 2, that Thomas Hearn copied it in the "Chronici Walteri Hemingford."[1] In each case it is a part of the text, and is written by the same hand as the rest of the manuscript. The scribes have not copied from each other, and there is very little doubt in my own mind that Arderne wrote it originally, and that it contains the story current in his day about the source of the feather, and Arderne was in a position to obtain the story at first hand. Incidentally it bears out an interesting point, for it says that both the King of Bohemia and the Prince of Wales bore the feather *above* his crest, not *as* his crest, so that it was used in exactly the same manner as was the Garter at first, viz. as an ornament to be worn at jousts or tournaments.[2] It only became a crest in later years, and so long as it was a mere ornament or distinguishing badge there was no need for it to be associated with a motto; indeed, in each of Arderne's figures the scroll placed upon the quill of the feather, which is single, is left blank instead of being charged. This use of the ostrich feather as an ornament at jousts further explains the passage in the Black Prince's will, in which he desired that his corpse should be taken through the City of Canterbury as far as the Priory, and that "two war horses, covered with our Arms and two men armed in our Arms and in our crests," should precede his corpse; that is to say, "the one for War, with our entire Arms quarterly, and the other for Peace, with our Badge of Ostrich Feathers," with four banners of the same suite.[3]

Dominus strenuus et bellicosus Princeps migravit at Dominum, scripsi libellum istum manu propriâ, viz. anno Millesimo ccclxxvi. Et Dominus Edwardus princeps obiit vi Idus Junii, viz. die Sanctæ Trinitatis, apud Westmonasterium in magno parliamento, quem Deus absolvat, quia fuit flos Miliciæ Mundi sine pare. Nastare species est clysteris sive enematis 'a glister pipe.'"

[1] Vol. 2, pp. 444, 446, in note.

[2] "Observations on the Institution of the Most Noble Order of the Garter, by Sir Nicholas Harris Nicolas." "Archæologia," vol. 31, p. 130.

[3] "On the Badge and Mottoes of the Prince of Wales," vol. 3. "Archæologia," vol. 31, p. 356.

"Et volons qe a quele heure qe notre corps soit amenez parmy la ville de Cantirbirie tantq'a la priorie, q'deux destreȝ covertȝ de nos armeȝ, et deuȝ homeȝ

The directions for making Nerbone plaister (p. 91) show the difficulties in reckoning small subdivisions of time. Arderne directs that the melted diachylon should be allowed to stand without moving by the space of a "pater noster" and an "ave maria." I asked a patient recently, the Mother Superior of a Convent, how long it would take to repeat these prayers, and she replied about three quarters of a minute. When I next saw her, after she had spent a sleepless night with a clock in front of her, she said that the question had interested her, and she found that a pater and an ave took exactly half a minute. Dr. Norman Moore draws attention ("The Progress of Medicine at St. Bartholomew's Hospital," 1888, p. 13) to a similar method employed by John Mirfeld, a Canon of the priory of St. Bartholomew, who wrote a general treatise on medicine—Breviarium Bartholomei—about the year 1380. He says, "Mirfeld treated chronic rheumatism by rubbing the part with olive oil. This was to be prepared with ceremony. It was to be put into a clean vessel while the preparer made the sign of the cross and said the Lord's Prayer and an Ave Maria, and when the vessel was put to the fire the Psalm, 'Why do the heathen rage,' was to be said as far as the verse 'Desire of me, and I shall give thee the heathen for thine inheritance.' The Gloria, Pater Noster, and Ave Maria are to be said, and the whole gone through seven times. 'Which done let that oil be kept.'" . . . "The time occupied I have tried," says Dr. Norman Moore, "and found to be a quarter of an hour."

The charm against Cramp (p. 102) was obtained from one who was at Milan when Lionel, Duke of Clarence, married Violante, the daughter of Galeazzo Visconti, at the door of the Cathedral, on June 5th, 1368. Five months of continuous jousts, feasts and revels were followed by the inevitable consequences of delirium tremens and epileptiform convulsions.

The sober testimony to the profligacy of the times given in the receipt for making confection of Sanguis Veneris (p. 89) is the natural outcome of the conditions described in Dr. Furnivall's "Early English Meals and Manners" (Early English Text Society, Original Series, No. 32). The boys and girls of the upper classes were transferred

---

armeȝ en nos armeȝ et en nos heaumes voisent devant dit n're corps, c'est assavoir l'un pur la guerre de noȝ armeȝ entiers quartelleȝ, at l'autre pur la paix de noz bages des plumes d'ostrace, ove quarter baneres de mesme la sute, et qe chacun de ceaux q'porteront les diteȝ baneres ait sur sa teste un chapeau de noȝ armes." "Nichols's Royal Wills," p. 68. See also "Notes and Queries," Series ii, 1861, vol. xi, pp. 224 and 294.

from their own homes to be educated in the houses of the nobility as pages and maids of honour. They were well fed, spent their lives in a round of pleasure, and were often badly looked after.

The account of juniper shows that Arderne knew London and its neighbourhood and talked with the countryfolk as he went amongst them. He says, "Juniper grows in Kent upon Shooter's Hill on the road to Canterbury, at Dorking also in Surrey as well as in many other places in that County, at Bedington too near Croydon, and the inhabitants of that country call it gorst because they do not know its proper name."[1] The Black Death does not seem to have left much impression upon Arderne's mind, because, like most contemporary medical writers, he only mentions it incidentally, and what we look upon as an appalling visitation had already faded from his mind, and its impression had been replaced by more recent epidemics.

Arderne lived through the most chivalrous period of English history, and in all probability he knew personally many of the peerless knights and splendid champions who survive for ever in the pages of Froissart. To have known such men was in itself an education, and to have lived in the household of Henry, Duke of Lancaster, and of John of Gaunt was sufficient to make Arderne the best type of an English surgeon—a scholar and a gentleman. The chivalry of the age is well brought out in the extant manuscripts of Arderne's treatises. In some cases he mentions the names of the patients, but in many instances he tricks their coat-armour instead of giving names, and thus some early shields are preserved, amongst others that of the great Douglas.

Arderne left a few traces on the sands of time, but very few. Johannis Argentin, a physician at Cambridge, wrote a treatise, which still remains in the Bodleian Library as Ashmol. MS. No. 1437. Tanner[2] thinks that it was written about 1476. He mentions Arderne no less than eleven times, and copies his style, especially his manner of quoting cases in illustration of his various subjects.

Arderne's fame as a pharmacist long outlasted his reputation as a surgeon. Tapsimel (p. 31), Pulvis sine pari (pp. 26 and 86), Tapsivalencia (p. 69), and the valences of Scabious and Wormwood (p. 97),

[1] "Et crescat in cancia super Scheteres hylde in viâ versus cantuariam, apud Dorkyng, eciam in Soþeray et eciam in aliis pluribus illius provincie, crescit eciam apud Bedyngton iuxta Croyden quam incole patrie illius vocant gorst, quia proprium nomen illius ignorant." (MS. Digby 161, leaf 23, in the Bodleian Library, Oxford.)

[2] "Bibliotheca," p. 48.

remained until the time of the first Pharmacopœia, 1618. Dr. Alleyne[1] speaks thus of them:—

"*Powers of Scabious, Valentia Scabiosæ.*—Take of the juice of green Scabious, pressed out and strained through a cloth, and of Hog's lard cleared of its membranes, each as much as you please. Let the Lard be beat in a stone mortar, and the juice poured in by little at a time, for the conveniency of mixture, and giving its tincture; and then put them together into a proper vessel, to be exposed to the sun, and so that the juice may cover the lard; after nine days put them again into the mortar as before, and throw away that thin and discoloured humidity, which separates upon beating, without rubbing them together; and again put into its vessel for five days. And afterwards beat it again and by little at a time, mix with it fresh juice of scabious, and after a fresh insolation of fifteen days in its proper vessel in the Sun, let it be cleared as before of its watery humidity. Let it then stand again in the same manner for fifteen days longer with fresh juice, and after a little beating let it be kept for use in a glass or earthen vessel. This, we are told by the first compilers of the College Dispensatory, was the contrivance of John Arden, an experienced surgeon at Newark in Nottinghamshire, who lived in the reign of Edward III. After insertion of this, which they had from an ancient manuscript, they particularly direct to repeat the processes with fresh juice till the Lard looks of a deep green; and that is made the measure of the repetition necessary. The powers and honey of Mullein were from the same author, and almost three hundred years ago were in great esteem amongst the surgeons of our own country, though they have now been long in disuse."

"*The Powers of Mullein; Tapsi Valentia.*—Take of the juice of Mullen and of Hog's lard, each as much as you please; let the Lard be cleansed of its membranes and fibres, and broke into small parcels; then beat it with the expressed juice, press out and strain as directed in the preceding process. Let it afterwards be put into a proper vessel for nine or ten days, and then be twice more impregnated with fresh juice until it is quite green. Lastly, after all the humidity that will separate is poured off, beat it again briskly, and put it by in a proper manner for use."

The first contriver of these processes, as appears from the first edition of the College Dispensatory, directs the medicines thus made to be fresh beat once in a month.

[1] "A New English Dispensatory," 1733, p. 336.

"*Honey of Mullen; Tapsimel.*—Take of the juice of Celandine and one part Mullen, of despumated Honey two parts; boil gradually till the juices are evaporated, adding thereto, if the Operator pleases, calcined Vitriol and Alum with Copperas, and again boil secundum artem."

The first College Dispensatory adds from the Author, that "if occasion requires this should be at last boiled up to a pretty thick consistence; and says that it will certainly cure itchings in any part of the body, and is a most noble ointment. But it seems the present Practice hath not faith enough to rely upon it for anything, for neither this nor the foregoing are ever prescribed or made. However, it hath been thought fit to continue such extraordinary discoveries still upon record for the sake of any that may think proper to make trial with them."

It is my pleasant duty, in conclusion, to thank those who have given me much help in the preparation of this volume. First, to Dr. Warner, the Keeper of Manuscripts, who allowed me to study the Sloane MSS. at the British Museum in comfort in the room which is doing duty as the large room; secondly, to Mr. L. Galbraith, who afforded me similar facilities in the University Library at Glasgow; and, lastly, to Mr. Falconer Madan, who made me feel at home in the Bodleian. Lieut.-Col. Walter D. McCaw, Surgeon of the United States Army, responded kindly, promptly and fully to my questions about the only manuscript of Arderne which Dr. Harvey Cushing of Baltimore has been able to obtain tidings of in America. Miss Evaline G. Parker at Oxford, and Miss Margaret E. Thompson in London, have helped me by transcribing obscure passages which I was quite unable to decipher; whilst my friend, Mr. J. H. Noble, has assisted me with the heraldry of the various MSS., a subject of much interest, which I hope some day to consider in greater detail. My obligations to Mr. S. Armitage-Smith are great; and I have endeavoured to show my appreciation of the interest which Dr. Frank Payne has always taken in Arderne, and the help I have received by dedicating to him this edition of his treatises. I have tried to make the text literally accurate, and to elucidate it by such notes as were needed to explain to myself the various difficulties which occurred in reading it. No one can be more conscious of the defects in the notes than myself, but the work has been a labour of love, and if they seem extremely bad it must be remembered that, after all, I am but a surgeon, whose business in life is to act and not to write.

BIBLIOGRAPHY.

The following table shows the manuscripts which I have examined personally at the British Museum, and in Oxford, Cambridge and Glasgow. There is said to be a French version in Paris and a Latin one at Stockholm, but I have not yet been able to obtain any information about them: there is a manuscript in Washington and another in Dublin.

Arderne issued his writings in the form of treatises, written in Latin, and with his own hand. These treatises were afterwards collected and were sometimes translated. The manuscripts therefore contain different combinations. The collection here printed is one of the more usual groups, but the translator has not rendered the whole of the last part on the preparation of various remedies. It is given in greater detail in the Ashmole MS. 1434 in the Bodleian Library.

MANUSCRIPTS OF JOHN OF ARDERNE IN THE VARIOUS LIBRARIES.

I. Practica de Fistula in Ano, &c.

Sæc. xiv. Brit. Museum, Sloane MSS. No. 341, ff. 41–69 b.
„ „ „ No. 3844, ff. 2–16 b.
„ „ „ No. 3548, ff. 65–88.
„ University Library, Glasgow, No. 339.

Sæc. xiv–xv. University Library, Glasgow, No. 112, ff. 38–98.
„ Surgeon-General's Lib., Washington, U.S.A., ff.41–138.

Sæc. xv. Brit. Museum, Sloane MSS. No. 6, ff. 141–154 b. [English].
„ „ „ No. 76, ff. 143 and 144. [English].
„ „ „ No. 238, ff. 99–214.
„ „ „ No. 277, ff. 60 b.–75 b. [English].
„ „ „ No. 347, ff. 122–240.
„ „ „ No. 563, ff. 63–121 b. [English].
„ „ „ No. 795, ff. 96 b.–163 b.
„ „ „ No. 2002, ff. 1–180.
„ „ „ No. 2122, ff. 10–32.
„ „ „ No. 29301, ff. 22–32 b.
„ „ „ No. 8093, ff. 140–174 [English].
„ „ Harleian MSS. No. 3371, ff. 13–39 b.
„ „ „ No. 5401, ff. 34 b.–52.
„ University Library, Glasgow, No. 251, formerly Sloane 2.
„ Bodley's Library, Oxford, Ash. 1434, ff. 11–107.
„ St. John's College, Oxford, No. 132, ff. 68.
„ Emmanuel Coll., Cambridge, No. 69.
„ Royal College of Surgeons, Ireland.

Sæc. xvi. Bodley's Library, Oxford, Ash. 829, ff. 76–80 and 81–115.
„ University Library, Glasgow, No. 135.
„ „ „ „ No. 403.

Sæc. xvii. Brit. Museum, Sloane MSS. No. 1991, ff. 142–159.
„ Bodley's Library, Oxford, Rawl. No. 355 c.

II. Liber Medicinarum sive Receptorum Liber Medicinalium.

Sæc. xiv. Brit. Museum, Sloane MSS. No. 56, ff. 1–100.
„ „ „ No. 335, ff. 1–78 b.
„ „ „ No. 341, ff. 1–40 b.
„ „ „ No. 3548, ff. 26–99.
„ Bodley's Library, Oxford, Digby 161, ff. 16–23 b.
„ St. John's College, Oxford, No. 86, ff. 53.
„ University Library, Glasgow, No. 339, ff. 232.
„ Royal College of Surgeons, Ireland. ? date.

Sæc. xiv–xv. University Library, Glasgow, No. 112.

Sæc. xv. Brit. Museum, Sloane MSS. No. 76, ff. 1–143.
" " " No. 238, ff. 8–96 b.
" " " No. 347, ff. 2–75.
" " " No. 795, ff. 20 b.–96 b.
" " " No. 962, ff. 123 b.–248 b.
" " " No. 2122, ff. 32–74.
" " " No. 29301, ff. 3–22, and 32 b.–47 b.
" Bodley's Library, Oxford, Ash. 1434, ff. 117–131.
" University Library, Glasgow, No. 251.
" Caius Coll., Cambridge, No. 219.
" University Library, Cambridge, No. 292.
" Trinity Coll., Cambridge, No. 1153, ff. 99 + 3.
" Emmanuel Coll., Cambridge, No. 69 [English].

Sæc. xvi. Brit. Museum, Sloane MSS. No. 563, ff. 122–129 b.
" University Library, Glasgow, No. 403.

Sæc. xvii. Brit. Museum, Sloane MSS. No. 1991, ff. 168–224.
" " " No. 2271 [English].
" Bodley's Library, Oxford, Rawl. 355 c.

Sæc. xix. Royal College of Surgeons, England. Transcript of E. H.'s [Sloane 2271] abstract.

III. Commentary "De Judiciis Urinarum."

Sæc. xiv. University Library, Glasgow, No. 328 [English].

IV. Hoc est Speculum Phlebotomiæ.

Sæc. xiv. Brit. Museum, Sloane 56, ff. 1–2.
Sæc. xiv–xv. University Library, Glasgow, No. 112.
" *xv.* " " " No. 251.
" " Emmanuel College, Cambridge No. 69 [English].

V. Scala Sanitatis.

Sæc. xv. Brit. Museum, 1080 A, ff. 31 b.–36 b.

[Sloane MS. 6, leaf 141.]

A tretis extracte of Maistre Iohn Arden of fistula in ano and of fistula in o*þer* placeȝ of þe body and of aposthemeȝ makyng fistuleȝ and of emoraideȝ & tenasmon and of clistereȝ: of certayn oyntementeȝ poudreȝ & oyles.

Fistula in ano.

Fistula in the limbs.

Of Mormales.

Of Piles.

Of Tenesmus.

Of Prolapse.

Of Clysters.

Of Powders.

Of Oils and Waters.

Of Valences.

Sloane MS. 2002, leaf 24, back.

PLATE I.—A Master of Surgery in the fourteenth century.

John Arderne's Treatises on Surgery.

[Sloane 6, leaf 141, back.]

Of the ploge of fistula in ano, and of þe manere of þe leche, and of instrumentis necessary for þe fistule.

[I, I]ohn Arderne fro the first pestilence that was in the ȝere of oure lord 1349 duellid in Newerk in Notyngham-shire vnto the ȝere of oure lord 1370, and ther I helid many men of fistula in ano. Of whiche the first was Sire Adam Eueryngham of laxton-in-the-clay byside Tukkesford; whiche Sire Adam, forsoth, was in Gascone with sir Henry, that tyme named Erle of derby and aftir was made duke of lancastre, a noble and worthi lord. The forsaid sir Adam, forsoth, suffrand fistulam in ano, made for to aske counsel at aƚƚ the lecheȝ and cirurgienȝ that he myȝt fynde in Gascone, at Burdeux, at Briggerac, Tolows, and Neyrbon, and Peyters, and many other places. And all forsoke hym for vncurable; whiche y-se and y-herde, þe forseid Adam hastied for to torne hom to his contre. And when he come home, he did of al his knyȝtly clothinges and cladde mornyng clothes, in purpose of abydyng dissoluyng, or lesyng, of his body beyng niȝ to hym. At last I, forseid Iohn Arderne, y-souȝt and couenant y-made, come to hym and did my cure to hym and, oure lord beyng mene,[1] I helid hym perfitely within half a ȝere; and aftirward, hole and sounde, he ledde a glad lif by 30 ȝere and more, ffor whiche cure I gatte myche honour and louyng þurȝ al ynglond. And the forseid duke of lancastre and many othir gentileȝ wondred ther-of. Aftirward I cured hugon derlyng of ffowick of Balne by Snayþe. Aftirward I

Sir Adam de Everyngham Arderne's first patient.

He had lost all hope of recovery,

but lived in health and strength from about 1346 until 1387 after an operation.

1 Domino mediante.

Patients cured by Arderne,

knights and priests,

merchants and friars.

[* leaf 142]

Arderne gives the glory to God and humbles himself.

cured Ioħn Schefeld of Briȝtwell a-side Tekyll. Aftirward I cured sir Reynald Grey, lord of Wilton in Waleȝ and lord of Schirlond biside Chesterfelde, whiche asked counsel at the most famose leches of yngland, and none availed hym. Aftirward I cured sir Henry Blakborne, clerk, Tresorer of the lord Prince of Waleȝ. Aftirward I cured Adam Oumfray of Shelforde byside Notyngham, and sir Ioħn, preste of the same toune; and Ioħn of holle of Shirlande; and Sir Thomas hamelden, p*ar*sone of langare in the Vale of Beuare. Aftirward I curid frere Thomas Gu*n*ny, custode of the frere Myno*ur*s of Ȝorke. Aftirward, in the ȝere of oure lord 1370, I come to london, and ther I cured Ioħn Colyn, Mair of Northampton, that asked counsel at many licheȝ. Aftirward I helid or cured Hew Denny, ffisshmanger of london, in Briggestrete; and William Polle, and Raufe Double; and oon that was called Thomas Broune, that had 15 holes by whiche went out wynde with egestious odour; that is to sey, 8 holeȝ of the to[ne] p*ar*ty of the ersse, and 7 on the tothir side; Of whiche some holeȝ was distant fro the towell by the space of the handbrede of a man, so that bothe his buttok*is* was so vlcerat and putrefied with-in that the quitour and filthe went out ich day als mych as an egg-shel miȝt take. Aft*er*ward *I cured 4 freręȝ p*re*chours, that is to sey ffrere Ioħn Writell, ffrere Ioħn haket, ffrere Petre Browne, ffrere Thomas Apperley, and a ȝong man called Thomas Voke. Of whiche forseid som had only on hol y-distau*n*te fro the towel by oon ynche, or by two, or by thre. And other[s] had 4 or 5 holeȝ procedyng to the codde of the testicleȝ; And many other mane*rs* of whiche the tellyng war ful hard. All thise forseid cured I afore the makyng of this boke. Oure lord Ih*es*u y-blessid God knoweth that I lye not, and therfore no man dout of this, þof-al old famo*us* men and ful clere in studie haue confessed tham that thei fande nat the wey of curacion in this case. ffor god, that is deler or rewarder of wisdom, hath hid many thingis fro wise men and sliȝe whiche he vouchesaf aftirward for to shewe to symple men. Therfore al men þat ar to come aftirward witte thai that old maistreȝ war noȝt bisie ne pertinaceȝ in sekyng and serchyng of this forseid cure. But for thai miȝt noȝt take the hardnes of it at the first frount, thei kest it vtterly byhinde þair bak. Of whiche, forsoþ, som demed it holy for to be incurable; oþer applied doutful opinions. Therfore for-als-miche in hard thingis it spedith to studiers for to perseuere and abide, and for to turne subtily thair wittes. ffor it is opned not to þam that ar passand but to tham þat ar perseuerand.[1] Therfore to the honour of god almyȝti that hath opned witte to me that I shuld fynde tresour hidde in the felde of studiers that long tyme and [with] pantyng breest I haue swette and trauailed ful bisily and pertinacely in diuanudiis.[2] As my faculte sufficeþ without fair spekyng of endityng, I haue brouȝt for to shew it openly to tham that cometh aftur, our lord beyng me[ne] and this boke. Noȝt that I shewe myself more worthi of louyng of suche a gifte than other, but that I greue not god, and for the dragme that he hath giffen to me that I be not constreyned for treson. Therfore I pray that the grace of the holy gost be to this werke, that he vouch-saf for to spede it; that tho thingis whiche in wrokyng trewly I am ofte tymes experte, I may plenerly explane tham in this litel boke. And this I sey that I know noȝt in al my tyme, ne hard not in al my tyme, of any man, nouþer in yngland ne in partieȝ biȝond þe see, that kouthe cure fistula in ano; outake a frere minour that was with the prince of Waleȝ in gascon & gyan, whiche rosed & bosted hym that he had cured the forseid sekenes. And at london he deceyued many men; and when he miȝt noȝt cure som man, he made suggestion to tham that no man miȝt cure tham, and that affermed he with sweryng that ȝif the fistule war dried, that the pacient at the next shuld noȝt eschape dethe; whiche, forsoþe, y-lefte & forsake of hym I cured perfitely. And to remoue false opinions of ignorant men, for witnes I putte experience. Auicen, forsoþ, seiþ, 'experience ouercomeþ reson'; and galien in pantegni seiþ, 'No man *ow for to trust in reson al-oon but ȝit it be proued of experience.' And he seith in anoþer place, 'Experience without reson is feble, & so is reson withoute experience fest vnto hym.' Neþer-

The old masters in surgery neglected cases of fistula,

but Arderne devoted himself specially to their study, and fears to hide his talent in a napkin (Matt. xxv. 14–29).

No one in England or abroad undertakes cases of fistula except one minorite in the retinue of the Black Prince, and he is a fraud.

Avicenna's opinion of the value of practice and theory.

[* leaf 142 back]

[1] non transeuntibus sed perseverantibus pulsantibus aperitur.

[2] "diu avidius" says the best Latin text.

Arderne recognises that some fistulæ are incurable.

The qualities required in a good surgeon: piety, charity, modesty, wariness, gravity, careful in the company he keeps; studious, sober, not gluttonous, nor cynical;

lesse I afferme no3t that I mi3t hele al ffistulae in ano. ffor som ben vncurable as it shal be seid [more fully][1] within when I shal trete of tham. ffirst it bihoueth hym that wil p*ro*fite in this crafte that he sette god afore eu*er*more in all his werkis, and euermore calle mekely with hert and mouth his help; and som tyme visite of his wynnyngis poure men aftir his my3t, that thai by thair prayers may gete hym grace of the holy goste. And that he be no3t y-founden temerarie or bosteful in his seyingis or in his dedes; and abstene he hym fro moche speche, and most among grete men; and answere he slei3ly to thing*is* y-asked, that he be no3t y-take in his wordes. fforsoth 3if his werkes be oft tyme knowen for to discorde fro his wordes and his byhestis, he shal be halden more vnworthi, and he shal ble*m*myssh his oone gode fame. Wherfore seiþ a versifio*ur*, 'vincat opus verbum, minuit iactantia famam'; 'lat werke ou*er*come thi worde, for boste lesseneþ gode lose.' Also be a leche no3t mich laughyng ne mich playing. And als moche as he may withoute harme fle he þe felawshippe of knafes and of vnu[n]este persones. And be he eu*er*more occupied in thingis that biholdith to his crafte; outhir rede he, or studie he, or write or pray he; for the excercyse of bokes worshippeþ a leche. ffor why; he shal boþ byholden and he shal be more wise. And aboue al þise it profiteth to hym that he be founden euermore sobre; ffor dronkenne3 destroyeth al vertu and bringith it to not, as seith a wise man, 'Ebrietas frangit quicquid sapiencia tangit': 'Dronkenes breketh what-so wisdom toucheth.' Be he content in strange places of metes and drinkes þe*r* y-founden, vsyng mesure in al thing*is*. ffor the wise man seith, 'Sicut ad om*ne* q*uo*d est mensuram pon*er*e p*ro*dest, Sic sine mensura dep*er*it om*ne* q*uo*d est': 'As it p*ro*fiteth to putte mesure to al thing that is, So without mesure p*er*issheþ all þing þat is.' Skorne he no man. ffor of that it is seid, 'Deridens alios non inderisus abibit': 'He that skorneþ other men shal not go away vnskorned.' 3if ther be made speche to hym of any leche, nouther sette he hym at nou3t ne preise hym to mich or *com*mende hym, but thus may he curteysly answere; 'I haue

[1] "Plenius" says the Latin text.

noȝt vrey knowleche of hym,[1] but I lerned noȝt ne I haue not herd of hym but gode and honeste.' And of this shal honour and thankyngis of eche p*ar*ty encresse and multiplie to hym; aftur this, honour is in the honorant & noȝt in the honored. Considere he noȝt ou*er* openly the lady or the douȝters or oþ*er* fair wy*m*men in gret me*n*nes[2] [houses] ne p*ro*fre tham noȝt to kisse, ne touche not p*ri*uely ne ap*er*tely thair pappes, ne thair handes, ne thair share,[3] that he renne noȝt into the indignacion of the lord ne of noon of his. In as moche as he may, greue he no seruant, but *gete he thair loue and thair gode wille. Abstene he hym fro harlotrie als wele in wordes as in dedes in euery place, for ȝif he vse hym to harlotery in priue places som tyme in opene place ther may falle to hym vnworship of yuel vsage; aftir þat it is seyde, 'Pede super colles pedes vbi pedere nolles.' 'ffart vpon hilleȝ and thou shalt fart whar thou wolde noȝt agayn thi willeȝ.' And it is seid in anoþ*er* place, 'Shrewed speche[4] corru*m*pith gode man*er*s.' When seke men, forsoth, or any of tham bysyde comeþ to the leche to aske help or cou*n*sel of hym, be he noȝt to tham ou*er* felle ne ou*er* homely, but mene in beryng aftir the askyngis of the p*er*soneȝ[5]; to som reu*er*ently, to som comonly. ffor aft*er* wise men, Ou*er* moche homelynes bredeþ dispisyng. Also it spedeþ þat he haue semyng excusacions that he may not incline to þair askyng*is*, without harmyng or without indignacion of som gret man or frende, or for necessarie occupacion. Or feyne he hym hurt, or for to be seke, or som other couenable cause by whiche he may likely be excused. Therfor, ȝif he will fauou*r*e to any ma*n*nes askyng, make he couenant for his trauaile, and take it byforehandeȝ. But avise þe leche hym-self wele that he giffe no certayn answer in any cause, but he se first þe sikenes and the maner of it; and whan he haþ seen and assaied it, þof-al hym seme that the seke may be heled, neþ*er*lesse he shal make p*ro*nosticacion to þe pacient þe p*er*ileȝ to come ȝif the cure be differred. And ȝif he se þe pacient persewe bisily the cure,[6] þan after that þe state of þe pacient askeþ aske he boldly more or lesse; but eu*er* be he warre of scarse askyng*is*, ffor

courteous, and not jealous of other leeches;

continent,

friendly to servants, [* leaf 143]

chaste;

easy of address, neither too rough nor too familiar

not too ready to undertake a case, and always to see it before giving advice;

to have a clear understanding about the fee before operating.

[1] "non habeo de eo veram notitiam" says the Latin version.

[2] in domibus magnatum.

[3] aut pubem.

[4] colloquia mala.

[5] nimis severus nec nimis familiaris sed in gestu mediocris secundum exigentiam personarum.

[6] et si viderit patientem attentius curam prosequi.

ou*er* scarse askyngis setteþ at not both þe markette and the thing. Therfore for the cure of fistula in ano, when it is curable, aske he co*m*petently, of a worthi man and a gret an hundred marke or fourty pounde, wi*þ* robeȝ and feeȝ[1] of an hundred shillyng terme of lyfe by ȝere. Of lesse men fourty pounde, or fourty marke aske he without feeȝ; And take he noȝt lesse þan an hundred shillyng*is*. ffor neuer in all my lyf toke I lesse than an hundred shillyng for cure of that sekenes. Ne*þer*lesse do another man as hym þink bett*er* and more spedefulle. And ȝif the pacientes or thair frendeȝ or seruauntȝ aske by how moche tyme he hopeth to hele it, eu*er*more lat the leche byhete þe double þat he supposeth to spede by half; that is ȝif the leche hope to hele þe pacient by twenty wekes—that is the comon course of curyng—adde he so many ouer. ffor it is better that the terme be lengthed þan the cure. ffor p*ro*longacion of the cure giffeþ cause of dispairyng to the pacienteȝ when triste to the leche is moste hope of helthe. And ȝif the pacient considere or wondre or aske why that he putte hym so long a tyme of curyng, siþe þat he heled hym by the half, answere he that it was for that the pacient was strong-herted, and suffrid wele sharp þingis, and that he was of gode complexion and hadde able flesshe to hele; & feyne he othir causes pleseable to the pacient, ffor pacienteȝ of syche wordeȝ are proude and delited. Also dispose a leche *hym that in clothes and othir apparalyngis be he honeste, noȝt likkenyng hymself in apparalyng or berying to mynistralleȝ, but in clothing and beryng shew he the maner of clerkes. ffor why; it semeth any discrete man y-cladde with clerkis clothing for to occupie gentil me*n*neȝ bordeȝ. ¶ Haue the leche also clene handes and wele shapen naileȝ & clensed fro all blaknes and filthe. And be he curtaise at lordeȝ bordeȝ, and displese he noȝt in wordes or dedes to the gestes syttyng by; here he many þingis but speke he but fewe. ¶ For a wise man seith, 'It semeth more to vse the eres than þe tunge'; And in an-o*þer* place, 'ȝif thou had bene stille thou had bene holden a philosophre.' And whan he shal speke, be the wordeȝ short, and, als mich as he may, faire and resonable

The cost of an operation.

Prognosis as regards the duration of cure and the reasons thereof.

[* leaf 143, back]

The leech to be dressed soberly,

to be clean in his person,

to cultivate silence.

[1] cum robis et feodis.

and withoute sweryng. ¶ Be war that ther be neu*er* founden double worde[1] in his mouthe, ffor ȝif he be founden trew in his wordes ffewe or noon shal doute in his dedeȝ. Lere also a ȝong leche gode p*ro*uerbeȝ p*er*tenyng to his crafte in counforty*ng* of pacienteȝ. ¶ Or ȝif pacientes pleyne that ther medicynes bene bitter or sharp or sich other, than shal the leche sey to the pacient thus; "It is redde in the last lesson of matyns of the natiuitè of oure lord that oure lorde Ih*esus* criste come into this world for the helthe of mannes kynd to the maner of a gode leche and wise. And when he cometh to the seke man he sheweth hym medicynes, som liȝt and som hard; and he seiþ to the seke man, 'Ȝif þou wilt be made hole þise and þise shal thou tak.' ¶ Also in another place in an omely vpon the gospel of the soneȝ of Zebedee, wher þer moder askid seying, 'lord, sey þat my two sones sitte in thy kyngdome, þe tone on þi riȝt hand and the toþ*er* on the left.' And Ih*esus* answeryng seide, 'Ȝe wote neuer what ȝe aske'; þan seid he to the soneȝ of Zebedee, 'May ȝe drink þe chalice þat I am to drink?' Þai seid to him, 'We may'; as ȝif he seid to þam, 'ȝif ȝoure soule or mynd couaite þat deliteþ, drinke þe first þat soroweþ or akeþ.' And so by bitter drink*is* of confeccion it is come to the ioyes of helþe."[2] Ou*er* that hym ow to comforte þe pacient in monysshyng hym that in anguissheȝ he be of gret hert. ffor gret hert makeþ a man hardy and strong to suffre sharp þingis and greuous: And it is a gret vertue and an happy, ffor Boecius seiþ, De disciplina scolariu*m*, 'He is noȝt worþi of þe poynt of swetnes that kan noȝt be lymed with greuyng of bitternes. ffor why; a strong medicyne answerith to a strong sekenes.' And þ*er*on seiþ a wise man, 'Be no cure sene heuy or greuous to the to whiche foloweþ ane heleful effecte.' ¶ And in anoþ*er* place it is seid, 'happy or blessid be þat day þat ordeyneþ mery ȝeres.' And anoþ*er* seith, 'he may neuer be in reste of body þat is oute of reste of soule; I wil suffre lesse þingis þat I suffre noȝt more greuous.' It semeþ a gret herted man for to suffre sharp þingis; he, forsoþ, þat is wayke of hert is noȝt in way of curacion, ffor *why; for-soþe in al [* leaf 144]

and not to be foul-mouthed or lying.

He should have a store of comfortable sayings.

The effect of mind on body.

[1] dupliciter sermo.

[2] Si mens vestra appetat quod demulcat, prius bibite quod dolet et sic per amarum poculum confectionis pervenitur ad gaudia salutis.

my lyf I haue sene but fewe laborante in þis vice heled in any sikenes: þerfore it is to be-war to wise men þat þei entremette noȝt with sich. ffor whi; þe wise man seiþ, 'All þinges ar hard to a waik hert man, for þai trow euermore yuelleȝ to be nyȝe to þam; þei drede euermore, þai suffre no þingis, þai are euermore vnstable and vnwise; þerfore a versifiour seiþ of tham, '*Quominus*[1] nil pacior paciendi me tenet horror': þat is þof-al I suffre no-þing, vgglynes of suffryng holdeth me. ¶ Also it spedeth þat a leche kunne talke of gode taleȝ and of honest that may make þe pacientes to laugh, as wele of the biblee as of other tragedieȝ; & any othir þingis of which it is noȝt to charge whileȝ þat þey make or induce a liȝt hert to þe pacient or þe sike man. ¶ Discouer neuer the leche vnwarly the counselleȝ of his pacienteȝ, als wele of men as of wymmen, ne[2] sette noȝt oon to anoþer at noȝt, þof-al he haue cause, þat he be noȝt gilty of counsell; ffor ȝif a man se þe hele wele anoþer mannes counsel he wil trist better in þe. Many þinges, forsoþe, bene to be kepte of a leche, wiþoute þese þat ar seid afore, þat may noȝt be noted here for ouer moche occupying. But it is noȝt to dout þat if þe forseid be wele kepte þat-ne þai shal giffe a gracious going to þe vser to þe hiȝte of worship and of wynnyng[3]; for Caton seiþ, 'Virtutem primam puta esse compescere linguam': The first vertu trow you to be to refreyne þe tong. Aftur al þise it houeth that he knowe þe names of þe instrumentis þat perteneth to þe cure of þe fistule, withoute whiche a leche may noȝt wele spede hym. Of whiche þe first is called 'Sequere me'—'follow me'—whose shap is shewed wher þe instrumenteȝ ar paynted [fig. 1]. And it is called 'Sequere me' for it is þe first instrument pertenyng to þat werk; for a lech ow for to serche þer-with þe way of þe fistule whider it goþ, wheþer by þe middeȝ of longaon or noȝt. And it ow to be made on þe same maner as wymmen vseþ in þair heuedeȝ,[4] and of þe same metal; and it ow to be smal þat it may liȝtly be plied & replied. And be þe heuedeȝ[5] als little as þai may wele be, elleȝ þai miȝt noȝt wele entere þe mouþ of þe fistule for þe streitnes of it.

The leech should have also a good stock of merry tales,

and should most strictly keep his own counsel about the patient.

The names of the instruments used in the operation for fistula:

the probe,

[1] Quamvis.

[3] quia ea exercenti ad culmen honoris et lucis aditum præbeant generosum.

[4] in capitibus.

[5] capita.

[2] MS. þe.

ffor why; oft tymeȝ ffistule in ano hath riȝt smale holeȝ, so þat som tyme þai shew noȝt but þat þ*er* appereth bolnyng in þe mouþes of þam. Aft*er*ward is þ*er* anoþ*er* instrument, þat is called 'Acus rostrata,' a snowted nedle, for it hath þe tone heued like a snowte, and in þe toþ*er* an yȝe like a nedel by whiche þredes ow to be drawen agayn by middeȝ of þe fistule, as it shal be seid *with*in in his place. And it ow to be of siluer, as it is paynted; and it ow to be no grett*er* ne lenger in þe snowte þan as it is paynted, but it ow to be longer atte þe left, þat it contene in al 8 ynches in lenghþe.[1] ¶ Þe þrid instrument is called 'tendiculu*m*,' and it ow to be made of boxe or of anoþir competent tree, nouþ*er* lenger ne gretter þan his shap is paynted. And it ow to haue an hole þurgh in þe side, as it is peynted, In whiche hole be þer putte *[2] in a wrayst,[3] by middeȝ of whiche wraiste in þe ouer ende shal be a litel hole þurgh whiche shal be putte þe two endeȝ of grete þrede four folde, goyng atte firste by þe towel[4] and þe hole of þe fistule; whiche þrede is called ffrenu*m* cesaris, and the whiche also goyng atuyx þe wraiste, in wraistyng þe skynne atuyx þe tewel & þe fistule be faste constreyned aboue þe snowte of þe nedel, vnto þat kittyng be done. 'Siringa' is an holow instrument by þe middeȝ, and it ow to be made of the shappe as it is peynted here, nouþ*er* gretter ne lenger, but euen aft*er* þe shappe as it is peynted here; ne haue it noȝt but oon hole in þe neþ*er* ende or smaller ende, as it is peynted here [*see p.* 10, Plates II and III].

the grooved director,

the dilator,

the peg.

[* leaf 144, back]

the "Syringe."

[1] ad minus octo pollices contineat.

[3] "unum vertile Anglicè 'a wrayste' imponatur."

[4] per anum.

[2] The words from here to the end of this page are reproduced in facsimile in Plate III.

Of þe apostemeȝ in þe lure causyng þe fistu*le*, and þe cure of tham.

[leaf 145]

Ischio-rectal abscess a common cause of fistula.

2. [T]hof-al þe principal entent was for to trete de fistula in ano, Neþ*er*les it spedeþ first for to touche somwhat of aposteme bredyng þ*er*-in or niȝe,[1] siþe oft tyme apostemeȝ bredyng þ*er* bene cause of fistule or of cancre. ffor, after aucto*ur*s, Aposteme y-bred in any place of þe body, if it be not y-helid by þre or four moneþes, it is turned into a fistule or a cancre. Therfore when ther falleth ane aposteme in þe lure or niȝe[1] þou shalt knowe it by þese signes; þat is by bolnyng, akyng, bry*n*nyng, ȝekyng & prikkyng.[2] And the pacient for akyng and anguissh may nouþer sitte ne ligge ne slepe. Whiche apperyng, ffirst it is to labo*ur* to þe slakyng or esyng of the akyng and brennyng and of oþ*er* accidenteȝ wi*th*out rep*er*cussione. ffor in þe lure ow noȝt to be rep*er*cussion, siþe it is ane emu*n*ctory, and in emu*n*ctorieȝ ow it noȝt to be done; þese bene emu*n*ctorieȝ:—þe armeholes, þe þeholes, þe chawelleȝ,[3] &c. And witte þou aft*er* Gilbertyne þat ane aposteme beyng wi*th*in þe lure is cured wi*th* þe infusion of oile roset in which is ceruse distempred, or led brent, or litarge, or all þise if þai be hadde, or with þe ȝolk of an ey. And he be euermore warre of paynyng of egestion. And ȝif his wombe be costyue[4] be it softned þat þe hardnes of þe ordure bryng noȝt in anguissh in egestion doyng. And be it softned wi*th* ane emplastre of malueȝ & swynes grese; Or with wat*er* of decocciou*n* of malueȝ and branne, with oile or butter fressh, or suche other, and be it ȝette in by a clisterye. Therfore take oyle roset and medle it with þe ȝolke of a rawe ey in euen porcion. Aftir putte it in a little bleddere, þan take a Nastar of tree[5] and putte it in þe bladder and bynde it aboute wiþ a strong þrede, and enoynt þe for ende wele with oyle roset, and softly putte it in þe lure and presse þat is in þe bleddre wi*th* þi fyngres in-to þe lure. þis, forsoþe, swageþ and softeneþ þe bry*n*nyng, þe prikkyng, smertyng & akyng, and comforteþ þe membre in boþe cause,[6] þat is

Signs of an ischio-rectal abscess.

Gilbertyn's treatment with litharge and rose oil.

A plaster of mallows and pork fat is good if injected through a glyster pipe.

[1] vel exterius prope anum.

[2] per tumorem et dolorem, ardorem atque pruritum et puncturam.

[3] "axillæ inguina et fauces," says the Latin text.

[4] et si venter constipetur.

[5] tunc accipe unum instrumentum ligneum, concavum per medium, quod Nastare ligneum vocatur.

[6] in omnibus membris corporis.

boþe in hote and colde. ffor, after auctores, Oile roset coldeþ ane hote membre and hoteþ ane colde membre[1]; and it doþ many oþer profites þere and in al þe membres of þe body. And þerfore a gode leche puruey[2] hym þat he want neuer oyle roset, siþe þer procedeþ of it many helpyngis to mannes body; for why; after Galien to euery akyng hote oile roset is mytigatif. Vpon þe aposteme, forsoþe, vtward be putte a gode emplastre and riȝt maturatif of diaquilon resolute with oile roset, or oile of lilieȝ, or of camamill, or dialtred,[3] or comon oyle, þat is oyle of olyue, or swyne grese, or gandres,[4] or maulerdes,[5] or hennes grese. ffor whi; diaquilon þus y-ordeyned and put-to matureþ colde materieȝ & resolueþ & mollifieþ hard materies. Also be þer made suche a vntment þat is riȝt mitigatiue. Recipe: tame comon malueȝ[6] M. i or M. ij, & brisse þam in a morter, and put þam in a quart of oyle of olyueȝ and lat þam putrifie þerin 7 dayes or 9. After boile þam long at þe fire vnto þe oile be wele grene; after cole it and * kepe it: þis oyntment is ryȝt mitigatiue of akyng of aposteme3, and mollifieȝ þan if it be put vpon [tham] hote with lana succida. Lana succida is wolle þat groweth atuix þe leggeȝ of ane ewe about þe vdder, ful of swet,[7] noȝt y-wasshe, and it opneþ strongly and consumeth; oyle, forsoþe, of propirte holdeþ opne and draweth and swageþ akyng. If, forsoþ, þou haue noȝt lanam succidam þan dippe a lyn clout in þe forseid oyntement and putte it hotte vppon and bynde it warly þat it fal not away. Also ane emplastre of þe forseid malueȝ is a ful gode maturatif and mitigatif of akyng in apostemeȝ of þe lure and of wymmenȝ pappeȝ, and to al oþer apostemeȝ þat nedeþ maturacion. And it is made þus. Recipe: malueȝ tame M. i. or ij; seþe þam in watir to þai wax softe, þan put þam out of þe watre and presse oute þe watre of þam, and aftir hakke þam small wiþ a sharp knyf on a clene borde; þan frye þam in a panne ouer þe fire with comon oyle or butter or swynes grese, Or, if þe pacient be riche or noble, with som of þe forseid oileȝ. And aftir vpon clene stuppes be it put on þe aposteme. And witte þou here þat if þou may haue wormed it profiteþ mich in curyng if it be

A prescription for a soothing ointment.

[* leaf 145, back]

Lana succida what it is

Prescription for an ointment for an abscess of the breast.

[1] oleum ros. membrum supercalescens infrigidat et super infrigidatum calefecit.

[2] "provideat."

[3] dialthæa.

[4] anatis.

[5] mallardes.

[6] "Malvas domesticas communes."

[7] sudore imbuta.

Nota. Pappis [of] wommen.

soden & made wiþ þe forseid malueȝ, for þat emplastre is best mitigatiue of akyng of pappes, & bryngeþ in quytour and conforteþ þe place, and makeþ þe mater for to vapour by þe poreȝ. And for certeyn it availeþ in al aposteneȝ in eu*er*y place of þe body, and also in many brissureȝ. With þis emplastre in cures of pappes I haue y-gette many worshippeȝ and benefetes, for certaynly it is soue*r*aynly mitigatyue. But witte þou aft*er* all auctours—and I haue p*ro*ued it for certayn exp*er*ience—þ*at* ane aposteme bredyng nere þe lure owe not to abide to it breste by itself, but þe leche owe bisily for to fele wiþ his fynger þe place of the aposteme, and wher-so is founden any softenes, þ*er*, þe pacient noȝt wittyng, warly, be it boldely opned wiþ a ful sharp lancette, þat þe quitour and þe corrupte blode may gone oute. Or elleȝ, forsoþe þe gutte or þarme þat is called longaon, þat deserueþ to þe lure, shal be bristen wiþ-in þe lure, and p*re*sed byfore þat þe aposteme be bristen withoute-forþe. Whiche case byfallyng, if it al-oonly brest within it is of hard cure, and þan shal þ*er* be ragadieȝ or frousingeȝ, fforsoþ if it briste boþe w*it*h*in* and with-out, þan may it neu*er* be cured but by a ful exp*er*te cirurgien in his crafte. ffor than may it þe firste day be called a fistule; siþe a fistule is noȝt elleȝ þan ane vlcus vndesiccable, and for it is vndesiccable, þ*er*fore by consequens it is vncurable, siþe no wonde ne vlcus may be heled but if it may be dried. Som tyme it bifalleth som men for to haue ane hole apperyng outward al-oonly, p*er*syng þurȝ þe longaon w*it*h*in* þe lure by þe space of ane ynche or of tuo, and bisyde þat anoþ*er* hole w*it*h-out, noȝt p*er*syng þe longaon w*it*h-in-forþ. And I haue sene som haue 7 or 9 holeȝ on þe tone p*ar*ty of þe buttokkis, and 6 or 5 on þe toþ*er* p*ar*ty, of whiche noon of þam, outake oon, p*er*sed longaon. And I haue sene som haue 2 or 3 holeȝ on þe buttokke, and 2 or 3 descendyng *doun into þe codde of þe testiculeȝ. And I haue sene som haue oon hole or many in þe tone buttok, and oon or tuo on þe p*ar*ty of þe ȝerde p*er*syng als wele longaon as þe ȝerde. And in þis case, as by my demyng, sich pacientes bene vncurable, and þat for fistulyng of þe

Arderne has used this ointment with benefit in many cases.

An ischio-rectal abscess should not be allowed to burst, but should be opened as soon as it softens,

otherwise chronic ulceration and fistula may follow,

for a fistula is only an ulcer that cannot be dried up.

The results of a fistula.

[* leaf 146]

Arderne cured a priest of a urethral abscess at Master Geoffrey Scrope's house in Lincoln.

ȝerde. And þat may be knowen, for som-tyme þe sp*er*me goþ oute by þe hole of þe ȝerde infistulate, and som-tyme vryne or bothe. Neþ*er*lesse I cured a preste, at lincolne in þe house of Maistre Giffray Scrope, þat had aposteme in his ȝerde, of whiche als wele vryne as quitour come doune into his codde, and sometyme blode went oute by þe hole of þe ȝerde, and his testicules war bolned out of mesure. Therfore, first, I putte on his testiculeȝ oon oyntement ruptorye, and I made an hole by whiche went out bothe vryne and quit*our*; þis i-do, þ*er* shewed ane bolnyng vnderneþe in þe ȝerde riȝt be þe lure, whiche I opned wiþ a ruptorie; whiche y-opned, þ*er* went out boþe quitour and vryne. Whom y-cured p*er*fitely, oure lord beyng mene[1]; but for certeyne his lure & longaon war vnhurte. And witte þou þat þis cure was ful hard. Þ*er*fore in suche þingis be a leche avised and discrete. Also a leche owe to be circu*m*specte in his askyng*is*, þat he enquere bisily of þe pacient if he fele ony tyme ventositeȝ or egestionȝ go out by þe holes of þe fistule. Also enquere he of þe pacient ȝif he fele any heuynes or greuousnes in his heued; Or if it appere to hym þ*at* þe house some-tyme is turned vp-so-doune[2] as it shuld falle, and þe pacient may noȝt for drede of fallyng enclyne to þe erthe; And if þe pacient fele akyng and heuynes or greuousnes in his lendeȝ[3] and feblenes in his stomake. Also sey he to þe pacient þus: 'I wote þat þe kynde of þe fistule is soche þ*at* somtyme it is opned by itself and putteþ out quitour, somtyme þikke and somtyme þynne, somtyme watery and somtyme blody. And somtyme it is closed be itself, & so by a moneþ or more þ*er* renneþ no-þing out; and eft-soneȝ it bigynneþ to ake or þat it caste out quit*our*. And aftirward it is opned by itself, and renneþ as it is seid afore, and aftirward it is sperred.'[4] ffor suche p*ro*nosticacions sheweþ and tokneth to þe pacient þat þe leche is exp*er*te in þe knowyng of þe fistule, and so þe pacient wil better trist vnto hym. And witte þou, aftir Bernard of Gordon, þat þe synoweȝ closyng and openyng þe lure haþe festnyng *with* þe stomake and wiþ þe ventriculeȝ of þe brayne, And for this cause suche

Urethral fistulæ are sometimes associated with uræmic symptoms,

which Bernard de Gordon teaches are due to a connection between the muscles of the pelvic floor, the stomach, and the brain.

[1] Domino mediante.

[2] ut si appareat ei quod domus subvertatur.

[3] "et si sentiat gravitatem in lumbis."

[4] et postea clauditur.

pacienteȝ ar som tyme vexed in þe heued[1] and in þe stomak. When þe leche, forsoþe, haþ talked þus to þe pacient, as it is seid, and þe pacient aske & p*er*sew for to be cured of hym, aske þan first þe siȝt of þe sekenes; Whiche y-sene, be þe leche war þat he put noȝt his fynger in þe lure of þe pacient, ne shewe no pryue instrumenteȝ wher-of þe pacient myȝt wonder or be aferd; or if p*er*auenture þe pacient haue wilyly broȝt in w*ith* hym any leche for to aspye, as I haue oft tyme sene. But considere þe leche bisily þe maner of þe fistule, & p*er*ceyue if it be curable. Ȝit[2] a leche ow for *to feyne p*er*ileȝ and hardenes of curyng, and for to make p*ro*nosticacions wilely þat þe sikenes askeþ long tyme of curyng, for þat þat þe medicyneȝ y-putte to may not abyde long for purgyng of þe wombe, and for moche moystenes goyng out of þe lure, and for many oþir lettyngis, as for þe lure is to streyte, or þe buttokkes be to grete or hard, or for þe pacient is waike of herte or vnobedient for to p*er*sew his cure or for to kepe his diete, and for many oþ*er* þat hym ow for to feyne on his owne heued þat he supposeth be necessarye.[3] And þise p*ro*nosticated, if þe pacient stond stedfastly þat he be cured, or aske if he may be cured, þan sey þe leche þus: 'I dout noȝt, oure lord beyng mene,[4] and þi gode pacience folowyng, ȝif þou wilt c*om*petently make satisfaccion to me, as sich a cure—noȝt litle to be co*m*mended—askeþ, þat ne þing*is* y-kept þat ow to be kepte, and y-lefte þat ow to be lefte, as it is seyde, I shal mow bryng þis cure to a loueable ende and heleful.' And þan acorde þay of couenant, of whiche couenaunt—al excusacione y-put abak—take he þe half byfore handeȝ[5]; And þan assigne a day to þe pacient when he will bygynne. In þe mene tyme, forsoþe, ordeyne þe leche redy his medicynes and his instrumentis; þat is to sey þat he haue first two spongieȝ or þre at þe lest, & a rasour or a ful sharp launcet, and oþ*er* instrumentis named afore, as Sequere me, Acum rostratam, Tendiculu*m*; And silke þredes, and lyn cloutes, and girdelleȝ, and oþ*er* þat ar seid afore and to be seid here-after. Haue he also redy a medicyne restrictyue of blode, and warme or leuke watre, and all

The method of operating not to be revealed to the patient or to his leech.

[* leaf 146, back]

Questions to be answered before operating on a fistula.

The prognosis of an operation.

Arrangements for the payment of the fee.

Preparations for the operation.

[1] in capite.

[2] Nihilominus.

[3] quæ debet capite proprio figere quæ sibi constiterit fore necessaria.

[4] Domino mediante.

[5] Quo peracto medium pretii præ manibus capiat omni excusatione propositâ.

oþir necesarieȝ, þat no-þing wante þat the leche may nede in his wirchyng. And ou*er* al this it is best & most sikir þat he kutte noȝt in þe lure ne do no violence ne greuousnes to it in þe tyme þat þe mone is in Scorpion, or Libra, or sagittari*us*, for þan of astronomyeȝ is forbede þer kuttyng. ffor as wille sou*er*ayne astronomieȝ and astrologiens, þat is to sey Ptholome*us*,[1] Pictagoras,[2] Rasis, and Haly, &c. A cyrurgien ow noȝt for to kutte or brenne in any membre of a mannes body, ne do fleobotomye whiles þe mone is in a signe gou*er*nyng or tokenyng þat membre.[3]

Choice of a day for operating.

[1] Ptolomæus, [2] Pythagoras.

---

[3] The Latin texts contain a chapter headed

Nota de cognitione signorum Lunæ.

Si quis scire et invenire voluerit in quo signo cœli fuerit Luna omni die, primo sciat signum in quo Luna soli conjungatur et diem conjunctionis per kalendarium. Quo invento tunc scias quod ab illa hora diei vel noctis in qua fuerit conjunctio usque ad talem horam diei sequentis completur, prima dies Lune. Postea computa quot sunt dies ab imprimatione prædicta usque ad diem de quo queris in kalenderio. Tunc videndum est in tabula precidente ubi invenitur numerus ille. Quo invento, queratur in superiori capite tabulæ sub quo signo Luna fuerit pr'ma sub quo recte descendens transeas donec directe perveneas ad signum correspondens Linealiter numero ætatis Lunæ predictæ, et in illo signo existit Luna eodem die. Et nota quod in ista computatione dies naturalis ad meridiem diei incipit secundum Astronomos. Qui, igitur, de tempore certificari voluerit tabulam sequentem de 12 signis discat et agnoscat; sic, incipit Aries, Taurus, Cancer, Virgo, &c.

A method for finding the position of the moon on any given day by means of the calendar and the table.

[*The Table given on pages* 18, 19 *follows here in Latin Text.*]

Sicunt volunt Astrologi summi videlicet Ptolomæus, Pythagoras, Rhasis, Haly, &c., non debet cirugus incidere vel urere in aliquo membro corporis humani nec facere phlebotomiam dum Luna fuerit in signo regnante illud membrum. Nam secundum est quod 12 signa zodiaci regunt 12 partes humani corporis prout patet in imagine predicta, ubi aries quod est signum igneum temperate siccum caput regit cum suis contentis. Luna vero in ariete existente cave ab incisione in capite et facie et [ne] incidas venam capitalem. Luna vero in tauro existente, cave ab incisione colli vel gutturis, nec incidas venam in his locis. Luna existente in geminis cave ab incisione spatularum brachiorum et manuum nec aperias venam in his locis. Luna existente in cancro cave ab incisione in mammis vel pectore aut stomacho, et a læsione pulmonis, nec incidas arteriam seu venam ad ipsam directionem. Luna existente

The best astrologers declare that no operation, not even bleeding, should be undertaken whilst the moon is in the sign governing the part to be operated upon.

Luna in cancro bonum / Luna in

leone indifferens / Luna in virgine indifferens / Luna in libra bonum / Luna in Scorpione malum / Luna in sagittario bonum / Luna in Capricorn: malum / L. in Aquar. malum / Luna in pisce bonum /

in leone cave a læsione laterum, costarum et ne incidas in dorso neque per apertionem neque per ventosam. Luna existente in virgine cave in ventre aut in locis interioribus occultis, nec minuas matricem mulierum deservientem. Luna existente in libra cave ne umbilico aut in natibus et hanc [in ano] nec in renibus, nec venam renibus servientem aperias, nec ventosam apponas. Luna existente in scorpione cave testiculorum, virgæ virilis, colli vesicæ, nec aperias venam testiculorum deservientem nec ventosam apponas. Luna in sagittario existente cave ab incisione femorum nec incidas maculas vel superfluitates quascunque in corpore humano existentes. Luna existente in Capricorno cave in genibus et a læsione venarum et nervorum in his locis. Luna existente in aquario cave ne incidis in tibiis aut in nervis earum a genibus usque ad inferiora cavillarum. Luna vero existente in pisce cave in pedibus, nec venam aperias in eorum extremitatibus.[1]

A note on the recognition of the Signs of the Moon.

The influence of the Moon on the body.

To ascertain the house of the Moon.

If any one wishes to know and to discover in which sign of the heaven the moon is on any day, he must first discover in the almanac the sign in which the Moon is in conjunction with the Sun and the day of the conjunction. When this is found you know the first day of the moon because it is from that hour of the day or night when the conjunction occurs to the same hour of the next day. Then calculate by the almanac the number of days from the new moon thus obtained to the day you want. Look next in the previous table where the number is found, and when it is found look in the upper line of the table for the sign in which the moon is. Coming straight down from this you cross until you come directly to the sign corresponding lineally with the number of the age of the moon, and this gives the sign of the moon on that day. And note that in this calculation the natural day begins at midday according to the Astronomers. If any one wishes therefore to be sure of the time let him learn and understand the following table of the 12 signs. It begins thus—Aries, Taurus, Cancer, Virgo, &c.

[The table is given on pp. 18 and 19.]

The influence of the Moon in surgery.

The highest Astrologers, viz.: Ptolomy, Pythagoras, Rhasis, Haly, &c., aver that a surgeon ought not to cut or to cauterise any member of the human body nor to breathe a vein so long as the moon is in the house ruling that member. For the 12 signs of the Zodiac rule the twelve parts of the human body, as is clear from the aforementioned drawing, where Aries, which is a fiery sign moderately dry, governs the head with its contents. But when the moon is in Aries beware of operating upon the head or face and do not open one of the head veins. When the moon is in Taurus refrain from operating upon the neck or throat and do not bleed from a vein in these parts. When the moon is in Gemini beware of operating on the shoulders, arms or hands, and do not

[1] Supplied from Rawlinson, C 355, in the Bodleian Library.

Table for finding the Moon's house.

Ætas Lunæ	Martius	Aprilis	Maius	Junius	Julius	Augustus	September	Octob'	Novemb'	Decemb'	Januarius	Februar
1 2	Aries	Taurus	Gemini	Cancer	Leo	Virgo	Libra	Scorpio	Sagittarius	Capricorn.	Aquarius	Pisces
3 4	Taurus	Gemini	Cancer	Leo	Virgo	Libra	Scorpio	Sagittarius	Capricorn.	Aquarius	Pisces	Aries
6	Gemini	Cancer	Leo	Virgo	Libra	Scorpio	Sagittarius	Capricorn.	Aquarius	Pisces	Aries	Taurus
7 8 9	Cancer	Leo	Virgo	Libra	Scorpio	Sagittarius	Capricorn.	Aquarius	Pisces	Aries	Taurus	Gemini
10 11	Leo	Virgo	Libra	Scorpio	Sagittarius	Capricorn.	Aquarius	Pisces	Aries	Taurus	Gemini	Cancer
12 13	Virgo	Libra	Scorpio	Sagittarius	Capricorn.	Aquarius	Pisces	Aries	Taurus	Gemini	Cancer	Leo

14 15	Libra	Scorpio	Sagittarius	Capricorn.	Aquarius	Pisces	Aries	Taurus	Gemini	Cancer	Leo	Virgo
16 17	Scorpio	Sagittarius	Capricorn.	Aquarius	Pisces	Aries	Taurus	Gemini	Cancer	Leo	Virgo	Libra
18 19	Sagittarius	Capricorn.	Aquarius	Pisces	Aries	Taurus	Gemini	Cancer	Leo	Virgo	Libra	Scorpio
20 21	Capricorn.	Aquarius	Pisces	Aries	Taurus	Gemini	Cancer	Leo	Virgo	Libra	Scorpio	Sagittarius
22 23	Aquarius	Pisces	Aries	Taurus	Gemini	Cancer	Leo	Virgo	Libra	Scorpio	Sagittarius	Capricorn.
24 25	Pisces	Aries	Taurus	Gemini	Cancer	Leo	Virgo	Libra	Scorpio	Sagittarius	Capricorn.	Aquarius
26 27	Aries	Taurus	Gemini	Cancer	Leo	Virgo	Libra	Scorpio	Sagittarius	Capricorn.	Aquarius	Pisces
28 29 30	Taurus	Gemini	Cancer	Leo	Virgo	Libra	Scorpio	Sagittarius	Capricorn.	Aquarius	Pisces	Aries

The influence of the Moon in surgery.

open a vein in these parts. When the moon is in Cancer refrain from operating upon the breasts or chest or stomach and from injuring the lungs, neither open an artery or a vein in their neighbourhood. When the moon is in Leo take care not to injure the flanks or the ribs, and do not operate upon the back either by cutting or by cupping. When the moon is in Virgo take care not to operate upon the belly or the internal parts, and do not bleed from the veins supplying the womb in women. When the moon is in Libra refrain from operating upon the navel or upon the buttocks or upon the kidneys, and do not open the vein supplying the kidneys, nor apply a cup. When the moon is in Scorpio refrain from operating upon the testicles, the penis and the neck of the bladder; do not open the testicular vein and do not apply a cup. When the moon is in Sagittarius do not operate upon the thighs, do not remove spots or superfluous parts occurring in any part of the human body. When the moon is in Capricornus refrain from the knees and from injuring the veins and nerves in these parts. When the moon is in Aquarius do not operate upon the legs or upon their nerves from the knees to the bottom of the calves. When the moon is in Pisces do not operate upon the feet and do not open the vein in their extremities.

Of diffinicion of a fistule, and places þat it is bred in, and when it is curable or noȝt.

Definition of a fistula.

[N]ow it is to procede to þe curyng of þe fistule. And aftir auctours of cirurgie, a fistule is a depe aposteme, hauyng oonly oon hole somtyme, and ofte-tymes two or þre, and oftymes mo, and bredyng in eche membre of þe body of aposteme or of a wounde yuel y-cured, giffyng out quitour of diuerse colour and of diuerse substaunce; þat is to sey now white and þinne, now watrye, now as wasshyng of flesshe þat is rawe, now clotty; somtyme myche stynkyng, somtyme litle. And somtyme þe holes ar closed be þam-self, and aftir a fourteniȝt or a moneþ, akyng goyng afore in þe place, þai ar eft-sones opned. And when siche maner fistules is bredde in þe armes or in the brest, or in þe costes, or in þe þies, or in þe knees, or in þe legges, or in þe fete, or in þe hende, or in þe ioyntours [*of[1] þise, þat it corrumpeþ oft-tyme þe boneȝ and þai ycorrupte ar oft tymeȝ put out by þe holeȝ of þe fistule. ¶ Bot fistuleȝ of

Various kinds of discharge.

Fistulæ may heal and afterwards re-open.

[*Sloane MS. 277, leaf 66, col. 1]

Prognosis of fistulæ.

[1] The MS. Sloane 6 is defective here. The missing folios are supplied from another English version, Sloane 277, made early in the fifteenth century.

iunctureȝ noȝt comyng of outward cause ar called þe [festred] fistulat gout. And sich fistuleȝ almost bene all vncurable, and namely in Wymmen. In ȝong[1] men forsoþ or waxen men, I hafe seene few euer be cured, out-tak þat I haue sene tuyse or þrise som waxen men by long processe of tyme, þurȝ benefice of nature, be cured of þe fistula in þe leggeȝ and in þe fete; þat is to sey in þe seuent ȝere or fourtent or two and tuenty fro þe tyme þat þe fistule come to þam. And þat miȝt be for, after Ypocras, alle sekeneȝ ouþer is termyned after þe mouyng of þe mone or of þe son. ¶ If it be after þe mouyng of þe mone. so it is termined in þe fourtened day, which is endyng of acuteȝ sekeneȝ and bygynnyng of croniceȝ.

Festred gout bad in women, sometimes cured spontaneously in young men.

An acute illness becomes chronic at the end of a fortnight.

If it be after þe mouyng of þe son þan þe first schal be in þe seuent moneþ or seuent ȝere and so ascendyng vpward by seuen, &c. *¶ And witte þou þat al ȝong men hauyng sich forseid fistuleȝ, if þai be in febreȝ and lene of body, ful seldom abideþ þe fourtened ȝere. To which for-soþ noieth most vse of milk and of fruyte and lichery. ¶ If þe fistule for-soþ be in a fleschy place of þe body al-only, it is possible to be cured and þer-for *fistula in ano* or bredyng niȝe may wele be cured. Whileȝ neþerlesse it be noȝt ouer olde or depe,[2] þat may be knowen by þe hardnes of þe place and discoloryng of þe skynne and mich goyng out of þe egestionȝ, and feblyneȝ of þe pacient, and if it haue perced þe waieȝ of þe vryne. ¶ þerfor wake ȝe þat couaitise blynde noȝt þe siȝt of ȝour eiȝen,[3] þat it may noȝt deme atuix curable and vncurable.

[* leaf 66, col. 2]

Milk, fruit and lechery bad for long-standing fistulæ.

Take care not to operate for the sake of the fee only.

2 dummodo tamen nota fuerit nimis inveterata vel profundior.

3 vigilate ergo ne cupiditas oculorum aciem exteret.

Of a maner of wirchyng in fistula in ano and þe curying þer-of.

When for-soþ thou knoweȝ þat he þat haþ fistule in þe lure, or niȝ biside, is strong and þe place of þe sekeneȝ wele colored and þat the pacient is gode herted and abydyng, it is noȝt to drede þat-ne þe lech schal spede wele in þe cure of it if he be experte. ¶ Which perceyued, when þe pacient and þe lech ar

Selection of patient.

1 ȝong *written above*, olde *deleted*.

acorded in al þings, þan be þe pacient ledde to a place made redy Where þe lech schal do þe mynysteryng of cure. And all men amoued away out-take one or tuo, þat þe lech will haue with hym to his helping, ouþer of his owne men or of oþer; þan sey þe lech þus to þe pacient, reward[1] yhadde to þe person of þe pacient. ¶ 'Witte ȝour gentilnes and ȝour hiȝnes, and also ȝour godehertynes, þat þe gracious perfeccion *of þis cure ow not only to be recced as now to þe possibilite of my gode bisynes, bot also to ȝour gode and abydyng pacience. ¶ And for-alsmich be it noȝt hidde to ȝow þat if ȝe be vnobedient and vnpacient to my commandyngs, lustyng þe tyme of wirchyng, ȝe may falle in-to a ful gret perile or tary longer þe effecte of þe cure. Therfor beþ-war, For he þat is warned afore is noȝt bygiled. Paynful things passeþ sone when at the next foloweþ glorious helthe.'[2] ¶ Þise things yseid, be þe pacient putte vp-on a bedde bifore a liȝt Wyndow, and be he putte after þe maner of þe sekenes þat is if þe holeȝ of þe fistule be in þe lefte side lye he on þe lefte side. And if þai be in the riȝt side vp-on þe riȝt side, or if þai be to-ward rigebone[3] lie he þan wide opne boþe his leggeȝ or þe tone raised vp after þat it semeth more spedeful and be þai hungen vp with a corde or with a towell festned aboue to a balk or a beme. ¶ Þe felaw of þe lech sitte at þe bakke of þe pacient, aboue on þe bedde þat þe pacient lieþ in, and hold fast with his handeȝ þe ouer buttoke in raisyng it vpward þat þe lech may haue gode siȝt in his wyrchyng. ¶ Þan at first putte the leche þe schewyng[4] fynger of his left hande enoynted with oile, or som oyntment, in-to þe lure of þe pacient. Which ydo with þe tother hand putte he þe heued of þe instrument þat is called sequere me in-to þe hole of þe fistule *þat is next to þe lure, if þer be many holeȝ, and assay bisily on þe fynger beyng in þe lure if he fele with it the instrument or fynger with-out any þing atuix. Which if byfall witte he with-out dout þat þe longaon is persed. ¶ And þan witte he for certayn þat it byhoueþ noȝt to cure þe pacient with no cure bot cuttyng with yren, or fretyng with a threde strengely yfestned.

To be taken to the operating room.

Advice to patient at [* leaf 67] time of operation to be brave and obedient.

Patient to be in a good light;

position to be adjusted.

The leech's mate to be told what to do.

The rectum to be explored with a finger. [Cf. frontispiece]

The fistula to be deemed incurable if the rectum is perforated.

[* leaf 67, col. 2]

[1] habito respectu ad personam patientis; "sciat generositas vestra et celsitudo necnon vestra magnanimitas."

[2] Cito transiebunt penosa, cùm in proximo salus succedit gloriosa.

[3] versus caudam spinæ dorsi, i. e. "rigbon" ejusdem.

[4] digitum manus sinistræ . . . qui index dicitur.

Incision to be preferred to the ecraseur.

¶ If þat hole for-soþe be noȝt distant fro þe lure bot by a nynch al-one, þan schal kuttyng be þe moste kynde and sonest cure; þat if it be so, þan tak þe lech Acu*m* rostrata*m* and putte he þe end hauyng þe eiȝ thurȝ þe hole next to þe lure þe lefte fynger yputte, as it is seid, in-to þe lure. And when he feleþ þe nedle wiþ his fynger, labor he warly þat he may bring out with his fynger þe heued of þe instrument þurȝ þe lure appliyng and wryþing. ¶ Whiche ydo, be þer taken a fourfold þrede of silk white or of strong lyne or tuyne and it is called ffrenu*m* Cesaris. And be it put in þe eiȝ of þe nedle And with þat þrede anoþer single threde and at oneȝ and to-gidre be þe nedle drawen þurȝ þe lure and þe hole of þe fistule. Afterward þe single þrede be fest by itself noȝt co*n*streynyng, bot þat it go noȝt out þe lech noȝt willyng, þar-if parauentur frenum cesaris be kutte or brusten þan schal þer anoþer frenum cesaris mow be broȝt in with þe forseid þrede with-out any anguisch. ¶ Therfor be þe lech witty in þis wirchyng þat he may do, and kon do, tuo things þan he fyndeþ in wrytyngs, *For al þings þat ow to be done about sich werk may noȝt be expressed in lettreȝ, and þerfor it byhoueþ a crafty [lech] to be wise and slyȝe wele ymagynyng subtile þings, þat in þose þings þat perteneþ to þe perfitenes of þis werk and aboue þo þings þat he has lerned in þis boke he may availe hym þurȝ benefice of his ovne witte; For Boecius seith ¶ *De disciplina scolarium*, He is of moste wreched witte þat euer more vseþ þings yfounden and noȝt things to be founden.[1] ¶ þerfor þe frene and þe þrede ydrawen, as it is seid, þan may þou chese wheþer þou will kutte it or fret it with þe þred. ¶ Iff thou will kutte it þan schalt þou take acum rostrata*m* and] [2] putte it þurȝ þe middeȝ of þe lengþe of þe instrument þat is called tendiculu*m*, bygynnyng at þe gretter ende. Aft*er* take boþe þe endes of freni cesaris, drawen þurȝ þe middes of þe lure and of þe hole of þe fistule, and þurȝ þe middis of þe hole of þe instrument þat is called vertile—a wraiste—. Be þai drawen þurȝ, and be þai faste y-knettid in p*ro*porcionyng þe lengþe of þe

A pilot thread to be used in case the main ligature should break or be cut.

The directions here given are merely hints [* lf. 67, bk., col. 1] which the leech may elaborate if he have the ability.

[leaf 147]

The cure of fistula by cutting.

The use of the ligature,

[1] Sic igitur medicus ingeniosus in hac operatione ut plura quam in scriptis inveniat agere sciat: quia omnia quæ circa tale opus fieri debent non possunt litteris exprimi. Et ideo oportet artificem esse providentem, subtilia bene imaginantem, ut in his quæ ad hujus operis perfectionem pertinent super ea quæ in hoc libello didicerit ingenii beneficio valeat prævalere. Dicit enim Boëcius "de disciplina scholarium," "Miserrimi est ingenii qui tantum utitur inventis et inveniendis."

[2] MS. Sloane 6, leaf 147, continues.

freni cesaris as it bihoueth, þat is aft*er* þe distance of þe hole of þe tendiculi to þe hole of þe fistule; þan take þe tendicule and putte þe snowte of þe nedle in þe hole of þe fistule in-puttyng it strongly.

which is to be tightened by the peg.

Aftirward take þe wraiste wiþ freno cesaris, and put it in þe hole of þe tendicule, þat is þe side of it; whiche y-putte in, putte þi fynger in þe lure, and wiþ þe toþ*er* hand þrist faste þe tendicule with þe snowt toward þy fynger. And when þou see3 tyme, be þe wraist turned aboute þat frenu*m* cesaris hold fast þe tendicule þat it go no3t out.

The end of the snowted needle to be fitted into the hole in the spoon or protector to prevent injury to the bowel whilst the fistula is being divided.

And so labour þe leche vnto þat he bringe out þe poynt of þe snowte by þe middes of þe lure; and þat he streyne fast þe flesshe festned in þe frene wiþ þe wraiste and þ*e* frene. Whiche y-do, take þe instrument þat is called coclear—a spone—Of whiche þe holow heued be putte in þe lure agayn þe poynt of þe snowte, so þat þe poynt of þe snowte stand in þe hole þat is in þe spone, no3t þur3 p*er*sed, & be þat halden of þe felaw of þe leche; þis, forsoþe, shal defende þe lure þat it be no3t hurt, þru3 uncouenable mouyng and sodayn styrryng of þe pacient, wiþ þe poynt of þe rasour or of þe launcette. As soon aftirward—þe pacient *com*forted—putte þe leche þe poynt of þe rasour in þe holwnes of þe snowte þat is in þe spone, and, als sone as he may, boldly kutte þe flesshe festened in þe frene aboue þe snowte euen be þe middes; and it y-kutte by þe middes, þe snowte wiþ þe frene shal lepe out by it-self. If, forsoþe, þ*er* be many holes þat ow to be kutted, be it done as it is seid.

Don't try to do too much at a time.

Or if it be nede, differre it to anoþir tyme; ffor in som case þe toþ*er* holes beyng outward may be heled wiþoute kuttyng or byndyng of þrede. Of whiche it shal be seid aftirward, þan it is to labo*ur* to þe staunchyng of blode.

The methods of stopping the bleeding

by sponge pressure,

ffirst put a spounge wette in a litel warme watre and wele wrongen in þe place of the kuttyng, and hold it þer fast to receyue þe blode, and lat it abide þer a gode while; þ*er*fore when þou trowest þe sponge to be wele ful of blode, remoue it, and if it be nede putte agayn anoþ*er* sponge, or þe same ordeyned in þe forseid man*er*. And when þou hast doon þus, be þe pacient raised vp warly, and make hym to sitte fast in a redy place vpon þe forseid sponge; and dout not þat ne it shal be wele staunchid. Aftirward when þou deme3 dew tyme, be þe pacient put in a dewe place and þe sponge remoued; and wheþir þe blode be staunchid, or no3t, putte in þe kuttyng pulu*er* of boli, sangu*is* dracon), aloes epatic*us*, pulu*er* of hennes feþ*er*e3 y-brent, or of an old lyn cloþe y-brynt, asshen of heres of hares y-brent, *Iuyse or puluer of walwort, &c., Of whiche it shal be seid aftirward in þair place. But witte þou þat it is no3t required þat al þise at oone3 and to-gidre be putte to, but I putte þam here þat a leche, som wantyng or no3t y-had of þe forseid þingis, may competently spede wiþ þe toþ*er* his nede3 or occupacion. ffor why; eueriche of þise medicynes symply by hymself or medled wiþ þe white of an ey stauncheþ wele blode þer and in oþir places. But witte þou þat to worþi men and noble it semeþ to putte to more noble medicynes and more dere. And witte þou þat þe iuse of walwort or pulu*er* of þe same, if it be had redy, is namely in eu*er*y medicyne þat is restrictiue of blode. How, forsoþe, þe poudre of walwort ow to be made, or þe iuse of it to be kepte, it shall be seid aftirward. Þe medicyne restrictiue, forsoþe, y-put to wiþ clene stupes and smal, or wiþ coton wele y-tesed, or wiþ heres of hares no3t y-brent, and w*ith* lynnen cloutis put aboue, be it warly bounden; þat is to sey be he girded on þe bare naked wele streit wiþ a lynnen girdel. Afterward haue he a list of wolnen cloþe, and be it bounden byhynd at þe bak of þe pacient to þ*e* lynnen girdel, and lat it descende atuix his buttokes vpon þe cloutes cou*er*ying þe lure, and be it festned fast to þe girdel vpon þe womb, and lat it abide so stille to þe tyme come þat it be eft-sones remoued. If þe holes, forsoþe, be in þe buttok somdele remoued fro þe lure, þan most it oþerwise be bounden. And þat þus, haue þe pacient a wolnen girdel or a lynnen, wiþ þe whiche he be girded in þe flanke3, to þe whiche girdel be hongen a lynnen cloute hauyng in brede seuen or 8 ynches, and in lengþe als many or mo; þ*er*fore be þe pacient girded þat þe side of þe clout next to þe lure lye ri3t atuix

by styptic powders.

[* leaf 147, back]

The better class not to have too homely remedies.

Styptics to be applied on small pieces of clean linen.

How to apply the bandage.

A T-bandage is best.

þe buttokkes upon þe lure; and oþir cloutes y-putte atuix, þan be bounden two listis hyngyng about þe þie of þe pacient. And if boþe þe buttokkes bene hurt, ordeyne he anoþ*er* girdel to þe toþ*er*, and be it ordeyned as it is seid afore, and on þe same wise.

A well-applied bandage aids greatly in the cure.

ffor knowe the leche þat competent byndyng shal giffe noȝt litte help in curyng. But if medicyneȝ, forsoþ, may cleue to vnto dew tyme, þe cure shal longer be taried. fforsoþe when þou seest, in þe secound day or þe þrid, þe blode wele staunched,

Remedies to be used on the second or third day when the bleeding is stopped.

þan take þe ȝolke of a raw ey, and wiþ oile roset or of camomille, or wiþ sangu*is* ven*er*is, or, þise defailyng, distempre it wiþ comon oile, and put it in a littel bleddre, and wiþ anastar of tree ich day but oones be it ȝetted into þe lure, so þat þe wou*n*de be filled þ*er*of. And aftirward put aboue lynnen stupeȝ kutted smal wiþ shereȝ, and aboue þe stupes a lynnen cloute. And þan be it bounden as it p*er*teneþ, and lat it so lye vnto þe morne. And þis cure ow to be kepte by 8 or 9 dayes;

Arderne's own preparation "Pulv. sine pare" to be used about the eighth or ninth day.

whiche, forsoþe, y-fulfilled, þanne owe þe leche to putte in þe kuttyng of my poudre þat I, Ioħn Arderne, made, whiche I called 'pulu*er* sine pari,' an[d] on frenssh, 'poudre saunȝ pere.' I wist neuer, forsoþe, ne knew poudre like to it, Of whiche it shal be seid aftirward in his place.[1] Aboue þe poudre, forsoþ, put coton or stupeȝ and bynd it.

[Sloane MS. 277, leaf 68, col. 1]

The bowels not to be moved for 48 hours after operation,

¶ And so by tuo hole natural daies be it noȝt moued, bot if voydyng of þe wombe make it[2]; bot warne þe lech þe pacient that he dispose hym so þat he remoue noȝt þe medycyne in any maner in als-mich as he may abstene. Elleȝ þe fruyte and þe vertue with þe effecte of the medycyne schal be annulled.

[* leaf 68, back, col. 2]

but the wound to be cleansed and dried after a motion.

If þe pacient for-soþ may noȝt abstene hym fro þe pryue *In þe mornyng be it clensed with hote watre and a sponge and be it dryed and eft soneȝ be putte in of þe forseid poudre, And be it ordeyned as on þe day afore. And ȝitte be he comaunded for to abstene as afore, þat if he do noȝt eft-soneȝ þe þrid tyme be it ordeyned with þe same poudre as afore, And ȝitte he be amonysched to abstine.

Unguentum viride a useful applica-

¶ Afterward wheþer he abstene or not, þe place wele yclensed and dried, be þe lure enoynted with

[2] nisi ventris evacuatio cogerit.

[1] The MS. Sloane 6 is again defective, and the missing folios are again supplied from Sloane MS. 277.

þe fynger dipped in vnguento viridi hard molten in ane ostree schell att þe fyre. And on ich aside about the wounde and within the lure and where-so-euer he seeþ þe skynne flayne. ¶ For why; þis enoyntment doþe away alle smertyng and fleyng.[1] And þis enoyntment is called Salus populi, þe making of which shal be schewed afterward. ¶ Which enoynted, be þer ȝetted in as byfore with a nastare of tree of þe ȝolke of an ey and oile. And as it is seid in þe place afore, be it reparaled in al þings, renewyng eueryday oneȝ first with þe forseid oyntment molten in a schell. And be þer ȝette in with a nastare of tree oile with an ey. ¶ And þis wirchyng be continued by 9 daies at the lest. ¶ About the twenty day, forsoth, or 24 or 26, eft-soneȝ if þou see nede, þan it is gode þat þou putte bisily within þe lure of poudre sine pari, and fille þe place of þe fistule within and without and as it is seid be it redied.[2] ¶ When forso*þ* þe wonde is remoued . eft-soneȝ as it is seid afore be it wasched and dried and be it anoynted about with Salus p*opu*li And after be caste in by a nastare oyle and þe ȝolk of ane ey And, if þe pacient may abstene hym fro þe pryue, be it noȝt remoued by two daies. *Elleȝ forsoþ when it is nede be it remoued. And considere þe lech bisily þe wounde ymundified if it be wele tretable and with-out hardnes and bolnyng and yuel colour: and som what for to cesse þe superflue moistnes which þe wonde sent out first. þan witte þe lech þat at þe next he may putte to cicatrizatiues as bene þise, Puluer of alum ȝucarin combust, 'bole armenic,' sanguis draconis, Aloe, mirra, sarcocolla, meele of barly and of beeneȝ, puluer of galleȝ and psidie[3] and puluer tanny, gummy arabic, terra sigillata, &c. ¶ Suppose noȝt þe lech þat it byhoueþ him to haue in one receyte al thise forseid togidre for þai ar sette here togidre. Bot it is to vnderstand þat þai ar named here togidre þat a lech know al to be of þe same vertu in regeneracion of flesch an[d] cicatrizacione and þat þai bene al stiptik. And to þise may be added ceruse and litarge of gold and of siluer. ¶ Iff þe lech want any of þem take of þe toþer þat he may fynde, For nouþer it byhoueþ here ne in none oþer place, þat

tion for chapped skin.

An enema to be injected through a wooden clyster pipe.

Treatment on 24th–26th day.

[* leaf 69, col. 1]

The means to complete the healing process.

Many remedies suggested but only some to be used.

[1] Nam hujusmodi unguentum omnino pruritum "smertyng" delet et excoriationem,

[2] et ut dictum est præparetur.

[3] pulvis gallarum quercuum.

The remedies to be applied on soft rags cut into small pieces.

al þings named þat haþ þe same vertue be putte in every confection; bot tuo, or thre, sufficeþ als mich as alle. ¶ Tak þer-for þe lech of þise forseid, tuo, or thre, or foure and medle þam with þe ȝolk of a raw ey, a litle oile of lynsede putte to, if it be hadde, or of sanguis veneris or of melle rosat', and with soft stupeȝ of lyne kutte smal or with coton. be it putt warly in the wounde, For whi; it clenseth þe wounde and heleþ and dryeþ it wele

[* leaf 69, col. 2.]

Our author's unguentum arabicum.

* for certayne. ¶ Or þou may put to common vnguentu*m* albu*m* þat apotecharieȝ makeþ, þis neþerlesse yknowen afore[1] þat þou ow to medle þer-with poudre of bole armenic' and sanguis dragonis, if þou haue it, and oile roset with watre of rose in which be resolued gumme arabic', and bþ it wele ymedled togidre and þerof be putte euery day in þe wounde and about þe wounde with coton. And for certayn it heleth wele noȝt only þer bot in euery place of þe body. And þis oyntment wold I neuer want and I calle it vnguentu*m* arabicu*m* of gumme arabic þat entreþ þerin and þan schal it be of rede colour. ¶ And witte þou þat with þis oyntment without any oþer medicine, outtake *salus* pop*u*li þou may finaly hele þe wounde of þe fistule, if þer be in it no ded flesch, no hole caue, or bolnyng, or hardneȝ, or blones, or rednes, or any oþer instans þat may be-falle.[2] ¶ þat if þer be-falle any of þise accidenteȝ why þe wounde may noȝt perfitely be souded be þer put in of puluis sine par*i* and it schal bryng in þe desired effecte. ¶ And þis schal be to þe þe tokne of perfite curyng when þou seeȝ þe linne clouteȝ putte to with þe medicyneȝ to be drye when þou remoueȝ þam. And in-als-mych as þai ar more drye in-so-mych þai ar þe better. ¶ And þis sufficeþ of þe kuttyng of þe fistule and of the curyng of it. by þo þings þat thurȝ þe bisines of a gode lech and a witty may make þe forseid werk more.[3]

The best sign of a cure is that the dressings remain dry.

[1] hoc tamen prænoto.

[2] livor aut rubor aut aliquod aliud instans quod contingere poterit/

[3] Et hæc de incisione fistulæ et ejus iunctione sufficiunt præter ea quæ per industriam boni et ingeniosi medici prædictum opus valeant ampliari.

[leaf 69, bk., col. 1]

Of a-noþer maner wirchyng in þe same fistule and þe cure wiþ diuerse exempleȝ.

Reasons for preferring to cure by liga-

If it by falle forsoþ þat þe fistule be depe and haue grete distance atuix þe hole of þe fistule and þe lure.

Or if þe pacient be ferdful for to suffer kuttyng. Or for oþer notable causeȝ being þer, þan may þe lech wit*h* kuttyng of þe þrede ydrawen thurȝ þe middeȝ of þe hole of þe fistule and þe lure kutte þe flesch, and þat availeþ even to kuttyng with iren, outtake þat it askeþ a longer tyme of curyng. For why; þof-al it be bounden riȝt streitly at þe first tyme ȝitte vnneþe schal þe fretyng be complete in som men by a moneþ or thre wekeȝ. ¶ Sich cure þerfor ysewed and þe festnyng ydo on dewe maner,[1] þat is after þat þe pacient may resonably suffre, puruey þe leche if þe pacient be delicate or feble, or waike of hert, þat þe þ*r*ede by which þe fistule is knytte, be so bonden þat if it be nede þat it may be loused without kuttyng, þat is with a lache knotte or slyppyng knotte.[2] ¶ Which ydo, lye þe pacient on a bedde; or stande he or go he by þre oureȝ or 5, or 6, vnto þat þe payne ycaused of þe byndyng cese somwhat. And wheþer þe akyng cese at þe forseid tyme or noȝt, putte þe pacient on a bedde and with a naister of tree putte into þe lure of þe ȝolk of a raw ey, medled with oile of rose leuke,[3] and be þe lure wele enoyntid[4] *of þe same withouteforþe. And so wiþoute puttyng atuix of any-þing late it aloon by a niȝt; At morne, forsoþe, bifore þat þe pacient go to priuè, be ȝettid into þe lure by a nast*r*e som oyle, what-so pleseþ to þe, þat þe pacient may so moche more liȝt ese hym. Witte þou þat þus ow þou to chaufe þe ȝolk of an ey with oyle. Take þe nasta*r*e wiþ þe forseid medicyne putte in þe bledder, and þe bledder putte in some vessell wiþ hote water, þat þe medicyne may be chauffed by þe hete of þe watre; ffor why; hote þing eseþ better þe akyng. Þan afore þe pacient go to þe priuè, take þe leche þe forseid þrede in þe lure, and be þe vtter knotte loused, and aftir be þe þrede more strongly constreyned if it may wiþout anguissh of þe pacient. Elleȝ, forsoþe, be it bounden wiþ tuo knott*is* or þre vnlouseable, and be þe heuedeȝ of þe þredeȝ kutte away so nere þe knotte þat þai may noȝt be p*er*ceyued of þe pacient or of oþer men. And witte þou þat þe leche

ture rather than by incision.

The details of treatment by ligature.

[* Sloane 6, leaf 148]

A method of giving a clyster by means of a bladder softened in hot water and attached to the end of the nastar or glyster pipe.

1 Prosecuta ergo tali cura et innexione debito modo facta/

2 Cum nodo currente Anglice "large knot" vel "slippyng knot."

3 et cum nastare ligneo infundatur in anum de vitello ovi crudo cum oleo ros. mistum.

4 Sloane 6, leaf 148, continues.

The leech to keep a stock of ligature material, and to be very careful to keep his methods secret.

shuld haue euermore þrede of white silke, small and strong; if he haue noȝt, forsoþe, þan take he strong þrede of lyne or of tuyne. And in no maner aft*er* his miȝt shewe he noȝt his wirkyng, nouþer in kuttyng ne wiþ þrede byndyng, þat his werke be p*er*ceyued of strange men, þat his cure be noȝt litle sette by, or þat any oþ*er* witty man p*er*ceyuyng his werk mow vsurpe it to hymself; for þus did I, þ*er*fore wake ȝe, for he þat is warned aforne is noȝt bigiled. It byhoueþ a leche vse many cauteleȝ, þat he ado*ur*ne[1] his faculte, whiche I may noȝt note to þe laste. It seemeþ, forsoþe, vnworþi for to vse wele þingis y-giffe þat kan noȝt gette hym mo þingis. Þ*er*fore when þe pacient has clensed his wombe, be he putte vpon a bedde, and be his lure wele clensed and wyped wiþ hote watre and wiþ a sponge. Aftirward be it enoynted wiþ þi fynger atuix þe buttokeȝ and on ich aside about þe lure wiþ Salus pop*u*li hette in an ostree shell. Aftirward be þ*er* ȝetted in by a nast*are* þe ȝolk of an ey as aboue wiþ oile. Aftirward be þ*er* putte aboue siche ane Emplast*re*:

A prescription for a good clyster,

Recipe—þe Iuyse of smalache or merch, wormode, Molayne, walworte, Sparge, waybrede, Mugworte, auance, petite consoude, wodbynd. Of alle þise herbes, if þou may haue þam, take euen porcion, outtake of wodebynde, of whiche, if it may be hadde, be taken þe triple or quadriple. If al, forsoþe, may not be hadde, take þe toþ*er* þat þou may haue, and namely þe þre first named wiþ wodebynd if þou may haue it. The confeccioɳ is þus:—Take þe Iuse of þe herbes, and be it medled wiþ als mich of wele clarified hony, al-wise mouyng on an esy fire, and boile tham so long vnto þat þe watrynes of þe Iuyse be somewhat þikned; whiche, y-take of þe fire and keled, kepe it in a gode potte.[2] It may laste al one ȝere or tuo; þ*er*fore when þou wilt vse þ*er*of, take of it als mich as it is nede, and putte þ*er*to als miche of whites of eiren, wele y-bette and scomed,[3] and moue þam togider. Aftir be þ*er* put to þam of subtile mele of whete als moche as sufficeþ, and medle þam wele to-gidre; þan putte * to a litle oyle of olyue, or of fressħ buttre scomed at þe fire, wiþ als miche virgine wax

and another for a plaster.

[* leaf 148, back]

[1] ut facultatem suam decoret.

[2] ab igne deposita et infrigerata, reservatur.

[3] prius ad ignem despunati.

togidre dissolued at þe fire by it self; þan first putte aboue þe iuse to þe fire wiþ hony and white of eyren, and moue þam all wayse wiþ a sklyse[1] þat þai cleue not to þe panne. When forsoþe it is wele hote but not wele y-soþen, be þe wax molten wiþ oile or buttre, as it is seyde aboue; whiche y-molten and þe forseid þingis beyng hote—þat is to seye þe hony, þe iuse, and þe white of eyren—be þai ʒetted togidre, and so eu*er*more mouyng strongly wiþ a spatour, seþe þam on a softe fyre vnto þey be made oon body: whiche y-do, sette it of þe fire, and it beyng hote, putte to of terebentyne als moche as sufficeþ and moue it strongly wiþ a spature vnto þat þe terebentyne be dronken in. And if it be nede for to chaufe it more for þe terebentyne, loke þat it suffre noʒt mych hete, for in seþing loseþ terebentyne his myʒtes. Þise y-do, be it yputte in a box and y-kepte to vse. Take of þis and wiþ a spatour or *with* þi þombe strech it vpon clene lyn stupeʒ and softe, and put it vpon þe lure, and aboue put a lyn cloute and bynde it, as it is seyde, in þe cure of cuttyng. Þis emplastre, forsoþe, is called 'diaflosmus,' for molayne þat is called flosmus. And not oonly it availeþ in þis forseid cure but also in cuttyng of þe fistule; ffor why; it heleþ wele alle woundes, þof-al þai be horrible, & also bolnyngis in woundeʒ and in brissures; and it seseþ wele þe akyng*is* of woundes and of brusours. And it eseþ wele þe akyng*is* and þe bolnyng*is* of ioyntures; þis, forsoþe, haue I ful ofte proued. I sey, forsoþe, þat þis emplastre i-had, it is noʒt nede in þe forseid caseʒ to renne to oþ*er* medicynes. And witte þou þat þ*er* is a naturel vertu in walwort þat moste wele re-streyneþ blode of woundes, and akyng and bolnyng of woundes and of al membreʒ it doþ best away. Witte þou þat þat confeccion aboue þat receyueþ Smalache, wormode, moleyne, sparge, &c, wiþ clarified hony soþen togidre at þe fire and kept by itself in a vessell is called 'Tapsimel.' When, forsoþe, þ*er* is added þ*er*to white of eiren and oyle, wiþ wax and whete floure and tereben-tyne, and ar soþen togidre, þan it is called 'diaflosmus.' And þus ow þam to be p*ro*porcioned :—R*ecipe*. tapsimel,

Be careful in heating preparations which contain turpentine because heat dissipates its strength.

The preparation of "diaflosmus."

Its uses.

"Tapsimel, its preparation and uses.

[1] cum spatulâ.

white of eiren—an*a* ℥ iiij ; whete floure ℥ iij ; oyle, wax—an*a* ℥ iij ; t*er*bentyne ℥ ij. And witte þou þat if in þe tyme of þe makyng of Tapsimel may be founden a litel pety morel[1] whiche bereþ white flo*ur*s and blak grapes or berieȝ, it shuld for certayn make riȝt noble þe emplastre diaflosmus. And petite morel is called in fflaundres 'Naghtstach.'[2] And witte þou þat þe iuse of it doþe best awey þe pustules in childres[3] mouþes.

Treatment of complicated fistulæ.

If, forsoþe, þ*er* be many holes p*er*sed to-gidre, þan owe þe leche als sone as he may for anguissh of þe pacient, aft*er* þe rep*er*acion of þe first wounde, as it is seid afore, for to knytte wiþ a þrede, as it is seyde afore, þe toþ*er* holes strongly. Or, if he may, þat is bet*ter* þat þey be kutte al fro oon hole to an-oþ*er*, acu rostrata, þe snowted nedle y-putte in þe hole, or som lynne tent, kutte þam to þe grou*n*de wiþ a raso*ur* or wiþ a launcete. Whiche holes, *forsoþe, y-brouȝt into oon, be þe wou*n*de als soon y-filled of pulu*er* sine pari ; Aboue the poudre, forsoþe, I putte stupes kutte small, or coton, or carpe of lynnen cloþe. Aftir putte aboue þe forseid emplastre diaflosm*us*, and be it bounden as it is seid, and ich day ooneȝ reparailed. I sawe a man of Northamptou*n*[4] þat had þre holes in þe lefte buttok, and þre in þe testicleȝ codde, and al p*er*sed fro oon to anoþ*er* by þe middeȝ of longaon ; whom I cured wiþ cuttyng of al þe holes at oon tyme, of longaon as wele as of oþ*er*. Of þe kuttyng, forsoþe, of longaon, blode went strongly out, for þe fistule was riȝt depe ; wherefore þe pacient swowned ; p*er*fore I putte to a sponge wette in cold watir and receyued þe blode. Aftirward I put in þe kuttyng of longaon restrictyues of blode, of whiche it is seid aboue, and a gode sponge y-wette in cold watre. I made þe pacient for to sitte in a chayer, and als soon þe blod was cesed. And aftir refetyng of mete and drink, he went into his bedde and sleped wele all þe niȝt, wiþoute goyng out of blode. In þe morne, forsoþe, he had hym wele ; þe seconde day, forsoþe, aft*er* þe kuttyng I filled all þe woundes of pulu*er* sine pari, and as it is seid afore in all þingis, w*ith* oile and an ey and salus pop*u*li and diaflosm*us* I helid hym finaly wiþ

Lay all the openings into one.

[* leaf 149]

A successful case.

[1] solanum parvum possit haberi.

[2] Naght-sarth.

[3] childreȝ Sloane MS. 277, lf. 70, back.

[4] Vidi et alium hominem sc. Iohan : Colyn de Northampton.

[1] Qui vero, ut dixit, viginti medicorum curam subegit.

in 14 wekes. Whiche, forsoþe,[1] as he seid, he vnder-ȝede þe cure of meny leches, And suffred it ten ȝere. And witte þou þat I saw neu*er* man vnder my hand suffre swounyng, outake hym þis; he was forsoþe corpulent and waike of hert, but neþ*er*lesse aboute þe fourty day aft*er* þe kuttyng he rode. I heled anoþ*er* man þat had a fistule in þe same maner in all þing*is*, outake þat longaon was noȝt persed; whom I cured wiþ kuttyng in þe same man*er* as it is seid of þe first. I haue sene som men hauyng oon hole aloon niȝ þe lure þat p*er*sed noȝt þe longaon, whom I heled wiþ pulu*er* sine p*ar*i finaly; but for þe mouþe of þe vlcere was ou*er* streit, first I put aboue of vnguento ruptorio of calce viue & sape for to large þe mouþe of the fistule; of whiche it shal be treted afterward among oþ*ir* confeccions. I haue sene som men haue tuo holes byside þe lure, of whiche oon p*er*sed þe longaon and þe toþ*er* p*er*sed in no place, but it was oonly symple by itself in þe flesshe, hauyng no pass-yng to þe tot*her* hole. Of whiche was such a cure:—The hole nerre þe lure was cured wiþ kuttyng or byndyng; þe toþer, forsoþe, wiþ poudre sine pare y-put in and diaflosmo, and oon emplastre þat is called Neyrbone put aboue, whos confeccion shal be shewed aftirwarde. I saw also, and, oure lord beyng mene, I heled p*er*fitely a man þat had ffistula in ano on þe riȝt side and on þe lefte side; whiche, forsoþe, had on þe lefte buttok 8 holeȝ, and þre in þe riȝt buttok; and wiþin was longaon p*er*sed toward þe riȝt side oonly. But neþ*er*lesse all þe holes of aiþer p*ar*ty of þe lure answered togidre in þe grounde þat was proued þus. I toke a siryng of siluer and a bleddre y-bounden aboute ful of sang*uis* ven*er*is, and þe siryng y-putte in þurȝ oon hole and þe bleddre com-pressed wiþ þe fyngers, þe oile inȝetted *went out by al þe holes togidre on boþe sides, and neþ*er*lesse þe hole of longaon answered noȝt but to oon hole oonly, and þat in þe riȝt buttok; þe soþefastnes of whiche þing was proued wiþ þe instrument þat is callid sequere me, and wiþ acu rostrata, wiþ ful gret hardnes and bisynes; þe cure of whiche was suche: ffirst eu*er*y day in þe lefte buttok þurȝ oon of þe holes I ȝetted in sang*uis*

Another case.

Cases of fistulæ with many openings.

[* leaf 149, back]

A method to discover the real fistula when there are many external openings.

Treatment by tents.

ven*er*is wiþ þe forseid siring and bledder; whiche y-do, I putte in tuo tentes or þre, or lard of pork or swyne in þe larger holes; after þat þe depnes of þe fistules asked, þe heuedes, forsoþe, of þe tentes war tokned *with* þredes drawen þurȝ þe middes wiþ a nedell, þat þe tentes shuld noȝt be drowned in þe grounde of þe fistules when þe tentes war put in. And I putte aboue þe emplastre þat is called Neyrbon strecchid vpon ly*n*ne cloutes, and dewly y-bounden aboute þe lendes wiþ a girdill and cloutes y-shapen as it is seid afore. I lefte it in pece vnto þe morne. At morne, forsoþe, þe emplastre remoued, þ*er* appered aboue ȝe emplastre ful putrid quitour in sup*er*flue quantite. Eftsones in þe secounde day I reparailed it in al þing*is* as in þe first day, and it bifell as in þe firste day; and so it continued almost by a moneþ. When þe quito*ur*, þerfore, bigynne to lessen somwhat, and the bolnyng somwhat to cese, and þe colo*ur* and þe substaunce of þe skynne for to turne to his ovne naturel habitude, þan at þe first turned I to þe p*r*incipale cure of þe fistule with p*er*syng of longaon, whiche I cured finaly wiþ byndyng of a þrede in þe hole of longaon. Þe toþ*er* holeȝ, forsoþe, beyng bisyde it I cured wiþ cuttyng and with puluer sine p*ar*e. Eu*er*more continuyng þe cure wiþ þe siryng in þe lefte side, and wiþ tentes als long as þay wolde entre in, and þe emplastre Neyrbon y-putte aboue, and salus pop*u*li and vnguento arabico, vnto a loueable ende wiþ goddes help aboute half a ȝere I cured hym, and lefte hym in pece. Also þ*er* bene som men þat haþ fistules noȝt apperyng outward, but þay putte out miche putred & watrye humo*ur*, and som-tyme clere blode, and somtyme blode y-medled wiþ quitour. And þai disese myche þe pacientes and febleþ þam. And oft-tymes suche maner sikenes bene toward þe rigbone of þe bak niȝ þe lure, þat þay may be feled wiþ a fynger. But wheþ*er* þay may be feled or noȝt be þ*er* done suche a cure wiþ whiche I haue cured many men. Be þe pacient putte vpon a bedde wyde opne agaynes a wyndowe, liȝt shynyng, and þe legges y-raised vp and wiþ a towel y-hungen or wiþ a corde ordeyned to þis werk; whiche y-do, be þe lure y-opned wiþ

Blind internal fistulæ.

Arderne's operation good,

tonges so y-shape þat when þe vtward endes bene streyned togidre þe inner endes be opned & agaynward. Or if þe leche kanne ymagyne more couenable instrumentis to þe forseid werk to be done, for so moche loued be god þat streyngþes ma*n*nes witte in godes. Þe lure, forsoþe, y-opened, and þe sikenes bisily y-sene, be þe hole of þe sikenes y-filled wiþ pulu*er* sine pare, and coton y-putte aboue; be þe tonges warly drawen out þat þai spill noȝt þe poudre, or þat þei hurt noȝt þe pacient. Whiche y-drawen out, and þe legges laten doun, late þe pacient long reste or þat he go, þat þe poudre be *noȝt letted for to go; and abide it so stille vnto þat þe pacient clense his wombe; and if þe pacient may abstene hymself fro þe pryuè by two dayes, it war full necessary to hym. When þe pacient, forsoþe, ow to be reparaled, þan be þe lure wasshen and dried; whiche y-wasshen, be *þer* ȝette in of a ȝolk of an ey wiþ sang*uis* ven*er*is to esyng of þe ake þat comeþ of puluer sine p*ar*e, and to þe clensyng of þe vlcer of flessh mortified by þe forseid poudre. And þis cure continue þe leche by fife dayes or mo, þat is to sey of þe ȝolk and of sanguis ven*er*is, vnto þat he se þe pacient wele alegedde[1] of þe first akyng. Whiche y-do, þan owe þe leche in þe best maner þat he may for to opne þe lure and bisily biholde wiþin, and considere if þe sikenes be mortified; whiche is knowen if þat þe vlcer seme depper þan it was sene afore þe puttyng in of þe poudre, and also by oþ*er* tokenes þat a gode leche fyndeþ more exp*er*te of long exercise. In þis *þer*fore to be yknowen be noȝt þe leche slowe; for why; þer shal folow noȝt litle louyng *þer*of. *Þer*fore if it be noȝt mortified be it eftsones filled of pulu*er* sine pare, and be it sewed[2] in all þingis as it is seid afore, wiþ þe ȝolk of an ey, & wiþ sang*uis* ven*er*is, vnto þat he se efte-sones þe pacient wele alegged, as it is seid afore. When, forsoþe, he troweþ þat it is mortified, þan it is to turne agayne to anoþ*er* cure, þat is to sey þat he take þe ȝolke of an ey to whiche be added þe half parte of tapsimell, and als miche as sufficeþ of poudre of alu*m*me ȝucaryne y-brent. And be it so made þat it may be ȝetted in by a Nastar of tree; and

but he is not wedded to it.

[* leaf 150]

After-treatment.

Examine for gangrene.

Treatment for gangrenous inflammation of rectum.

[1] bene alleviatur.

[2] et prosequatur.

þis cure be continued al-oonly by þre or foure dayes: þe fourþe, forsoþe, or þe fifthe day aftir þis medicyne done to, be þe vlcer reparaled wiþ þe ȝolk of an ey and sang*uis* ven*er*is þre or foure dayes continued. And so owe þe leche for to chaunge his hande fro oon medycyne

Diminished discharge a good sign.

to anoþ*er*, vnto þat he se þe sup*er*flue moisteneȝ firste goyng out for to cesse; þat is tokne of cure or helþ beyng niȝe. þan, forsoþe, may he *with* vnguento arabico and salus po*pu*li finaly spede þe forseid cure aboute four & tuenty wekes, or more or lesse, aftir þat þe pacient be obedient and bisy; ffor why; gret spede of werk standeth in þe paciens and bisynes of þe pacient.[1]

The treatment of ulceration of the rectum.

And it is to witte þat in all vlc*er*ieȝ beyng wiþin þe lure, or moiste ragadiis puttyng out quitour or blode, þis I sey þat þe vlcereȝ be noȝt bubones, i. e. owles, of whiche it shal be seid aftirward, for þai be al vncurable[2]: þat if a leche may noȝt wiþoute grete anguissħ, als wele of hymself as of þe pacient, opne þe lure of þe pacient wiþ tonges, as it is seide afore, þan owe þe leche oonly putte in of tapsimell and pulu*er* sine p*ar*e medled togidre in suche þiknes þat

The applications are not to be too irritating.

it may be ȝetted in by a nastar*e* of tree. For why; þis medicyne mortifieþ wele and clenseþ putred flessh in an vlcere. But witte þou þat eue*r*more aftir þe ȝettyng in of tapsimel wiþ þe forseid poudre, þou ow in þe nexte reparalyng for to ȝette in wiþ a nastar*e* of tre of þe ȝolk of an ey wiþ sang*uis* ven*er*is or oyle rosette, or wiþ comon oile if þe forsaid wante. And þis cure be continued wiþoute leffyng

[* leaf 150, back]

*by þre or foure dayes. It spedeþ noȝt, forsoþe, þat medicynes bryngyng in akyng be to moche vsed or haunted, as is tapsimel wiþ pulu*er* sine pare.

Soothing clysters are best.

Neþ*er*lesse tapsimel wiþout pulu*er* sine p*ar*e, wiþ þe ȝolk of an ey and wiþ poudre of bole armonic ful smal y-broke and medled wiþ oile of lynsed togidre, oyle of rose added to, or of violett*is*, or of sanguis ven*er*is if it be had redy, And ȝetted in wiþ Nastar*e* of tre, heleþ wele vlceres, ragadyes, and excoriacions or fleyngis wiþin

[1] Nam magna operis expeditio in patientiâ et sedulitate patientis consistit.

[2] Nota de ulceribus infra anum existentibus. Et notandum quod in omnibus ulceribus infra anum existentibus, vel rhagadiis humidis saniem emittentibus vel sanguinem, hoc dico, quod ulcera non sunt bubones, de quibus inferius suo loco dicetur; Bubones namque sunt omnes incurabiles.

þe lure; þis supposed aft*er* þe sleyng of flessh putred,[1] wiþ enoyntyng of salus p*opu*li, þat availeth beste for certeyn in euery cause wiþin þe lure and wiþoute.

Of bubo with-in þe lure, and the impossibilitie or mych hardnes of þe cure of it.

6. [B]ubo is ane aposteme bredyng wiþin þe lure in þe longaon wiþ grete hardnes but litle akyng. Þis I sey byfore his vl*cer*acion þat is noþing elles þan a hidde canker*e*, þat may noȝt in þe bigynnyng of it be knowen by þe siȝt of þe eiȝe, for it is hid al wiþin þe lure; And *þer*fore it is callid bubo, for as bubo, i.e. an owle, is a best dwellyng in hideles[2] so þis sikenes lurkeþ wiþin þe lure in þe bikynnyng, but aft*er* p*ro*cesse of tyme it vlcerate, & fretyng þe lure goþe out. And ofte-tyme it fretiþ and wasteth all þe circu*m*ference of it, so þat þe feces of egestiones goþ out continuely vnto þe deth, þat it may ne*uer* be cured wiþ ma*n*nes cure but if it plese god, þat made man of noȝt, for to help wiþ his vnspekeable v*er*tu. Whiche, forsoþe, is knowen þus: Putte þe leche his fynger into þe lure of þe pacient, and if he fynde wiþin þe lure ane hard þing as a stone, somtyme on þe to p*ar*ty al-oonly, som tyme of boþe, so þat it lette þe pacient for to haue egestion, it is bubo for certayn. Signes, forsoþe, of his vlceracion bene þise: þe pacient may noȝt abstene hym fro þe pryuè for akyng & prikkyng, and þat twyse or þrise wiþin ane houre[3]; and *þer* goþe quitour out *þer*-of as it war medled wiþ watrye blode and stynkyng. To þat also wele vnkunyng leches, as þe pacient,[4] troweþ þat þey haue þe dissenterie, þat is þe blody fluxe, when trewly it is noȝt. Dissenterye is eu*er*more wiþ flux of þe wombe, but bubo goþ out hard egestions, and som tyme þey may noȝt go out for streytnes of þe bubon but þai ar constreyned wiþin þe lure streitly, so þat þai may be feled wiþ þe fynger and y-drawe out. And in þis cas availeþ þe myche clisteries lenitiues of watre of decoccion of whete brenne[5] wiþ oyle or butter, or wiþ

Cancer of the rectum.

The diagnosis.

The signs

often mistaken for dysentery.

The way to distinguish between cancer and dysentery.

1 Hoc superposito post mortificationem putridæ carnis.

2 Bubo est animal latebras colens.

3 "et aliquando sæpius," adds the Latin text.

4 Tam medici ignari, quam patientis.

5 lenitiva ex aquâ decoct. furfuris tritici.

symple decoccion of branne wiþoute medlyng of any oþer þing. Neþerlesse vnkunyng leches ministreþ vnto suche restrictiues medicynes of dissenterie, of bole,

Read Bernard de Gordon's 'Lilium medicinæ.'

and sang dracon, mastik, coriandre, sumac, mirtilles, harde ȝolkis of eyren, gret wyne, and suche oþer þat aváileþ to restreynyng of flux of þe wombe, as þou shalt mowe fynde in 'lilio[1] medicyne,' capito "de fluxu ventris." And how moche more þat þai giffe restrictiues, so moche more þai noye to þe forseid in constipand, i.[e.] costyuenes, and in hardenand þe squilullam[2]; þat I haue oftymes bene experte of, And I haue lerned it in experience in whiche I was not bigiled: ffor why; constrictiues y-lefte als wele in diete as in þe forseid

The diet in cancer. [* leaf 151]

medicynes I esed mich wiþ vse *of clisterieȝ of branne symple or of malueȝ and branne wiþoute oyle or butter or any fatnes; ffor why; al fatte þingis and oile þingis norissheþ þe cancre and fediþ it. And it is to witte þat þise bene þe accidentes of þam þat haþ bubon in

The symptoms.

þe lure: þai may ete and drynk and go, and somwhat sitte and somwhat slepe; þai be menely hungry and þrifty in mete vnto þe ende; þai may noȝt abstene

Death in autumn.

þam fro þe priuè. And ofte tymeȝ comeþ perisshyng to þam aboute autumpne or heruest; and it neiȝyng nere,

The favourable signs.

þay bigynne for to haue febres as it war a softe febre; and þai lose as it war þair appetite; þai bigynne for to loþe ale and þai couaite wyne; þai ete ych day lesse and lesse; þai slepe vnesely; þai ar made heuy als wele in mynde as in body; and þe fallyng doune neiȝhyng nere, þai are made feble, and þai halde continuely þair bedde, and þay couayte watre aboue all þingis. þise þerfore y-sene, deþe is in þe ȝatis.[3] Neþerlesse þai may speke & raise þamself vp and moue almost to þe

Be careful only to use palliative treatment.

breþing out of þe spirit. þerfore wake ȝe þat ȝe putte noȝt ȝoure hand to þis but in giffyng clisteries, as it is seid afore; whiche alegeþe mych þe forseid pacientes, as I haue be experte, and makeþ euermore pronosticacion

Warn the friends.

to þam or to þair frendes als wele of deþ as of vncurablenes. Sich pronosticacion, forsoþe, shal worshipe þe bisynes of þe leche: þerfore flieþ auarice and abstene ȝow fro false byhestis. Witte þou þat þe fynger y-putte

[1] in lilio medicinæ capitulo.

[2] squibala.

[3] His ergo visis, mors est in januis.

into þe lure of hym þat has þe dissenterye, he shal fele noþing in þe longaon but to þe man*er* of oþ*er* hole menne. But in þe lure of þam þat haþ þe bubon) shal be feled a bolnyng riȝt hard, as if þ*er* war an ey of ane henne or of a gose. But neþ*er*lesse þe putrede, i.[e.] rote*n*neȝ, and þe blode þat goþe out of boþe bene mych liche; þat is þe quitour is citryne or ȝellow and blo or wanne medled wiþ watry blode wiþ gret stynk, and it goþe out to þe quantite of o sponeful or of tuo wiþout medlyng of egestionȝ, and som-tyme wiþ egestion. But in dissenterie he shal fele fretyng about þe nauyle and þe flankes; in bubon, forsoþe, noȝt so; but akyng, stirryng, and prikkyng, and tenasmon; þat is, appetite of egestion. I se oon of Northampton-shire whos lure was frete on eu*er*y p*ar*ty, so þat he miȝt wiþholde noþing of þe feces of egestions but þe grettest; ffor why; his lure was euermore stopped w*ith* a grete towell of lynne cloþe; but neþ*er*lesse þe þinner egestions went out continuely, so þat his cloþes about his buttokes war euermore moyste; and þe towel y-drawen out, in þe stede of þe lure was a rounde hole by whiche an ey of a dukke miȝt liȝtly be putte in, and I myȝt se ferre into his wombe. Whiche died aft*er*ward of þe forseid infirmite; ffor why; he was vncurable, for þe mouþe of þe lure wiþ þe lacertes and þe synowes speryng and opnyng þe lure was vtterly gnawen away.[1] And forþy [2] in suche like be it done avisily þat couaitise bryng noȝt forþe blame to þe leche. I saw neu*er* ne I hard noȝt any man þat miȝt be cured of þe bubon), but I haue knowen many þat defaileþ of þe forseid sikenes. Also I haue sene som hauyng a ful gret brennyng aboute þe lure wiþout, and vntholeful smertyng[3] wiþ ronklyng of þe skynne aboute þe lure closed to þe * maner of a purse, wherfore þe pacientes miȝt noȝt wele sitte, ne ligge, ne stonde euen, ne fynde reste in no place, but eu*er*more mònyng and stirryng þamself as it war wode men. And sup*er*flue watrenes swette out fro þe place þat was wonte for to file many lynnen cloþes putte atwix. To whiche sikenes availeþ mich colde þingis in power but hote in dede y-putte to, as bene aysel,[4] vinegre, hote by itself or wiþ

Make a rectal examination to distinguish between cancer and dysentery.

An advanced case of cancer of the rectum.

Cancer of the rectum incurable.

[* leaf 151, back]

Palliative treatment methods to be adopted.

[1] quod orificium luræ cum lacertis et nervis Luram claudentibus et aperientibus omnino corrodebantur.

[2] idcirco.

[3] pruriginem intolerabilem.

[4] acetum.

Local applications.

Iuyse of rubarbe, or plantayne, or virga pastoris, or of oþer cold þingis in power. But for þat ofte-tymes suche herbes may noȝt be had redy, þan it is to flye to oþer remedyes; þat is to sey, Take þe raw ȝolk of an ey and medle it wele wiþ þe poudre of bole armenic broken ful smal, or ceruse, or boþe, and anoynt it aboue þe sore wiþ a penne or feþer or wiþ a spatule; þis, forsoþe, seseþ þe brennyng and þe akyng, and be þis oft tymes done agaynȝ.

Fomentations.

Also in euery remouyng it aualeþ mich þat þe yuel or sore be wele fomented or soked wiþ vinegre and watre y-medled togidre and chaufed; ffor why; þis gretly euaporeth noyful hete. And aftir þe fomentyng, þe place wele y-dried, be it reparaled as it is seid afore, wiþ þe ȝolk of an ey and bole.

An ointment for pruritus ani.

When þe customable watrynes, forsoþe, is sene to cese, and þe pacient feleþ as it war vnsufferable ychyng, þan be þer putte to euery day oones ane oyntement made of blakke sope and poudre of bole and sulphur and frankensence ymedled to-gidre. And þis oyntment shal drie, and shal make skales to rise fro þe sore; whiche y-sene, be þe lure anoynted als wele wiþin as wiþout wiþ vnguentum album sharped wiþ bole and wiþ quik-siluer, and þis shal cese þe hete and it shal cicatriȝe þe fleeng.[1] And if it bene anoynted wiþ salus populi, it profiteþ mych.

Another ointment.

At þe last, forsoþe, agaynȝ þe disesyng ychyng be it anoynted wiþ tapsimel, In whiche be pulueresȝ of alume ȝucarine brent, of attrament, and of vitriol; þis, forsoþe, doþe heste away ychyng for certayn, als wele wiþin þe lure as wiþoute. Or if þou haue noȝt redy þe forseid tapsimell, be þe same done wiþ scomed hony, and þe ferseid pulueres medled þer-to. Or þer may be made a medicyne to þe maner of þe forseid tapsimel of þe Iuyse of celidone and scomed hony, to þe whiche þe forseid pulueresȝ ymedled, I haue proued þat it doþe heste awey ychyng.[2] Also þe Iuyse of celidone y-medled wiþ vinegre and warmed at þe fire, and wiþ a fether anoynted up þe foreseid sore, þat is to sey in þe bigynnyng of þe sikenes, it quenchiþ wele þe wickid hete and keped fro recidinacion,[3] þat is fallyng agayne.

A treatment for erysipelas.

And it quenchiþ wele herisiptam, þat is wilde fir

[1] et hoc calorem sedabit et escoriationem cicatrisabit.

[2] Pruritus

[3] bene calorem noxium extinguit et a recidinatione preservit.

or few sawage[1] in euery place of þe body. And þe same doþ leuke vinegre[2] put aboue by itself; Or vnguentu*m* albu*m* sharped wiþ quicsilu*er*. Also oile of citonior: cureþ þe herisiple and wickid vlcereȝ.[3] Also þe Iuyse of celidone, imbibed in a sponge or in ly*n*ne cloþes, and y-putte leuke to þe front and to þe temples, it ceseþ þe akyng of þe heued. And þis I proued oftymes in þe second pestilence. Þer come a man fro Burdeux in Gascon vnto Newerk, þat had ane horrible sore, þat is to sey peces or gobett*is* of rede flesshe and rawe in p*ar*ties hyngyng dovne to þe lengþe of ane ynch. And þai occupied boþe his buttokes on aiþ*er* p*ar*ty of þe lure to þe *brede of þre fyngers; and þ*er* went out þer-of riȝt mich watrinesse and some-tyme blode wiþ gret hete and stynk, so þat his buttokkes war cauteriȝid; and þei grew to þe liknes of þe womb of a fissh þat is seid creuyse or lopster when he sp*er*meþ or frieþ. And þose sup*er*fluites p*ar*tyngly grew in þe hole skynne; and when þei war mortified euen to þe rotes, þer appered holes fro whens þai went out. I mortified, forsoþe, þe sup*er*fluities wiþ a poudre þat is called Pulu*er* greke, þe confeccion of þe whiche shal shewe aftir. And for þat þe mich watrynes goyng out in þe bigynnyng ouercome þe forseid poudre, þ*er*fore I putte aboue, aftir þe puttyng of þe poudre greke, of þe moste subtile mele of barly abundandly, þat is called alfita, aboue þe poudre greke; and so I quenchid þe forseid sup*er*fluites wiþin þre or four puttyng to, so þat þai bigan to dry and to welk and fall away. Pulu*er* grek, forsoþe, is riȝt desiccatiue and wele cleuyng[4] to; and noȝt oonly it restreyneth wele watry moistenes but also blode, and it mortifieþ þe curable canc*er* and þe blody fike[5] in eu*er*y place. A man had vpon his buttok a blody fyk puttyng out blode and somtyme quit*our*, and it was like to a Mulbery; to þe whiche I putte aboue pulu*er* grek by oon niȝt, and in þe mornyng I pulled out riȝt liȝtly wiþ my fyngers þe fike half mortified; þe whiche y-drawe out, blak blode went out aft*er*. Aft*er* a litel goyng of þe blode, forsoþe, I putte to pulu*er* grek, and þe blode was restreyned. Aboue þe

Recites a case, and its treatment.

[* leaf 152]

Pulvis Græcus and its uses.

A case of bleeding piles and its treatment.

1 "feu sauvage."
2 Acetum tepidum.
3 Ulcus perniciosa.
4 bene adhærens.
5 ficum sanguineum.

poudre, forsoþe, coton y-put atuyx, I putte aboue þe emplastre Nerbon vpon a lyn cloute, to kepe þe poudre þat it shulde noȝt falle away. And þus, þis forseid cure continued, he was hole wiþin a shorte tyme.

Of fistules in þe fyngers, and hardnes of cure of it.

7. [I] haue sene oft-tymes þe fistule be in þe fyngers and in þe þombes, als wele of men as of wy*m*men; als wele of ȝong men as of olde men; þe cure of whiche many men knoweþ noȝt: ffor why; it bredeþ oft-tyme in þe fynger or þe þombe of som men in þe extremitè of þe flesshynes mortifying al þe oue*r*more iuncture, þat is þe flesshe wiþ þe bone. And somtyme it brediþ in þe middes iuncture, and þat is more pe*r*ile; and somtyme in þe lawer iuncture by þe hande, and þat is werste. Neþe*r*lesse þe fistule bredyng in þe extremitè of þe fynger deceyueþ so*n*ner þe pacient þan in oþer places; ffor vnku*n*nyng men seiþ þat it is þe whitflowe, whiche þou shalt knowe þus. If þer byfal to any man in þe extremitè of his fynger akyng wiþ inflacion, and when þat it bristeþ it makiþ a litel hole, and oute of þat hole þe*r* goþ out a litle docelle of putrified flessħ or rede, to þe gretnes of a whete corne, and þe*r* goþ but litle quitour or noon out þerof, þan witte þou þat þer cleueþ a fistule to þe fynger. And wiþoute doute if it be wiþoute help any long tyme, as by a moneþ or fourty dayes, it shal noȝt mow be cured wiþoute lesyng of þe oue*r*more iuncture wiþ þe bone, and pe*r*auenture of þe ouermore and þe neþer-more boþe; þat I haue oftymes proued. ffor why; oftymes þe bone of þe fynger is frete or gnawen or it bigynne for to ake, þat is proued þus. fforsoþe I haue heled som men þat seid þat þei feled noon yuel but by a fourtniȝt; *And when I saw þe forseid tokne of þe fistule, þan al-sone I depa*r*ted in-als-mych as I myȝt þe skyn of þe fynger riȝt foule wiþ a rasour and sheres; and þe skynne y-put of, I fonde al wiþin putrefied, and neþe*r*lesse þe fynger was noȝt but a litle bolned. And poudre creoferoboron y-putte

Fistulæ in the fingers not to be mistaken for whitlows;

they take a long time to cure.

[* leaf 152, back]

Some cases seen early.

Their treatment.

to mundefye þe corrupcion by al a niȝt, and aboue þe emplastre sang*ui*boetos. In þe mornyng when þe filþe was dissolued and drawen out, I p*er*ceyued þe bone of þe fynger to be tabefacte, i.[e.] corrupte, and frete & loused fro þe toþ*er* iuncture, and þat was meruaile. And in som men I haue p*er*ceyued þe bone corrupte in p*ar*ty and noȝt in all fully; and somtyme two iunctures vtterly mortefied and corrupte. ffor why; it is certayne þat bones shul noȝt be corrupte wiþin a fourtniȝt if þai war vncorrupte afore þat tyme. Þe cure of þe forseid is such: If sich ane yuel or sore come of newe, and he haue had no cure afore, and if þou p*er*ceyue þe forseid tokne of fistulacion, þan alsone be þe skyn flayn wiþ a rasour, as it is seid afore. Aftirward if þ*er* be any filþe þ*er*in, be pressed out. Aftirward, forsoþe, be þe wounde filled of þe pulu*er* creoferoboron; þat y-do, be þ*er* putte aboute of the emplastre Sang*ui*boetos wiþ stupes, and so be it lefte by oon day and a niȝt hole. Aftirwarde whan þou remoues þe emplastre and haþ mundified þe filþe y-fonden, If þou fynde þe bone of it blak and putrefied in þe hiȝe p*ar*ty, it bihoueþ of necessite be drawen out. Or if þe vtter p*ar*ty of þe bone be losed al aboute fro þe flesshe and þe naile, þof-al it be noȝt blak, it bihoueþ be departed and þat alsone as it may, þat þe bone þat is corrupte aboue infecte noȝt wiþ his corrupcion þe bone þat is festned to hym; whiche if it bifal, it bihoueþ boþe be drawen out. ffor why; a corrupte bone or a lesed may noȝt dwelle or abide in þe flesshe, for no cure beyng mene, þat ne it corrumpe ouþ*er* þe flesshe or þe synowes. Or þe flesshe shal caste it out when it is in a wounde or in aposteme, or in a cancre or fistule. Þe bone forsoþe y-drawen out, be þe place y-filled of þe poudre creoferoboron, and aboue þe emplastre Sang*ui*boetos; and be it lefte þer by als long tyme as it is seid afore. Aftir forsoþe, þe emplastre remoued, if þou se þe hole y-clensed wiþ þe forseid poudre, þan be þ*er* putte eftsones of þe forseid emplastre wiþ þe poudre, renewyng þe emplastre ych day tuyse. And so wiþ þe forseid emplastre, or wiþ vnguent*um* viride lefe noȝt to hele it vnto þe ende. If

The signs not obvious at first.

The dead bone should be removed.

Treatment after the dead bone is removed.

A means of recognizing the growth of proud flesh.

þ*er* growe, forsoþe, any sup*er*flue flesshe in þe hole, as it falleþ oft tymes, þat þ*o*u shalt know þus: þe sup*er*flue flesshe bygynne for to growe fro þe bone in middes of þe hole, and noȝt fro þe sides of þe flessħ. And wiþin þre dayes or foure, if it be not mette or agayn-standen it passeþ þe sides of þ*e* gode flessh, for it groweþ wiþ hastines; whiche flessh, forsoþe, may be drawen out in þe bigynnyng wiþ þe poudre of creoferoboron. If it excede in grete quantitè, þan it bihoueþ for to putte to poudre of arcenek, or ane hote iren.

Treatment of the fistula

Aftir þe puttyng to of þe poudre, or of þe hote iren, þ*er* is to be putte-to larde enoynted wiþ þe iuse of porres, for to lese [* leaf 153] *þe mortified flessħ; whiche y-lesed, þe fynger is to be enoynted wiþ ane oyntment made of sape & brymston. In þe hole, forsoþe, be putte vnguentu*m* viride vpon a stupe; and eu*er*y day be it tuyse remoued, and þus eu*er*more sewe þe forseid man*er*.

by operation.

If þe bone, forsoþe, of þe fynger or of þe þombe be corrupte in p*ar*ty bot no3t lesed fro þe naile, þan aftir þe mi3t be þe corrupte shauen away, and þan be put þ*er*to liciu*m*, þat is carpe wette, in ane oyntment þus y-made: Take liciu*m*, þat is þe iuse of wodbynde, i.[e.] caprifoile, and hony and poudre of white glasse an*a*; be þai medled togidre and made ane oyntment; þis oyntment engendreþ flessh; it fleeþ þe fistule; it mu*n*difieþ þe filþe or putrifaccion of þe bone. ffor why; glasse makeþ flessh for to grow vpon þe bone; hony purgeþ and remoueþ þe stynk; liciu*m* haþ vertu for to mu*n*difie þe filthe or þe putrefaccion of þe bone, and for to hele þe wonde, and for to sle þe cancre and þe fistule.

Licium is made in this way.

And liciu*m* is made þus: Take þe leue3 of caprifoile and brisse þam in a morter, and þriste out þe iuse, and putte in a brasen vessel or of glasse, and drie it at þe sunne, and kepe it to vse. It is þe beste medicyne; If þe fynger, forsoþe, of any man haue be long vnheled of vnwise cure, or of negligence of þe pacient aft*er* þat þe bone is take out—

A case treated by a lady was so neglected that

As somtyme it bifell of oon þat was vnder þe cure of a lady by halfe a ȝere, aft*er* þat þe vppermore iuncture of þe bone of þe fynger was drawen out. ffor why; þat lady entended for to haue heled hym al-oonly wiþ drynk of Antioche and oþ*er* pillul*es*; and for cause þat the naiȝ of þe fynger abode stille, she trowed þ*er*fore for to haue souded þe place of þe fynger in whiche þe bone þat was drawen oute stode bifore; whiche, forsoþe, miȝt noȝt be, for þe flessħ and þe skynne wiþ þe naile þat went aboute þe bone bifore war infecte and putrefacte of þe bone; wherfore of necessite al mortified and corrupte bihoued to be drawen out of þe flessh and þe skyn or þat it shulde come to helþe. Þ*er*fore a long tyme ou*er*passed, when he come to me and þe fynger ysene, first I putte in poudre creoferoboron, and aboue þe emplastre Sanguiboetos in þe man*er* seid afore. Aftirward, it remoued, I p*er*ceyued þat it was of hard substance and inobedient to þe poudre; þan putte I to poudre of arsenek. In þe day, forsoþe, folowyng, I biholdyng þe fynger I p*er*ceyued þat þe arsenek had wrouȝt litel or noȝt. ffor þe place wher arsenek is putte in, if it wirch p*er*fitely, shal bycome blo & bolned aboute þe extremites wiþin a niȝt and a day; Aftir in þe þrid day þ*er* shal departe in sondre in þat blones, þat is to sey mortified fro þe quik. But þat worchyng shal better done and soner if þe secounde day aft*er* þe puttyng to of arsenek be putte to larde wiþ þe emplastre sanguiboetes. The place, forsoþe, of þe forseid fynger strongly agayn-stode to þe poudre of arsenek. ffor þe place was drye and inveterate, or olde, in substaunce. Þis y-sene, wiþ som men it is to wirche wiþ cauteries; þan, forsoþe, a cauterie putte þ*er*-to, I brent þe fynger in þe extremite of it wiþin vnto þe bone; þe pacient, forsoþe, almost feled noþing. Aftir þe brennyng, forsoþe, I putte in to þe hole þe fattenes of lard wiþ þe iuse of porres; þe second day, forsoþe, a gret quantite y-mor*tified, þe flesshe and þe skynne went away wiþ þe naile; þan þat tyme I putte-to þe emplastre Sanguiboetes; In þe mornyng, forsoþe, þe poudre Creoferoboron wiþ þe same emplastre. And so aftirward by seuen dayes, ich day wirchyng as it is seid, þer was ȝitte þ*er*fore in þe wounde þe endes or heuedes of synowes; whiche, þe bone remoued, war festned, apperyng wiþ a man*er* blaknes, and þe flessħ mortified on þe to partye. Þis y-sene,

it had to be dressed with arsenic

and touched with the actual cautery

[* leaf 153, back]

for seven days before the dead bone could be removed,

eft-sones I couchid softly þe heuedes of þe synowes and þe side mortified *with* ane hote iren, puttyng in þe shauyng of lard wiþ þe iuse of porres. In þe mornyng, forsoþe, þat sup*er*flue flessħ was remoued, and þan I putte in poudre of Creoferoboron for to mundifye it, and aboue þe emplastre forseid, and so aft*ir*ward *con*tinuely by þre dayes: þan, forsoþe, putte I to þe enoyntment made of liciu*m*, seid afore, continuely by nyen dayes. I enoynted, forsoþe, al aboute þe fynger vpon aiþ*er* side wiþ ane enoyntment made of sope and sulphur*e*, and als sone þe fynger was flayne, and put out as it war scales; and als sone þe bolnyng biganne for to cese; þan, forsoþe, I putte-to vnguentu*m* viride vpon stupes, And þe fynger bigan for to soude. But a litel after þe puttyng to of vnguentu*m* virid*e*, þer bigan for to growe vpon þe heued of þe bone of þe iuncture rede flessħ to þe gretnes of a pese; and þat y-sene, I distroyed it wiþ a cauterie; And þan I made hym suche ane oyntement desiccatiue. R*ecipe*: Sulphu*r*. auri-pigment*i*, tartar., alume, vitriol, sape and oyle; whiche ich day puttyng to oones, he recouered helþe p*er*fitely.

and for nine days with ointment,

and the patient recovered perfectly.

8. Of fistul in þe lawe ioyntour of þe fyngers, and in þe legges, knees, fete, & ankles, wiþ corruptyng of þe bones, and þe hardnes of þe cure.

Cases of Spina ventosa.

[S]um-tyme also the fistule gutte byfalleþ in þe fyngers of ȝong men, and oft-tymes of ȝong wy*m*men, in þe lower ioynture by þe hande, and it makeþ holes in þe skynne som-tyme on þe to p*ar*ty and som-tyme on boþe p*ar*tyes. When þe knowes, forsoþe, þe holes to be on þe boþe p*ar*ties, witte þou þat þe pacient is incurable, But if þe fynger be holy cutte away be þe iuncture where it is festned to þe hand. If þe bone, forsoþe, of þe hand niȝe to þat fynger be corrupte also, he is incurable but if it be drawen out. But witte þou þat it is noȝt mich to entremette of þe cure of suche þat þe helþ of þam be vndertaken. ffor I haue but seldom

Amputation is best.

sene any suche scape wiþout deþe whan þe sikenes was helped. ffor þe fluxe or þe rynnyng þ*er* y-dried, or stopped, or staunched, þai dye sone after. Suche þingis shalt þou knowe þus: þe fynger or þe hand, or þe fote, or þe legge, or any oþer membre in whiche is sich a fistule stynkeþ gretly; it haþ streite holes; þe wondes haþ hardnes wiþ whitenes and redenes; and when þe wondes be rennyng þan þe pacient haþ hymself miryly and glad; and when þai ar stopped þe pacientes bene pale in þe face and lene and feble. Also it falleþ of-tyme in þe legge, in þe knee, in þe fote, and in þe ankle. In þe legge and in þe fote I haue cured it, and in þe ankle; But in þe ankle and þe kne also it bristed out agayn aftir litle tyme.

Signs of incurable fistulæ.

9. Of þe man*er* of cure of oon þat had þe fistule in þe legges aboue þe ankle.

[O]on tyme I heled a man þat had a fistule goutte in þe legge aboue þe ankle and þe fote wiþ þe emplastre Sanguiboetes, and wiþ a poudre þat is *made þus: R*ecipe* auripigment*i*, sulphur, calx viue, and black sape an*a*; be þai poudred and putte to tuyse in þe day. Aboute þe wounde, forsoþe, I anoynted it wiþ comon oyle or vnguent*um* alb*um* vnto þat he come to p*er*fite helþe. Also I gaffe hym drynk of Antioche. Aftir þe cure, forsoþe, I sawe hym neu*er*, þ*er*fore I know noȝt how long he liffed.

A powder for fistulous gout.

[* leaf 154]

10. Of þe maner of cure of ane enposteme in the buȝt of the knee that was disposed to the fistule.

[O]on aposteme come to a man in the bowyng of þe kne, þat was hard to breke for vncouenable emplastres putte þ*er*-to first; þ*er*fore I putte first þ*er*to þe skynne of lard þat diffieþ wele apostemeȝ; And neþ*er*lesse aft*er* þre dayes I miȝt noȝt perceyue signe or tokne of rupture or of brystyng. Whiche y-sene, I wold þrieȝ haue opned it wiþ a fleobotome or wiþ a raso*ur*, but þe pacient for-

Treatment of a patient with an inflammation in the ham,

who would not have it opened.

soke it; þan, forsoþe, put I to ane herbe y-brissed þat is called pede lyon, þat it miȝt make a rupture in þe skyn, for it was to þikke; and in þe niȝt þe pacient put it

The plaster used.

away. Þan made I ane emplastre to hym of mele of whete and of clene hony medled togidre, and I putte it to; & aftir þe second puttyng to it brest in þe niȝt, and þer ranne out þerof quitour wiþ-out mesure; þe quitoure y-þristed out, I putte in tentes of larde to þe lengþe of a fynger, þat þe hole shulde noȝt be stopped byfore þat þe aposteme war purged. In þe mene tyme

The discharge ceased when he became feverish,

þe pacient felle into þe febres agueȝ, And als sone þe flux or þe rennyng of þe quitour in þe aposteme cesed, in partye for negligence þat tentes was noȝt put in bycause of þe sikenes, and in party for distemperaunce of hete þat dried it. And so, þe hole y-closed or stopped, it biganne eft-sones for to bolne bineþe and for to gedre to a newe aposteme; þe whiche y-sene, I opned þe hole wiþ a spature and expressed þe quitour gedrid to-gidre. Aftirward I putte in ich day of lard, renewyng it ich, by a fourtniȝt and more. And neþerlesse I perceyued

and the inflammation nearly became a fistula.

noȝt þat þe aposteme dried any-þing, but more and more for to harden and wax rede, and putte out quitore, liquide and watry, somtyme mych and somtyme noþing. Þerfore I perceyued þat þe place was disposed to þe fistule, for it had ane hole or a mouþe and a depe wonde, and it putte out quitour of diuerse coloures and liquide, wiþ hardnes of þe place and yuel habitude or hauyng; þerfore I putte in tentes anoynted wiþ anoyntement þat is made agayns þe fistule, þat is þus made: R*ecipe* auripigment, sulphur, calx viue, blak sape; þe whiche, forsoþe, y-putte in fyue tymes or seuen, I perceyued it noþing to amende. I made a ventose to be putte to, and it wolde noȝt drye; þis y-sene, I perceyued þat rewme—þat is a flowyng or rennyng—miȝt noȝt cese, for þe place in whiche was þe aposteme is of moiste substaunce. And it is to witte þat in þe place byside þe bowyng of the kne

Arderne has seen the popliteal space in dead men.

in þe neþer party is a place þat haþ no flessh but fatnes aloon; As I haue sene þer in dede men, þe skyn of þe flessħ y-persed and þat fatnes bene eten or wastedde. Þan I putte in þe hole vnto þe ground a tent of tre, somwhat brode, and aboue I cutted þe skyn by þe middes wiþ a rasour. In þe wonde, *forsoþe, I putte a cloth depped in þe white of an ey. In þe morne, forsoþe, it remoued, I put in a poudre þat is þus made: R*ecipe* vert-grese, vitriol, auripigment*um*, alume; Aboue, forsoþe, carpe, And aftirward ane emplastre þat is þus made: R*ecipe*: apii, i.[e.] smalach, Mogwort, Walwort &c. as aboue. And so wiþ þis poudre and þis emplastre he wás sone aftir cured. Or if þou wilt, aftir þe cuttyng þou may hele w*ith* diaquilon. But it is to witte þat he þat owe to make incision in þis place þat he be-war of þe grete veyne þat is called sophena, þat comeþ doun by the þ[i]e to þe legge, þat it be noȝt kutted, for it liggeþ niȝe þat fatty flesshe &c.

[* leaf 154, back]

The patient was cured by a stimulating powder and plaster.

Beware of cutting the vessels in operating on the ham.

11. [þ]e arme of a certane manne biganne sodenly for to ake & prik in þe buȝt of þe arme[1] and aft*er*ward gretly to bolne fro þe shulder to þe fyngers; þe pacient, forsoþ, hauntyng or vsyng þe medycineȝ of ladieȝ, as it war by a moneþ, euermore had hymself worse. At þe last he soȝt & asked my help. And when I biheld his arme gretly bolned & replete of redenes & of brennyng & hardneȝ & akyng, ffirst I made hym ane emplastre of tartare of ale, i.[e.] dreggeȝ, & of malueȝ, & hony, & salt, & bran, & schepeȝ talowe boiled togidre to thikneȝ, & streched vpon stupeȝ and folden w*ith* a lynne cloþe. I put þe emplastre on his arme, and alsone he feled alegeance of akyng. Þe 3 day, forsoþ, remeuyng þe emplastre, þe bolnyng in p*ar*ty was slaked. Bot in þe buȝt of þe arme al þe colleccion or gedryng abode stille, schewyng as it schuld gadre to ane heued. Þe which y-sene, I putte to ane emplastre maturatyue of malueȝ y-soþen and y-brissed, w*ith* grese 3 daies or 4, and neþ*er*les I p*er*ceyued neu*er* þe son*er* for to be matured, bot þe bolnyng abode mych stil. And in þe buȝt of þe arme þe skyne appered rounde w*ith* diu*er*se colou*r*s to þe man*er* of a tode,[2] alwaieȝ denying tokne of rupture. And in þe ground or bothme of þat gedryng was felt ane hard þing, as it war ane nutte riȝt in þe buȝt vnder [a]vena epatica.[a] Which y-sene, I putte to al a niȝt ane

[leaf 155 (*in a different hand*)]

Another case of a man who was treated by ladies.

Arderne treated him with a plaster until the swelling subsided,

and afterwards a mallow plaster.

1 in flexu brachii.

2 ad modum bufonis.

a—a "i.[e.] lyu*er* vayne" *overlined*.

The arm blistered,

emplastre of colu*er*ȝ dong[1] & porris[a] & garlek y-brissed w*ith* þe iuyse of apii and a gode handful of salt. And in þe mornyng remeuying it, þe place was ful of litle bladders in man*er* of pustuleȝ, and þer went out as it war water; þis y-sene, where þe sore semed þikker I putte vpon a cloþe schapen to þe brede of þe sore ane vntement made of blak sope and sulphure & of arsenec; aboue þat, forsoþe, þe emplastre seid afore. Þe second day, forsoþ, þat emplastre & oyntement remeued, þe skyn was vtterly bristen, and þ*er* appered a litel hole of þe arme, and þ*er* went out vnder blak water and holdyng in man*er* of groute. Þan I made putte aboue þat place chauy*ng* of lard; aboue, forsoþe, ane emplastre þus made. R*ecipe*: Iuyse of apii, wormode, Mugwort, netle, walwort, hony, white of ane ey, an*a*, and tempred w*ith* mele of ry. And if þ*o*u may noȝt haue al þise þings, þe iuyse alon of apii[b] w*ith* hony and white of ane ey and mele availeþ mych. And þan bigan þe ded flesch for to disseuere, And in þe arme wher war bifore þe bladders eu*er*more went out droppes of white watire when þe arme was bare w*ith*-out þe emplastre. And in middeȝ of þe more wonde appered pappeȝ of gret flesch; and eu*er*more þ*er* appered (a certayne ?[c])[2] rednes in þe skyn. To þe pappeȝ, forsoþe, I made sich a poudre; R*ecipe* viridis [æris], vitriol, auripigmentu*m*, alum an*a*; And I put it to ich oþ*er* daie; aboue þe poudre, forsoþe, I putte carpe, and at þe last aboue þat I put a litel clouth to þe qu*an*tite of þe wounde enoynted w*ith* vnguento fusco or albo or viridi. Þe rednes, forsoþe, and þe watry placeȝ I enoynted w*ith* ane oyntement made of blak sape, and poudre of sulph*ur*; aboue, forsoþe, a dry lynnen cloute, whiche I lete lye stille to þat it wold fall away bi it-self. And þan þat place put away from it al dry skynneȝ; than eftsoneȝ I anoynted w*ith* þe forseid vntement vnto þat þe rednes & þe water went vtterly away. Þe forseid wonde, forsoþe, was fully cured in þe forseid man*er*. Witte þou þat þis anoyntme*n*t is best to al spotteȝ or filþeȝ of þe skyn which giffeþ oute watre and makeþ redneȝ, for it

and the skin broke at the place, discharging dark blood.

The arm was rubbed with lard and a plaster put on;

it healed by granulation.

The ointments used.

The patient got well.

[1] ex fimo columbino.

[2] et semper quidam rubor in cute.

[a] "lekeȝ" *overlined.*
[b] "smallach" *overlined.*
[c] *Obliterated.*

drieþ mich and doþe away rednes in eue*r*y place of þe body, out-tak in þe eiȝen.

[leaf 155, back]

Bot witte þou þat aft*er* þe puttyng to of þe oyntment þat is þ*us* made—R*ecipe* sape, sulph*ur* & arsenec—þer appered a blak litel cruste to þe þiknes of a seme of a scho, þat was hard for to parte w*ith* þe forseid corrosiueȝ for it was mich ritted. To which I putte aboue a cautery, i.[e.] a bry*n*nyng iren, þat þe pacient almost feled it noȝt. Aft*er* þe cauteriyng forsoþe, I putte to þe schauyng of larde, as it is seid aboue, in sewyng al þings vnto þe ende.

The cautery used.

12. [A] man was smyten on his legge vpon þe shynbone, but ne*þer*lesse þe skyn was noȝt cleuen[1] alsone aft*er* þe smytyng. Aft*er*ward, forsoþe, þe þrid day it bolned and bigan to ake. *þer*for he went to a man þat haunted or vsed sich cure vnto þe tyme þat *þer* come in his legge ane hole, rounde and depe, and ful of blak filth in man*er* of brent flesch; whome whan he come to me I heled hym þus. ffirst I wasched þe wounde w*ith* hote wyne, or water in which was decocte þe croppeȝ or þe iuyse of plantayne or sich, or in vryne. Aft*er*ward I putte to ane e*m*plastre made of iuyse of playntayne, of rubarb, of smalach, of hony, and whete or rie mele & white of eyren y-medled togidre; or ane emplastre þat is called sang*ui*boetes. Afterward, þe place su*m*what mollified, I putte to poudre Creoferoboron, w*ith* þe medicine of arsenec y-medlet; aboue þe poudre stupeȝ or carp; aboue al-togidre, forsoþe, þe emplastre of apii, mugwort, walwort seid afore. Aft*er* þe puttyng to forsoþe of þis poudre, I did þe cure in al þings w*ith* lard & w*ith* oþer þings, as it is seid aboue, vnto þe clensyng of þe wounde. Aft*er*ward, forsoþ, w*ith* vngue*n*to viridi & vnguento albo and carp I wroȝt in man*er* as it is seid aboue vnto þe ende. Aft*er*ward, forsoþ, when *þer* growed or wex any sup*er*flue flesch in þe wounde, I w*ith*stode it or mette it w*ith* poudre of creoferoboron or of litarge vnto þe fulle curyng of þe wounde. If any pustuleȝ wex in þe leg about þe wounde, þou may

A patient knocked his leg and an ulcer formed.

Arderne's plasters

and stimulating powder.

He treated the proud flesh.

[1] "Broke*n*" *overlined.*

Wounds with swords and axes must be treated like other injuries.

Bruises from the kick of a horse or from stones should first be scarified.

cure þam *with* vnguen*t*o albo, as it is seid aboue. ffforsoþ if þe wonde be in þe leg of swerd or ax or sich oþ*er*, be it cured as ben oþer woundes. If any man, forsoþ, be smyten in any p*ar*ty of þe legge violently and w*ith*out wondyng of þe skynne, as falleþ oft-tyme of þe smytyng of ane horse fote, or of a stone or of sich oþ*er*, þan is it gode sone in þe bigynnyng for to garse þe place y-smyten and for to draw out blode þ*er*-of, and aft*er*ward for to putte to emplastreȝ repressyng þe akyng and bolnyng.

A patient's leg swelled suddenly on a Christmas-day.

Arderne fomented it,

and by cock-crow the patient was relieved.

The juice of marigold is very useful in inflammation of the breasts and in whitlow.

[A] man in þe day of þe natiuite of our lorde sodenly had his legge gretly bolned fro þe kne to þe ankleȝ, w*ith* redenes and gret brennyng, so þat he myȝt noȝt stand. I (smeared?)[a] þe legge on ych side, and epithimated w*ith* þe iuyse of solseq*ui*, i.[e.] marigold, and a litil vinegre putte þ*er*to,[1] and made þam a litel leuke[b]; þe which y-do, lynnen cloþes wette in þe same iuyse I laide warme aboute his legge, and when þe cloþe was dronken of þe iuse I laid hym in his couche; And for certayn afor þe cok kraw þe akyng and þe brennyng was cesed and þe pacient rested wele. And w*ith*in þre daies w*ith*out any oþ*er* medicyne he was p*er*fitely cured, whar-of many men wondred. Also for certayn þe iuyse of solsiquii, marigold, epithimated bi it-self or w*ith* vinegre destroyeþ meruelo*us*ly apostemeȝ in þe pappes of wy*m*men, and þe felon,[c] and þe carbuncle and ȝekyng,[2] and rednes, and bloneȝ, and brennyng þat comeþ of þe forsaid þings.

[leaf 156]

A prescription for tartar water.

[A] chanon was on a tyme seke, and when he bigan to wex hole þar was made a grete gedryng to-gidre of humo*ur*s descendyng doune in his legge. Aft*er* a tyme, forsoþ, þ*er* wex pusceleȝ brovnysch and clayisch.[3] He, forsoþ, putte þat he schuld dry þe puscheȝ watre of tartar þ*us* y-made: R*ecipe* tartari ℔ i or ij, and putte it in ane newe erþen potte, and, þe mouþe of þe potte stopped w*ith* clay, putte it in a strong fire and lat it be þer a niȝt and a day or more if þou wiłł. Aft*er*ward tak þat tartar and hyng it in some place in a lynne*n*

[1] quem curavi cum succo solsequii addito parum de aceto et cum dicto succo tepido epithimiavi tibiam suam undique. [MS. Digby 161, leaf 22, back.]

[2] Pruritus.

[3] pustulæ fuscæ et latæ.

[a] *Obliterated.* [b] "warme" *overlined.*
[c] "antrace" *overlined.*

The treatment of an ulcerated leg in a Canon.

sacce or pokette, and vnder it putte a brasen vessel to receyue þe watre þat distilleþ droppyngly to þe maner of lye out of þe sak; þis watre is seid for to dry pusche3 wele, bot neþerlesse it availed no3t to hym. At þe last, forsoþ, þer grow in þat party of þe legge a large wounde, And about þe ankles þre or four smale wounde3 to þe brede of ane halfpeny. And þe legge semed of 3elow colour medled with rednes fro þe calf to þe ankele3, And þe skynne kast euermore out many skale3. When, forsoþ, he had vsed a certayne tyme lede or puluer incarnatyue and sawe þat it availed hym noþing, þan he vsed a long tyme ane entrete þat is called entractum nigrum,[1] blak entrete, which is made of white lede and rede and comon oile and tartarye &c.; bot neþerlesse he perceyued none amendyng þerof, for it come to a mormale; þe which, when I had sene it, I affermed it to be a mormale. And I did sich a cure to it: þis is þe cure to þe mormale—ffirst sewe þe pacient legge strongly with a lynne cloþe[2]; After wasche wele þat legge so sewed with hote watre, after þat þe pacient may suffre. And so after þe waschyng lat it lye by a naturel day, þat is ane hole day & a ni3t, kepyng þe legge fro aier and fro cold. Þe second day, forsoþ, remoue þe cloþe and mundifie þe wounde or þe woundes if þai be many, and putte in euery wounde a litel pece of lynne cloþe moisted in cold watre. Afterward putte of þe oyntement of dyuylyne in þe circuite of þe wounde[3] aboue þe hole skynne so þat it touche no waie3 þe wounde3 with-in, & couer it with a lynne cloþe y-wette. Do þus euery day tuye3, renewyng þe oyntment and mundifying þe wounde3 and fyllyng þam of a lynne cloþe y-wette, as it is seid aboue. Þis is þe oyntment: Recipe coperose, sal nitri, [a]cineris geneste,[a] cineris [b]nigri testudinis,[b] atramenti, ana, parte 1; viridis greci somwhat; Of quikke-siluer double to þe quantite of one of þe forseid; Of bore3 grese resolued at þe fire and mundified, þat sufficeþ. Þan medle first þe ashes with þe grese, afterward þe toþer poudre3, and when þou hast wele ymedled, put it in a

Arderne diagnosed the case as mormale or inflamed sore on the leg.

His treatment by bandaging and very hot fomentations,

then cold compresses,

afterwards mercurial ointment,

[1] Quæ titulum confert de Dyuelyn.

[2] Primo consere tibiam fortiter et aliquantulum stricte in panno lineo.

[3] Postea pone de isto unguento in circuitu vulneris.

a—a "aschen of brome" *overlined.*
b—b "of blak snaile" *overlined.*

and finally Lanfrank's ointment,

box and it schal be blak oyntment. *With* þis oyntment, forsoþ, I cured fully þe gretter wondeȝ of þe forseid legge, doyng in þe maner seid afore; þe lesse wondeȝ, forsoþ, cured I *with* vnguento viridi, i.[e.] grene oyntment of lanfrank. þer was dede flesch of blo colour to þe brede of a peny; þat dede flesch, forsoþ, was mich þikke, and, þat y-se, I kutte *with* a rasour a litel þe ouer party of þat flesch; Afterward I putte to larde, and so at þe last *with* larde & with cuttyng I dissolued, i.[e.] lesyd it vtterly. þat flesch þerfor remoue, eftsoneȝ *with* þe oyntment of dyuylyn[1] aforeseid and a cloþe wette in water I held þe wounde opne to þe brede of a peny,[2] And þan eftsoneȝ þer brest out a wounde aboute þe sideȝ, and it bygan to large it vnto þat it was almost of þe same gretneȝ as it was afore.[3] þat y-sene, I putted in four tymeȝ poudre of litarge and anoynted it about *with* vnguento albo, and putte in þe wounde a lynne cloþe wette in þe water of herb robert. Which cure semed to me more profitable, and sowded better þe extremiteȝ and gloweþ[4] þam vnto perfite halþe.

though he had to use the knife.

[* leaf 156, back]

It is best to cut away the dead flesh in an ulcerated leg,

and then to apply a powder.

Lanfrank in his book gives advice about the cure of a mormale.

* If þe mormale be euen aboue þe schyn-bone, þat it be more sikerly and more sone cured it is profitable to cutte þe dede flesch and putte it away if þe pacient consent. And if it be cutte, alsone after þe cuttyng is to be putte in a cloute wette in whyte of ane ay al a nyȝt. Afterward putte in poudre of white glasse and of alum ȝucaryne, i.[e.] alum glasse, or alum plume or of boþe. And if þou se þe bone mortified, witte þou þat it is incurable or vnneþ for to merowe be cured. If þou trow it be curable, it is to be helped *with* some cure of þe mormale in þe boke of lamfrank. Also, as it is seid aboue, som tyme a man is smytyn som party of þe legge violently *with*out wondyng of þe skynne, as of ane hors fote or of a stone or staffe or sich oþer, and þan is it gode sone for to scarific þe place y-smyten and drawe þe blode þenneȝ, and after put on enplastreȝ repressyng akyng and bolnyng. ffor oft-tymeȝ þe mormale comeþ of sich þings. Agayne þe mormale be þer lesnyng[a] of vena basilica, i.[e.] lyuer vayne, of þe riȝt arme or on þe left; after-

[1] cum unguento de Dyuelyn.

[2] usque ad festum Scti Matthæi Apostoli et Ecclesiæ proxime sequere operatus sum.

[3] circa festum Scti Laurentii.

[4] et conglutinavit.

[a] "minnuschyng" *overlined.*

ward, if it be nede, of þe sophene. At þe last be he scarified[a] in þe legge3.

[leaf 157]

A treatise on Piles.

Chiefly a compilation.

14. [A] tretys of þe emoraide3, y-drawen out after lamfrank, a discrete maistre of þe kyng3 of fraunce; which made tuo boke3 of cirurgie, þe lesse and þe more. Also after maister bernard de gordon in his lilie. Also after maister bartelmow in his passionarie. Also after maister Richard in his Micrologie. And after maister Roland, and mayster Guy; And after Roger Bawn And maister Iamarcii, And maister Gilbertyne; And after oþer experte men whos doctryne I haue beholden & sene, and which I haue founden moste experte in practi3ing, with helpe of our lord. I schal schew þam in þis boke. Emoroys on greke is said flux of blode, and it is seid of emak, þat is blode, and rois, flux. Greke3, forsoþ, calleþ emeroys flux of blode in what-euer parti of þe body it be; Bot anence latyne men [1] þis worde is appropriate to þe flux of blode of þe lure; And þe veynes apperyng in þe lure when þai flwe,[2] i.[e.] ren, and ar bolned and akeþ, þai ar called emeroyde3, bot neþerle3 vnproperly, sauand þe pece of þe comon puple. ffor when þai send out no blode, bot ar bolned, and akeþ, and ycheþ or smerteþ þai ar called by oþer names anence leche3. Lewed men and vnexperte men calleþ al þe infirmite3 bredyng in þe lure emeroyde3, or pile3, or fics. ffrench men calleþ emeroyde3 fics, men of London calleþ þam pile3. Neþerlesse it is no3t to strife agayne3 þe vse of spekyng, bot raþer it spedeþ þat lered men and experte knawe þe maner of spekyng and vse it. ffor John Damascen seiþ 'It is heuy for to chaunge noying custom, and most if it be olde.' Neþerle3 of þe name is no stryuyng while3 þe sekene3 bene knowen. Diuerse auctoure3, forsoþ, haþ putte diuerse names to þe sekene3 of þe lure, and also þai haue assigned diuerse causes and spice3, And þai haue ymagined many maners of curacions; Of whiche some more profitable and ofter experte bene sewyngly to be noted vnder compendiousne3 to þe vtilite[b] of helyng. þerfor for to trete schortly it is first to witte þat þe

Etymology of the word Emeroids. The Greeks use the word in a more general sense than the Latin writers.

The unlearned call everything piles. Frenchmen call piles "figs,"

but there nothing much in a name if all are agreed as to the condition.

[1] Apud Latinos.

[2] quando fluunt.

[a] "garsed" *overlined.*   [b] "i.[e.] profite" *overlined.*

Varieties of piles: "the deaf piles" of Avicenna.

emeroideȝ if þai sende out blode þai ar seid ryȝtfully emeroydeȝ. If þ*er* appere, forsoþ, in þe lure bolnyngs blo or blak, or redneȝ to þe qu*an*tite of a bene or gretter, þat is to þe qu*an*tite of a testicle of a cok or of a hounde, as I haue oftyme sene, som tyme occupiyng þe to half of þe lure only, and som tyme boþe, sich bene called of Avicen deef emeroydeȝ, for þer rynneþ noþing out of þam. And sich bolnyngs forsoþ, if þei be gretter, puttyng out no blode, þai ar called condilomata, of condilo of greke, þat is þe closed fist of a man. Condilomata, forsoþ, scheweþ þe schappe of a fist y-closed,

Condylomata, why so called. The cause of condylomata; their appearance.

And condilomata bredeþ of gret malicio*us* or malencolio*us* blode. Aft*er* lamfrank, forsoþ, þe lesse bolnyngȝ if þei be blak or blo þai ar called attritos,[1] or atreos, for þe blak colo*ur* of þam. If þai be rede þai ar called uve, i.[e.] grapeȝ, and þai haue þe schap of a rede vyne or grape. And þai þat bene of blode and of colre ar called moraleȝ,[2] and þai ar like to mulberieȝ when þai bigynne to wex rede.

Verrucæ, their causes;

And som bene called verucaleȝ[3] for þai ar like to warteȝ, and sich haþ þair bygynnyng of malencolye. And som bene of blode, þof it be bot seldom, which ar called fics, [4]If þai be made of ventosite[4] with grete strechyng of þe skynne. Al þe forseid may be reduced vnto tuo þings: Ouþ*er* of hoteneȝ of hum*our*s, or of mych aboundyng of blode. If þ*at* hoteneȝ be in cause, þ*at* is blode and colre, þise schal be þe signe—

the symptoms of the inflamed variety: of the chronic form.

brennyng *with* greuo*us* prikkyng, and smertyng, and vnslepyng, and som tyme *with* ychyng in þe lendeȝ and *with* tenasmon and gret costyueneȝ of þe wombe, and þrist, and febleneȝ of goyng. Signeȝ of cold cause, þat is of gret blode and malencolio*us*, bene þise—bolnyng *with* hardneȝ and derkneȝ and akyng—bot not scharp as of hote cause—þe colo*ur* of þe bolnyng blo or blak, smertyng in þe lure, *with* louseneȝ of þe wombe and akyng, and greuo*us*neȝ or heuyneȝ of þe þieȝ.

Piles due to congestion.

Signeȝ if þe em[er]oideȝ be of multitude of blode bene þise, þat is to sey of þe veyneȝ apperyng in þe leggeȝ. And if

[1] "blakeȝ" *overlined.* [2] "mulberieȝ" *overlined.*
[3] "warty" *overlined.*
[4—4] "after gordon, and þai ar as war white bledders" *overlined.*

þai ren, þat þai ren mych & oft-tyme, and þat þe pacient be of sanguyne habitude. ffor why; in þam is multitude of blode *þat vseþ not fleebotomye, and þat drynkeþ copio*us*ly and oftymeȝ wyne, and þat eteþ scharp þings, as onyons, lekeȝ, cauleȝ, comyne, and þat takeþ medicynes ap*er*tyueȝ of veyneȝ,[1] as bene scamonye i.[e.] aloe and euforbiu*m*, as wittenesseþ all aucto*ur*s togidre and exp*er*te men. Emeroideȝ ar caused of malencoli*ous* blode, which is þe fece of clene blode aboundand in our body; which blode, forsoþ, for his yuel qualitè and odio*us* to nature, discretyue v*er*tu enforceþ for to cast out to þe helpyng of al þe body, helpyng þe vertu expulsyue of al þe membreȝ togidre. And so þurȝ þe strengþe of nature it is putte out fro þe vayne kilyuz,[2] þat lieþ to rig-bone of þe bak, which p*ro*perly is receptacle of malencolio*us* blode. Which kylis, forsoþ, is diuided into fiue b*ra*ncheȝ þat bene ended about þe p*ar*ty of nature[a]; which veyneȝ, forsoþ, when þai ar som tyme filled of melancolio*us* blode þai distende, i.[e.] strecheþ, so þe veyneȝ þat ouþ*er* þe blode bresteþ out or þ*er* ar gendred bolnyngȝ of diu*er*se spiceȝ and schapeȝ. And also oþ*er* sinthomata,[3] i.[e.] p*er*ileȝ, as scharp akyng and prikkyng, brynnyng, ychyng, smertyng, thenasmon, i.[e.] inordinate appetite of egestion, wi*th* ful mich enforsyng and neþ*er*lesse he may do none egestion whan he comeþ to þe pryuè. If, forsoþ, þe blode brist out it is called þe emoroydeȝ; but if þat it flowe temp*er*atly it doþ many helpyngs and p*re*s*er*ueþ þe body fro many sekeneȝ aduste and corrupte, as is Mania, male*n*colia, pleuresis, lepre, morfe, ydropisy, mormale, quartane, passions of þe splene, and so of oþ*er* like. Bot as it p*re*s*er*ueþ fro þise when þat it fleweþ temp*er*itely, so when it is wont for to flewe and aft*er*ward ceseþ vtterly al þe forseid sekenes ar gendred. Also when þai flewe ou*er* temp*er*ance þai bene cause of ptisyk or of ydropisy. Wherfor seiþ Galiene and ypocras aft*er* lamfrank 'Ich long lastyng and ou*er*mych puttyng out of blode is moste miȝty cause for to make ydropisy.' þ*er*for in þam in whome malencolio*us* blode is multiplied temp*er*ite fluying

[* leaf 157, back]

Those who are subject to congestive piles.

The cause of piles.

The pathology of piles.

Anatomy of the vena cava.

Symptoms of piles.

Uses of piles when they only bleed moderately.

[1] et medicinas venarum aperitivas sumunt.

[2] κοῖλην vena cava.

[3] Symptomata.

[a] "i.[e.] lure" *overlined.*

What constitutes moderate bleeding.

How to stop the bleeding from piles.

The cause of the bleeding in piles.

[* leaf 158]

The impatience of the present generation.

Bleeding piles are often concealed piles.

of blode of þe emeroydeȝ helpeþ mych, ne it is noȝt vtt*er*ly to be restreyned. It is called temp*er*ite vse when þe pacientes feleþ þamself more liȝt þat þai war wont[1]; hauyng bett*er* appetite, and etyng and slepyng more swetely or softely, and sich oþ*er*. Bot when þe pacientes felen þamself more heuy, and þ*er* schewe malice of appetite and foule colo*ur* of body, þan is þe flwyng ou*er* mych; wherfor it is alsone successyuely to be restreyned and turned away. Þ*er*for siþe þ*er* is noȝt a litel hardneȝ in restreynyng of þe emeroideȝ, þ*er*for many þings ar be noted of þe restreyning of þam; þat is to sey þat þe leche wytte wheþ*er* þe flowyng be done of anathemasy or of diabrosi or of rixi; þat is wheþer þe flowyng be made of opnyng of veyneȝ, þat is called anaþemasis; or of fretyng of þe veyneȝ, þat is called diabrosis; or of cleuyng or twynnyng, þat is called rixis. Þerfor if þe blode ybroȝt to þe lure be aduste—for when blode is aduste it is scharped[2]—or if false flewme or colre be medled, þan oft-tymeȝ þe veyneȝ ar freted and þai make þe fluxe. And for certayne sich flux is of hard restreynyng. ffor why; þe substance of þe veyne yfreted may noȝt be *sonded[3] w*ith*-out disese and heuynes, siþe þat it nedeþ a medicyne corrosyue. And men now-of-daieȝ bene vnpacient and yuel tholyng, And for-þi flowyng of diabrosi[a] is of hard curying. And þe secundary is rixis[b] which also is cured w*ith* corrosyueȝ in þe bygynnyng. Anathemasis[c] is more liȝtly cured þan þe oþer, bot p*er*auenture noȝt w*ith*out corrosyueȝ. Þis I sey, if þe flowyng be olde, Anathemasis is made for aboundance of blode or for ventosite descendyng doune. Rixis, forsoþ, is made of ou*er* myche dryneȝ, of cause w*ith*in-forþe or of cause w*ith*out-forþe, or of hardneȝ of filþeȝ,[4] or for ane hote aposteme, or any scharpe flowyng. Also flowyng emoroydeȝ somtyme ar hidde w*ith*in, w*ith*out any bolnyngs schewyng outward, þat of som þai ar demed to be dissenterikeȝ and yuelȝ wrong.[5] ffor why, in þe inward emoroideȝ first goþ out egestion and aft*er*ward goþ out blode w*ith* egestion to-gidre. In ciliaca passion, forsoþ, goþ out blode and eft*er*ward egestion. Ciliaca

[1] cum patientes se sentiunt leviores solito et melius colorati.

[2] quia cùm sanguis aduritur acuitur.

[3] non consolidari.

[4] ex duritie fæcum.

[5] quæ a quibusdam judicantur dysentericæ} et malé.

[a] "fretyng" *overlined.* [b] "clyffyng" *overlined.*
[c] "opnyng" *overlined.*

passion is akyng of þe wombe w*ith* puttyng out of blode sewyng. Also aft*er* gordon, *scilicet* de morbo, 'In eu*er*y þing þat goþ out of þe body bene 3 comon cause3; Ouþ*er* by reson of þe membre, or of vertue,[1] or of humo*ur*. If it be bi reson of þe membre, þat is for þe membre is ou*er* þinne. If it be for vertue, þan it is for v*er*tue retentyue is feble, and v*er*tu expulsyue strong. If it be for humo*ur*, þ*at* is for ouþer it is malencoli*ous* or for it is scharp, or subtile, or watrye. Also emoroide3 ar caused of scharpnes of blode and ou*er* mych hete brennyng þe blode, as in colorik men þat bene of hote nature; for blode when it is brent it geteþ scharpnes, as it is seid afore. Also ou*er* mych flowyng of blode is made ouþ*er* for multitude of blode, as in þam þat drynkeþ mych wyne or oþ*er* mete3 or drynke3 þat multiplieþ blode, or in þam þat bene sangyne complexion. Also it is made for yuel qualitè of blode, as for it is ou*er* scharp or subtile or watry, as in þam þat vseþ rawe fruyte3, ffor raw fruyte3 gendreþ watry blode. Þe causes, forsoþ, y-knowen, p*ro*pre cure may be done to. Signe3 of dedly flowyng bene þise, þat is to sey:—ffowyng of blode bryngyng to swou*n*yng is mortale[a]; Also flowyng of blode w*ith* coldne3 of extremite3 is mortale; Also flowyng þat comeþ sodeynly and w*ith* hastine3 is mortale; Also flowyng of blode þat bryngeþ to pale colo*ur*, or grene, or blo, or browne is werst and mortale; Also quantitè of blode passing 4 pou*n*de is yuel, and if it come to 24 it is deþ. fflowyng of blode w*ith* li3tnyng of þe body is gode. In þam þat poleþ emoroide3 þe vryne schal be in colo*ur* remissed white with powdry resolucions blak or blo residente3 in þe bothme of þe vessel. Aft*er* Egidi de vrinis, white and remisse ow for to be of malencoli*ous* blode ou*er* aboundant in þe body, wherfor naturel hete is febled. ffor why; digestion waxeþ raw, and of rawnes of digestion is þe vryne discolored, *And it appereþ w*ith* poudry resolucions which bene resolued of malencoli*ous* blode blak and erþi abou*n*dyng, and by contynuel waie3 þai ar drawen to þe bladdar and putte out w*ith* þe vryne. And for þai ar heuy and erþi þai satle in þe grounde. Þe same vryne

They are to be distinguished from dysentery and passio iliaca.

Bernard de Gordon's Lilium Medicinæ quoted.

Piles are due to an excess of blood,

to eating and drinking too much,

to diseases of the blood.

Danger signals in bleeding piles. Sudden onset.

Pallor. Great loss.

Quotes Gilles de Corbeil de Urinis.

[* leaf 158, back]

[1] aut ratione membri aut virtutis.

[a] "dedly" *overlined*.

How noli-me-tangere and lupus are produced.

The blood is not confined.

Choler and melancholy are cribbed in the gall bladder and in the spleen.

The signs of melancholy.

Treatment of bleeding piles by herb pills.

Phlebotomy is best in the overfed and idle whose piles bleed.

also may betokne in men vice[a] of þe splene, and in wy*m*men w*ith*holdyng of menstrueȝ. And witte þou þat aft*er* gordon in 'clarificac*ione* de vicio splenis' þat innatural humo*urs* may be gendred in oþer place þan in þe lyuer, as in þe stomak colre peassyue,[1] i.[e.] grene, and also colre erugino*us*, of which is gendred 'noli-me-tangere,' and lupus. And also in þe veyneȝ ar gendred vnnaturale humo*urs*. Bot þe splene haþ no v*er*tu of gendryng anyþing, siþe it is noþing bot a receptakle of malencolie, which is ane odio*us* humo*ur* to nature and to al me*m*bris of þe body for his yuel qualitèȝ. Also witte þou þat þe blode haþe nouþer house,[b] ne receptakle, ne prison; but colre and malencoly haþ prisons, þat is to sey colre in þe chiste of þe gall and malencoly in þe splene. Also witte þou þat if þe pacient of emoroideȝ be of malencolio*us* complexion, þise bene tokneȝ:—smalneȝ[c] of body, discolo*ured*, erþi, angry, waike of hert, heuy, and only ferþful and couait*ous*. And witte þou þat if þe forseid pacient sende out blode blak and þikke and stynkyng, þat þis flowyng is noȝt to be restreyned, bot if it ou*er*flowe & þe pacient be febled. In eu*er*y-þing, forsoþ, þe vertu of þe body is to be kept bifor al oþ*er* þings. Agaynȝ þe flowyng of þe emoroideȝ distempre þou moste subtile mele of whete, w*ith* iuyse of millefoile, and make þ*er*of pilluleȝ, and giffe hym eu*er*y day in þe mornyng 3 or 4 of þam distemp*er*ed w*ith* wyne of decoccion of millefoile, or plantayn, or burso pastoris, or rede netle, or p*ar*uenc*is*. Bot if þe pacient be of sanguyne complexion, and lifyng delicately and in ydelneȝ, and blode be aboundand, þan þof þ*er* be sych flowyng it is noȝt to be restreyned bot if it ou*er* flow, þat is knowen by þe tokneȝ aforeseid. Þ*er*for if þer faH ou*er* mych flowyng, it is spedeful þat it be restreyned; for, aft*er* galien, blode is norischyng of al me*m*breȝ, als wele of sadde as of softe, and al haþ bigy*n*nyng or spryngyng of blode; and for-als-mych it is seid þe frende of nature, þ*er*for if þe frende be destroyed þe enemy waxeþ miȝty. Þ*er*for, aft*er* gordon, to þe curyng of þe emoroideȝ is fleobotomy competent, if v*er*tu and age suffre it,

[1] prasina.

[a] "sekenes" *overlined.* [b] "duellyng" *overlined.*
[c] "or leneȝ" *overlined.*

boþe for it avoideþ matery goyng afore, and also it *with*draweþ þe matery to þe co*n*trary.[a] And fleobotomy ow to be done of þe basilic veyne of þe arme for mater goyng afore, and aft*er*ward of þe sophenis at þe hele, þe vtter sophe turneþ þe flowyng of þe emoroideȝ and restreyneþ þe emoroydeȝ for eu*er*more. Whiche fleobotomy, forsoþ, continued * fro ȝere to ȝere, and namely about þe fest of seynt Michelł, bifore and aft*er* oneȝ or twieȝ, or when-someu*er* þe pacient feleþ tyklyng or ychyng or prykkyng in þe lure, þan be he minusched as it is afore seid, and alsoue he schal be cured. Also witte þ*o*u þat fleobotomye of þe inward sophenis of þe leggeȝ prouokeþ þe emoroideȝ and menstrueȝ; And of þe vtter sophenis streyneþ þe emoroideȝ and menstrueȝ, and p*re*serueþ for certayne fro þe forseid passions. Sopheneȝ bene þo grete veyneȝ þat ar streched fro þe kneeȝ vnto þe ankleȝ of boþe p*ar*tieȝ of þe leggeȝ. Þe man*er* of doyng of þis fleobotomye is þat it be done about þe hour of euensong or latter, þat is in þe regnyng of malencolio*us* blode, þat is fro þe 9 hour of þe daie vnto þe 3 hour of þe niȝt. Also witte þ*o*u þat fleobotomye to be done vnder[b] þe hele and in saluatella of þe handeȝ, oweþ noȝt to be done w*ith* a blode iren bot w*ith* a lancete, for hurtyng of þe syneweȝ, but if þat nede make it. Also witte þou þat he þat schal be laten blode oweþ for to putte his fete in hote watre, and eftsone þam owe to be putte agayn, þat þe blode go out bett*er*; And þe pacient ow to abide still in þe watre, vnto þat þe blode þat appered first blak chaunge into fair*er* col*our*. Be þis doct*ri*ne boldly kept, for if it be noȝt done competently it p*ro*fiteth noþing or litel; ffor certayne I haue cured for eu*er*more, w*ith* on latyng blode al-only of þe vtter sophene, many men þat þoled þe emoroideȝ many ȝeres, vnto þe feblyng of þe body. Bot witte þ*o*u þat, aft*er* gordon, þat þof-al fleobotomye make blode fluxible, neþ*er*lesse if it be done of þe vtter sopheneȝ it draweþ þe flowyng to þe opposite; and so it makyng[1] þe flowyng for to be turned fro þe lure þat it flow noȝt to þe costomable place; and forþi it profiteþ to al þat ar cured of þe emoroideȝ,

Blood to be taken either from the basilic vein or the external saphenous.

[* leaf 159]

The bleeding should be annually about Michaelmas.

Bleeding from the internal saphenous bad for piles and menorrhagia.

Anatomy of the saphenous veins.

Evening is the proper time for phlebotomy.

Treatment after phlebotomy.

[1] et ita facit.

[a] "opposite" *overlined.* [b] "at" *overlined.*

The patients should be let blood once or twice every spring and autumn even though their piles be cured.

and also to al þat ar disposed to þe emoroideȝ, for to be laten blode of þe outward sophenis, oneȝ or tuyeȝ in ver and alse ofte in autu*m*pne fro ȝere to ȝere. ffor why; sich fleobotomye for certayne p*re*s*er*ueþ fro þe emoroideȝ, and avoideþ pacienteȝ fro al yuel hum*our*s and kepeþ þam in hele. And þ*er* be no blode-later redy, be þ*er* made ventosyng w*ith* garsyng atuix þe buttokeȝ at þe rigebone ende or aboue þe veyneȝ, for it doþe þe same þat þe forseid fleobotomye, bot noȝt so exp*er*tly, bot nede haþe no lawe. [1] And it is to witte þat if þe leche may gette þe riȝt reule by al þings in eu*er*y wirching aft*er* crafte, fleobotomye owȝt neu*er* to be done in þe emoroideȝ byfore purgacion y-done, and þan sewyngly mynischyng. Also aft*er* gordon, in ou*er* mych flowyng of þe emoroideȝ, and also of menstrueȝ, is co*m*pete*n*t a medicyne laxatyue to purge corrupte hum*our*s þ*at* induceþ þe flowyng, þat þe cause cesyng, þe effecte cese. To which þing to be done al þe mir[obalan)] . . . . . .[a] [con]oueuie*n*t ffor mirabolan) laxeþ afore þam and streyneþ aft*er* þam . . . . .[a] and þai avoide al yuel hum*our*s. þ*er*for be þai prep*ar*ate . . . .[a] decocte byfor þat þai be taken, for bi decoccion þair . . . .[a] *and so þe strength of laxatiueyng shuld be febled, bot þai ow to be resolued in rennyng liquore, as in mylk or whey, w*ith* racyns & liquorice, elleȝ walld þai schrenk[b] þe stomake and lefe yuel tokeneȝ byhynd[c] þam; and so of þe racyns and of þe liquore ar þai reuled þat þai bryng in no harme. Which, forsoþ, resolued and þe kirnelleȝ cast away, lat þam lie al a niȝt in þe same liquor, and in þe mornyng þe colyng be giffen to drynk. þis medicyne, forsoþe, of mirobolan) is ful noble, siþe it purgeþ hum*our*s of niȝt placeȝ, þat is citrineȝ colre,[2] kebuliȝ fleume,[3] Indi malencoly, i.[e.] blak colre, bellerici and emblici colre aduste. And so may al þe hum*our*s be purged; wherfor be mirabolan) hadde in reu*er*ence, ffor þai availe mich to þe emoroideȝ and menstrueȝ to be purged. And þis medicyne for certayn cureþ eu*er*y flux of þe wombe, þat is to scy diaria, dissenteria, liencaria. Also it is to wytte þat

The patient must be purged before he is bled.

Myrobalans is the best purgative in piles;

[* leaf 159, back]

raisins and liquorice may be used,

[1] Ad quod faciendum myrobalani sunt multum convenientes, quia myrobalani ante se laxant, et post se constringunt h[oc] est comprimendo laxant et eos humores malos evacuant. Myrobalani, autem, hoc modo, præparentur:—Non debent myrobalani decoqui antequam fumantur, quia per decoctionem eorum gummitas in fumum resolveretur et sic vis purgandi debilitaretur.

[2] citrini choleram.

[3] kebuli flavam.

[a] A portion of the leaf is missing. [b] "ronkle" *overlined.*
[c] "aft*er*" *overlined.*

in pacientȝ of þe emoroideȝ be þ*er* neu*er* giffen medicyneȝ ap*er*tyueȝ of veyneȝ nouþ*er* be þe mouþe, as scamonè, or aloe, or euforbiu*m*, comyn, lekeȝ, onyans, garleke and sich oþ*er* scharp þingȝ; ne be þar noȝt putte opon þe place, out take aloen and comyn, which tuo, putte outward, streyneþ, and *with*-in-forþ taken opneþ veyneȝ. Bot it is to wytte þat in þe forseid fluxeȝ of þe wo*m*be mirabolan) ow to be dissolued in gote mylk,[1] if it may be had, or in iuse or wat*er* of fumitere or of playntane, or in rayne wat*er* or rose wat*er*, or of veruene, or of anoþ*er* stiptike herbe as millefoile or mynte. Also witte þou, aft*er* al aucto*ur*s, þat þose þings þat restryneþ emoroideȝ restreyneþ menstrueȝ, and e*converso*; And þe same sekeneȝ þat comeþ of þe vice of menstrueȝ, comeþ also of þe emoroid, & e*converso*; and so by sewyng[a] þat þai acorde in cure. Þerfor in cold cause be þai giffen: þat heteþ and ingrosseþ þe mat*er* of flowyng of blode, als wele of þe p*ar*ty of meteȝ as of medicyneȝ. Of þe p*ar*ty, forsoþ, of meteȝ be þ*er* giffen milk, mele of whete decocte, frese beneȝ, *with* canel, gret wyne, riȝe[2] and mynte. Of þe p*ar*ty of medicyne be þ*er* giffen note of cipresse[3] and þe lefeȝ, mirre, thure, mastike, ladanu*m*, storax calamita, anyse rosted, and sich oþe. And excercice and strong frotyngs and swetyngs aváileþ. And if þe cause be hote, be þ*er* giffen lentes[b] *with* vinegre, porcelane,[4] sour milk, soþen barly brede, substance of coleȝ þe tuo watreȝ[5] þat it is decocte in y-cast away, pereȝ, coynceȝ[6] & meldeȝ,[7] & sich oþ*er*. Medicyneȝ restrictyueȝ bene þise; Camphore, accacia, spodin, coriandre, sang*uis* dracon*is*, sandali, lap[is] omoptoes,[8] bole armoniac, ypoquistid,[9] galleȝ cupule, sumak, mirteƚƚ,[10] . . . .[c] plantane, cincfoile, q*u*inquin*er*uie, ribbewort, bursa pastoris, millefoil, ...[c] forsoþ

but never scammony or aloes.

The myrobalans may be given in goat's milk.

What is good for piles is equally good for menorrhagia.

Remedies to be used in the treatment of piles.

[1] dissolvi in lacte caprino.

[2] cum farina tritica, faba fera cum cinnamomo, vinum crassum, rutæ.

[3] nux cupressi.

[4] Portulaca

[5] caulis duabus aquis abjectis.

[6] Mespila.

[7] Cotonea.

[8] hæmat.

[9] Hypoquistidos.

[a] "it folweþ" *overlined.* [b] "growel" *overlined.*

[c] A portion of the leaf is missing.

[10] The Latin text of this mutilated passage runs:—pysidiæ, balaustia, plantago, quinqueneruia, sanguinaria, millefolia et similia. Corpore ergo patientis hæmorrhoides sine menstrua superflua existente pletharico i.[e.] pleno sanguine ex virtute forti præ ceteris attendendum est ut in initio phlebotomia fiat de utrâque basilica brachii. Deinde mulieri menstruosæ ponantur ventosæ magnæ sub utrâque mammillâ. Deinde mundificetur secundum exigentiam humorum peccantium. Deinde liga brachium ligatura dolorosa. Deinde fiant localia remedia. Et id quod intelligendum est, &c.

of þe pacientȝ emoroideȝ or menstrueȝ beyng plettorike. . . . . . .[c] beyng strong. Which is to be take hede to afor al oþ*er* þings . . . .[c] fleobotomy of basilica of boþe þe armes.

[leaf 160] And it is to vnderstond þat þis is wont to availe aboue al oþ*er* þingȝ: R*ecipe* Iuyse of plantane, muscilage dragau*n*te & gu*m*me arabic; be þai medled to-gidre, and o p*ar*ty be take be þe mouþe and anoþ*er* be cast in by a clistery; and be þis continued, and w*ith*out dout it schal cure p*er*fitely, vniu*er*sale purgacions goyng afore, aft*er* barnard gordon. Also corall brent and gu*m*me arabic, y-medled and y-dronke w*ith* cold watre, streyneþ þe flux of blode, of what place so-eu*er* it floweþ. Also canell haþe þis p*ro*pi*r*te,[1] þat if þ*er* be take of it to þe weȝt of 2 penys eu*er*yday w*ith* cold water, it streyneþ at þe best þe flux of emoroid*es* & of menstrueȝ. And if þe forseid poudre be giffen w*ith* watre of plantane it schal be more effectual. Also vitriol, i.[e.] coprose, streyneþ þe flux[2] of emeroi*des* and drieþ humo*ur*s, if it be made w*ith* Iuyse of moleyn, or of plantayne, or verueyn, or rubarbe, i.[e.] sengrene; ffor why; of þe medlyng of þe iuyse of any of þe forseid cold herbes þe hete of þe vitriol is repressed; wherfor it constreyneþ w*ith* d*r*ineȝ. Bot it is to wytte þat þe emoroideȝ hid w*ith*-in þe lure[3] ful seldome bene made w*ith*out fretyng of longaon or kynnyng[a] of it, And þ*er*for certaynly sich man*er* emoroydeȝ may noȝt p*er*fitely be cured bot w*ith* a medicyne cauteriȝatiue, as is vitriol combuste be it self or medled w*ith* quick-lyme, in a grete case, þat is in a grete fretyng. Also puluis sine pari in þis case putte in heleþ wele, bot disesily or angerfully; bot þat is noȝt to charge.[4] ffor to a strong sekeneȝ answereþ a strong medicyne, and namely in strong men. I calle, forsoþ, delicate men feble men. ffor al þingȝ bene hard to a waik hert man. To a strong hert man, forsoþ, is noþing grete. To emoroideȝ hid w*ith*in þe lure, wheþ*er* þai be w*ith* fretyng or clyffyng or w*ith*out, þe most noble cure schal be ich day to caste in in man*er* of clistre, or ich oþ*er* day, al

Local applications for piles.

Styptics for piles.

Concealed piles lead to ulceration of the rectum.

Delicate men are usually timid.

[1] Item cinnamomum habet hanc proprietatem,

[2] cum succo tapsibarbato

[3] sine corrosione longanonis & ejusdem fissurâ.

[4] sed de hoc non est notandum.

[c] See note on page 63. [a] "cleuyng" *overlined.*

medicyneȝ temp*er*atly liquide in s*u*bstance w*it*h a schort and no man*er* streit nastar of tre. To strong men þ*er*for tak pulu*is* sine pari, and medle it w*it*h a litel tapsimel, nouþ*er* to þinne ne to þikke, bot þat it may most competently be þristed out and ȝetted into þe lure. If forsoþ þou haue noȝt tapsimel, in-stede of it tak hony cotted w*it*h a litel vinegre and scomed, and medle it w*it*h þe forsaid pulu*is*, and vse it, for it euenly availeþ as tapsimel. If þe pacient, forsoþ, be delicate, þan tak of citrine oitment p*a*rte 1, vit*r*iol combust. p*ar*tes ij, alom ȝucarine als mich as of boþe, and be þai medled to-gidre and ȝetted in: þis, forsoþ, wirkeþ noȝt so violently as puluis sine pari for þe vertgreȝ þat entreþ not here. ffor-soþ when þou has done þus oneȝ, or tuyse, or þrise, aft*er* as it falleþ þe pacient for to w*it*hhold þe medicyne long or schort tyme, It bihoueþ þan for to chaunge þe cure and giffe clistereȝ mitigatiueȝ, of ȝolk of an ey, w*it*h oile of ros*et*, and pulu*is* of bole armoniac, and aloes epatici, or sang dragon, by 3 daies or more. When þe pacient, forsoþ, feleþ hymself aleged, þan assaye bisily wheþ*er* þe inner place nede ony man*er* of þe first medicyne, i.[e.] of þe pulu*is* w*it*h tapsimel, þat if it so be, be it eft-soneȝ done, as it is seid afore, als oft as it is nede; Aft*er*warde be it mitigate, as it is seid. When þe place, forsoþ, is mu*n*dified, þan be it heled w*it*h þe ȝolk of an ey & wat*er* of ros*et*, in which be resolued gu*m*me arabic, addid þ*er*-to pulu*is* bole, san*g* d*ra*gon, ceruse, aloes, galt, psidie, mu*m*mè, olivai[1] mastike; *and þe lure first enoynted w*it*hin w*it*h lynsede oile & oile of ros*et*, þe forseid medicyne be ȝetted in w*it*h a nastar*e* and so continue it vnto þe last ende, or on like man*er* aft*er* þin owne witte & bisines. And witte þou þat when þ*er* is putte vitriol, or puluis sine p*ar*i, or any pulu*is* corrosiue w*it*hin þe lure aboue fretyngȝ or cliffyngȝ, þan aboue þe pulu*is* corrosiue owe bole armoniac to be putte, for to defende þe pulu*is* corrosiue þat þe humiditè in þe lure quench noȝt & wesch away þe pulu*is* corrosiue. ffor why; bole w*it*h his drynes and viscositè consumiþ þe moisteneȝ, and vitriol wirkeþ bett*er* and more strongly. If, forsoþ, þou haue no bole, þan putte most smal meel of barly in his stede, for it is riȝt mich desiccatiue. þise

A strong local remedy for piles.

A milder remedy.

Examine the rectum as soon as possible.

Cleanse it with an ointment and get it healed.

[* leaf 160, back]

Vitriol is better than bole armoniac.

[1] olibani.

þings restreyneþ blode: ventosing putte w*ith* scarificacion,[a] putte ex antipasi,[b] and mirre, and Iasp*er* of grene colo*ur* hauyng in itself naturale droppes of blode, Saphir rede coralle rubye,[c][1] and fyme of wilde swyne. Also þise restreyneþ blode, of þe vertu of þair qualiteȝ: Iuyse of walwort, Iuyse of rede netelt broken[d] w*ith* al his substance, salt y-put þerto.

Nettle juice is a good remedy to stop bleeding.

Or Iuyse of nettel y-dronkyn restreyneþ blode in eu*ery* place of þe body and of eu*ery* cause, [e]and in boþe kynde.[e] Bot it is to wytte þat to a woman in menstrueȝ and to þam þat haueþ þe emoroideȝ owe þe rote of it to be giffen w*ith* þe croppeȝ of þe same[2] 3 daies continuly, w*ith* rayne watre or rennyng watre.

The hairs of a hare and a powder of burnt hen's feathers are both good to stop bleeding.

Also of þam þat restreyneþ blode bene þise: Mu*m*mè, bole armoniac, sang dracon, thure, aloe, vitriol co*m*bust, pulu*er* of heres of ane hare, brent or noȝt brent; pulu*is* of he*n*neȝ feþers brent, medled w*ith* white of ane ey; Alphita, i.[e.] subtile & clene meel of barly[3]; Also a been clouen by þe middeȝ and putte vpon a wonde and bounden faste, streyneþ.[4] Bot þis haþe no stede bot to so streyt a wounde þat þe been may take w*ith*in his extremiteȝ þe extremiteȝ of þe wounde, as of prikkyng of a smal knyfe or sich a þing.

Tinder, too, is good.

Also aschen of ane olde lynne cloþe y-brent streyneþ blode; þe white of an ey and barly mele y-putte aboue or w*ith*outen.

Acupressure stops bleeding, and so does the cautery.

Som-tyme it bihoueþ for to bynde þe heuedeȝ[f] of þe veyne w*ith* ane nedel putte vnder þe veyne, and aft*er* for to bynde w*ith* a þrede aboue þe nedel. Som-tyme it byhoueþ for to cauteriȝe þe wounde w*ith* an hote iron.

The application of cold is a styptic.

Also blode is stopped w*ith* coldyng of þe me*m*bre y-hurte, wherfor oft-tymeȝ is blode restreyned in som men w*ith* oneȝ drynkyng of colde watre. And som men putteþ þair testiculeȝ in cold watre; And som men lappeþ þair testiculeȝ in clay w*ith* vinegre or watre, or temp*er*ate w*ith* iuyse of plantayne;

Clay with vinegar may be used,

And þis is p*ro*fitable to þam þat bledeþ at þe nose. And it is better if þe fronte and templeȝ of þe pacient be emplastred of þe forseid clay, and also if it be putte vnder þe armeholeȝ; þis, forsoþ, quencheþ þe feruo*ur* of blode and draweþ to þe opposite. Also puluereȝ y-putte

1 corallus rubri, et stercus porci campestris.

2 radix ejus cum summitate ejusdem.

3 Item faba per medium fissa.

4 sanguinem stringit.

a "garsing" *overlined.* b "on þe contrary" *overlined.*
c "rubye" *has been crossed out.* d "brissed" *overlined.*
e—e "i.[e.] of man & woman" *overlined.* f "endeȝ" *overlined.*

in þe nose may more strongly streyne & availe. *Puluer of here3 of ane hare y-brent[1] aboue alþings streyneþ þe flux of þe emoroide3, y-medled *with* white of an ey and *with* here3 of ane hare no3t y-brent; coton of softe stupe3 y-putte aboue. And som men *with* þe forseid puluer alon and þe white of an ey anoynteþ þe emeroide3 *with*-out puttyng to of coton, and alsone ceseþ þe flux and þe akyng. Witte þou þat aloe and comyn, recepte bi þe mouþe, opneþ veyne3; and putte to *with*-out-forþ restreyneþ.[2] Þe same doþ leke3 and þe iuyse of þam þe lefe3 of moleyne y-brissed and put to *with* þe white of an ey streyneþ þe emoroid*es* and heleþ þam sone. Also Iuyse of orpyne[3] y-dronken *with* wyne heleþ al fics, *with*out and *with*in; wherfor it is called fics-herbe. Also lana succida y-dipped in þe iuyse of porre3,[a] þe lefe3 remoued away, and hote putte to bolned emoroid*es*, and when it is collde eftsone3 renewed, and oft tyme3 so y-done, it is a certayne remedy agayns þe bolnyng of emoroid*es*; And if pulu*is* of comyn be putte þerto, it schal spede better. To emoroide3 y-bolned and apperand as war a chykyn torde, brisse wele blak sope *with* þe tendrons of moleyne[4] and putte vpon; and þe þrid day þai schal no3t appere. Oile of violette *with* white of 3 eiren well stired to-gidre and putte to, on a wonderful man*er* mitigateþ þe akyng and brynnyng of þe emoroide3. Agayn3 ou*er* mych flux of emoroid*es* and of menstrue3 þe best medicyne *con*strictiue and desiccatyue is made on þis man*er*. In þe best lu*m*barde3 ynk be dissolued a gode quantitè of gu*m*me arabic; which dissolued putte in of pulu*is* of bole armoniac, mastic, mu*m*mè, sumak, rede coralle, bdellii, galle3, psidie, acacie, anteros[5] ypoquistidos subtily puluered and sarced,[6] an*a*; and medle þam to-gidre so þat þai may be 3ette into þe lure by a nastare. *With* þis medicyne was cured Demetri*us*, kyng of Perse3, of a cristen man þat was halden prisoner *with* þe same kyng; which criste*n* man was made ful riche, and was sent home to criste*n* me*n*ne3 lande by þe coma*n*dement of þe same kyng, and many prisoners of cristen men war late go free *with* hym. Panis cuculi

[* leaf 161]

but after all the burnt hairs of a hare are the best for stopping bleeding in piles.

Aloes and cummin taken internally cause bleeding from piles, externally they stop it.

Remedies for piles. Leeks.

Powdered cummin.

Black soap and mullein.

Gum arabic dissolved in ink

cured Demetrius, king of Persia, by the hands of a Christian.

[1] Pulvis ex pilis leporis combustis.

[2] Item facit porrus et succus ejus, item folia tapsi-barbati.

[3] Item succus ebulæ.

[4] cum summitatibus tapsi-barbati.

[5] antheæ.

[6] et cribrantur.

[a] "leke3" *overlined.*

Cuckoo bread wrapped in red dock leaves may be tried in piles, condylomata and dead flesh.

alleluya, i.[e.] wodsour, is a treyfole growyng vnder busche3 and bereþ white fl*oure*3, is a ful sour herbe. Ane handful of þis herbe w*ith*out any brissyng be lapped in a lyn clouth y-wette in wat*er* and þristed out, or in lefe3 of rede dok, and be it rosted vnder hote aschen þ*at* it be no3t dryed; aft*er*ward be it draw out and brissed, and put it vpon emoroide3, or fics, or co*n*dilomata, or dede flesch, wher-so-eu*er* it is It freteþ softly & remoueþ al þe forseid þing3, aboue any þing of þe world: þ*er*for when it may esily be had it noyeþ no3t for to assay. A Rial þing[1] exp*er*t, þat wonderfully and happily amendeþ þe err*our* als wele of þe first digestion as of þe seconde, and doþ away wicked col*our* & vnnat*ur*al, *and it restoreþ natural col*our* and makeþ it gode: R*ecipe* cynamom̄, *3in3ib* galang', reubarb an*a*; be þai subtily puluered, to which be done 3uccary[2] euenly, and brese þam to-gidre. Vse þe pacient þis pulu*er* in bygynnyng of his mete to þe we3t of 5 d*rams* in wyne; þis medicine is p*ro*fitable to þam þat haþe þe emoroid*es*, for þai ar oftyme discolored. And it is to witte þat if it may be done on gode man*er* þer oweþ neu*er* to be putte to in þe place remedie3 mitigatiue3 bot þe bodi war first mu*n*dified w*ith* farmacie, i.[e.] medicyne laxatiue, as is of þe forseid mirabolan̄ and fleobotomye, for elle3 þe mitigatiue3 availeþ lest. A mitigatiue of akyng to emoroide3 bolned, w*ith* prikkyng and brynnyng:—Make ane emplastre of comon malue lefe3 decocte in watre and aft*er* well y-brised, w*ith* swyne grese, oile of rose putte to, or of violete, or of lilie, or of camamille, or of comon oile if þe toþ*er* be no3t had. It schal be made þus: þe lefe3 of malues decocte and þe watre expressed, be þai wele fried in a pan w*ith* some of þe forseid oile3; aft*er*ward streche þam on wolle y-tesed or subtile stupe3 of line, and putte þam to hote; and wonderfully it mytigateþ þe akyng. If þe rote of lilie may be had and be soþen w*ith* þe forseid malue3 it schal be more effectuo*us*. Þis emplastre is comone yno3, ffor in wynter may lilye rote3 be hadde when malue3 faileþ, and þan may þou do w*ith* þe rote al-on as it is seid of þe malue3; if þai boþe may be had þe emplastre is more effectuo*us*. Also þe akyng and bolnyng of emoroid*es* is mitigate w*ith* þe 3olk

[* leaf 161, back]

A stomachic for those who have piles.

A soothing application for inflamed piles.

Lily roots should be added to it.

[1] experimentum regale.

[2] quibus additur sacchari.

of ane hard ey rosted, and oile of rose and croc*us* done to; which, y-brissed to-gidre and w*ith* wolle putte to, it mitigateþ wond*er*fully in eu*er*y cause. And it schal be better if þ*er* be added to opiu*m* in litel p*ro*porcion. Also ane emplastre of þe white of ane rawe ey and oile of violette bette to-gidre and putte to is seid wonderfully for to be mitigatiue. Also be eiren soþen hard, and þe white of þam w*ith* oile of rose or of violetȝ or of boþe w*ith* coton be putte to hote, it ceseþ þe akyng of þe emoroideȝ in one niȝt, and doþ it away. Þis is þe medycine which I, Iohn Arderne, made, þe which I wold neu*er* wante, for it mitigateþ wonderfully eu*er*y bolnyng of emoroid*es*, and akyng and prikkyng w*ith* brynnyng, and it doþ it away: which owe to be made þus:—R*ecipe* Moleyn and swyneȝ grese[1] wele y-clensed of þe litel skynneȝ and smal y-kutted; and be þai wele brissed togidre in a morter or in a basyn vnto þe grece be wele imbibed of þe iuyse; and þan lat þis grese w*ith* þe iuse stand stille 9 daieȝ or more vnto þe grese shew grene; which y-se,[2] eftsone soneȝ be it brissed w*ith* þe same iuyse, And when þe grese is p*er*fitely imbibed and colored of þe iuyse, putte away þat þ*at* is sup*er*flue of þe iuyse, and eftsoneȝ brisse þe grese w*ith*out any iuyse and putte it in an erþen vessel, and kepe it to þin vse; And þis medicyne is called tapsiualencia. And witte þou þat þis medicyne owe fro moneþ to moneþ oneȝ to be brissed, and in þe brissing for to putte in litel bi litel of oile of rose, or violet, or camamille, þat þe valence may co*m*pete*n*tly imbibe it. And if þ*er* war added to of gode popilion[3] þe helpyng of þe medicyne schal be more effectual. Þ*er*for when þ*ou* hast nede for to vse þ*er*of, tak lanam succida*m*, if *þ*ou* may haue it, and if þ*ou* may noȝt, tak oþ*er* clene tesed wolle and putte þ*er*-on of tapsivalencia w*ith* þi fynger or w*ith* a spature i*m*p*re*ssyng it, and be þer made ane emplastre more or lesse aft*er* þe discrecion of þe leche, and putte it on þe lure. Bot witte þ*ou* þat afore þe puttyng to þat þe lure be wele fomented w*ith* a sponge y-wette in hot watre of decoction of malueȝ and branne, and be it hote putte to and abide long þ*er*on. ffor whi; sich fomentacion availeþ mich more for certayne þan hote stuphis, and more hideþ þe rede bolnyngs and lesseneþ þam, as I

The recipe for Arderne's own ointment.

Arderne calls his ointment "tapsivalencia."

It can be kept, but should be stirred once a month.

[* leaf 162]

The ointment may be spread or applied with the finger or a spatula.

Fomentations to be used before the ointment is applied,

[1] succum tapsi-barb. et axungia porci a pelliculis mundata.

[2] quo viso iterum cum succo eadem bene contundatur.

[3] et si de bono Populeon additur.

haue of-tymeȝ p*ro*ued. Aft*er* þe fomentacion and desiccacion of þe lure, be þe bolnyngs anoynted *with* oile of rose chaufed in ane ostre scheƚƚ; and putte in wele *with* þi fyng*er* þe oile atuix þe runcleȝ of þe skynne; And aft*er*ward putte to þe forseid emplastre menely chaufed, And be it bounden, þat it falle noȝt away, *with* lynne clouteȝ and a girdel atuix þe bottokkeȝ, as it is seid in þe fistuleȝ. And *with*-in one niȝt þe akyng schal be cesed. Þis medicyne, for-soþ, passeþ all oþ*er* to þe akyng, bolnyng, brynnyng, prik-kyng, and smertyng in þe lure, of which blode renneþ noȝt; And he þat haþe þis medicyne, hym nedeþ none better. Bot neþ*er*les it is gode for to kune many liȝter,[1] þat one defailyng he may go agayne to anoþ*er*. And it is to wytte þat in akyng and bolnyng of þe emoroideȝ, þat nouþ*er* stupheȝ of hote stones, and thure & coluer fyme [2] and sich oþ*er*, ne syttyng aboue vesseleȝ *with* herbeȝ, as many foleȝ doþ,[3] be noȝt so competent as fomentacion. ffor certayn, fomentacion made *with* watre of decoccion of comon malueȝ or furfur colace,[4] hideþ wele and mitigateþ and dissolueþ þe emoroid*es* about þe lure. Also witte þou þat in akyng of þe emoroid*es* þ*er* owe to be putte noþing cold in acte bot hote. ffor aft*er* ypocras cold þingȝ in acte bene enemys to boneȝ, to synoweȝ, to teþe, to brayne, to þe lure, to þe bladdre, and to þe nerwȝ of þe rigebone.[5] And forþi þe medicyne when it is applied vpon þe wolle,[6] it ow a litel to be holden agaynȝ þe fire, þat þe actuale coldnes be done away, and þa*n* put it to. When a lech seþ any man hauyng grete ake and many bolnyngs or fewe, more or lesse, aboute þe lure *with*outen, *with* ful mych akyng and payne, þan it is spedeful þat aft*er* þe puttyng to of ane emplastre mitigatiue, and fomentacion done tuise or þrise—If þe forseid bolnyngs begynne noȝt to abate—þat þe leche *with* a lancet or a blode iren smyte warly þe bolnyngȝ ful of blode, þe pacient noȝt wittyng, and receyue he þe blode in a sponge wette in hot watre and expressed and putte to þe bolnyng. And do þe lech þis boldely, for þ*er* is no p*er*ile þ*er*-in. ffor why; I haue p*ro*ued þis ful oft tymeȝ for to be most sone helpyng. Þe fleobotomy y-done, be þ*er* putte vpon of valence or some oþ*er* equiualent medicyne, and be þ*er* done fomentacions

and it should be kept in place with a bandage.

The remedy is "sovran" for piles,

but the leech should know of others.

Fomentations for inflamed piles.

Hippocrates quoted.

Inflamed piles should be lanced freely

[1] Sed tamen bonum est plena scire leniora.

[2] et fimo columbino.

[3] sicut multi stolidi faciunt.

[4] vel furfuris coluti.

[5] vesicæ, ac spinali medullæ.

[6] super lanam.

and enoyntyngs vnto þe bolnyngȝ and þe akyngȝ vtterly defaile. If þe leche, forsoþ, may noȝt wirk þus, make he þe pacient for to be fleobotomed of þe vtter veyneȝ of þe leggeȝ in the euyng as it is seid afore. Also if þe leche se any men haue aboute þe lure wi*th*out rounde bolnyngȝ, in þe endeȝ [a] of which appereþ blak spotteȝ, witte he þan for certayn þat in þam is blak cluttered [b] blode; which forsoþ yknowen, be þer done *fomentacions and enoyntyngȝ. And aft*er*ward tarye noȝt þe leche for to opne wi*th* a launcet þe forseid bolnyngȝ in þe place of þe blaknes—þe pacient noȝt wittyng—ffor þe pacient schal fele no greuance þer-of; I haue p*ro*ued it forsoþe oft-tymeȝ, And wi*th* þis cure al-on I haue sene ful many for to haue be cured for eu*er*more, and þat riȝt sone. ¶ And be þe lech war þat none of þam þat standeþ about p*er*ceyue when he opneþ wi*th* þe lancet or sich oþ*er* þing sich man*er* bolnyngȝ. ffor if barbou*rs* knowe þis doyng þai wold vsurpe þis cure, appropriand it to þamself vnto vnworschip and noȝt litel harme of maystreȝ. ¶ If any man, forsoþ, haue as it war purseȝ [1] aboute þe lure wi*th*oute, hyngyng in man*er* of a welked gri[pe], which ar wont for to bifalle of inflacion and ou*er* miche extension of emoroid*es* had afore; þan if þe pacient consent þe lech may wi*th*out p*er*ile kutte away wi*th* a lancet or a rasou*r* al þo burseȝ, first y-bond wi*th* a þrede, and aft*er*ward sone hele þam wi*th* vnguento arabico.

and the patient afterwards let blood.

[* leaf 162, back]

Thrombosed piles should be incised.

The treatment by incision should be kept secret lest the barbers get to know of it, to the detriment of the Master Surgeons.

[1] pendentes instar uvæ marcidæ.

16. And for þat þai þat haþe þe emoroid*es* haþe ofttyme a sekeneȝ þat is called tenasmon, þ*er*for here we make mencion þ*er*-of. Tenasmon is a sekeneȝ wi*th*in þe lure þat makeþ þe pacient for to desire purgyng of his womb byneþ-forþ; ffor it semeþ hym eu*er*more þat he miȝt haue egestion, and when he comeþ to þe p*ri*uè he may noȝt haue egestion. ¶ Cause of þis seknes bene som tyme emoroid*es* hid wi*th*in þe lure, or pustuleȝ, or excoriacions in longaon, or for chynnyngs of longaon [2] which ar called ragadie, or for hote humou*r* imbibed in longaon, or for þat cold humou*r* is inuistate þer, or for apostemeȝ, or for vlcereȝ, or for takyng of laxatiue medicyne. Signeȝ of hote cause in thenasmon bene hoteneȝ, brennyng, and prikkyng. Signeȝ of coldneȝ is þat cold is

Tenesmus;

definition.

Causes are piles, ulceration, purgatives, or chronic constipation.

[2] vel propter fissuras longanoni.

[1] "heuedeȝ" *overlined.* [b] "coagulate" *overlined.*

The signs and symptoms of Tenesmus.

feled in þat place, and it is helpid of hotene3. ¶ If it be for apostem*es*, þ*er* is grete akyng & greuo*us*. ¶ And if it be for vlc*er*e3, þ*er* is gret akyng when any-þing is putte þer-in. And if it be for emoroide3, þ*er* apperep bolnyng and inflacion and akyng in þe veyne3 þat ar about þe circle of þe lure. And if it be for fece3, it is knowen forþi þat þe pacient long tyme afore went no3t to sege. ¶ And if it be for medicine laxatiue, it is knowen for þ*er* was in it Diagrediu*m* or scamonie or pulpa coloqu*in*tid*is* or aloe. ¶ And if it be for outward cause, it is knowen by schewyng of þe pacient.

The prognosis.

¶ Pronosticacion is þis: If þat þe thenasmon last long, it bringeþ to þe colik and iliaca passion, and to vnslepyng and feblenes of vertu, and malice of þolyng, and to passions of þe heued, and to swownyng. And cause of þise is continuel akyng.

The treatment of Tenesmus.

¶ If it be for outward cause, Sitte þe pacient in ane hote bath of swete watre w*it*h oleo laurino and sich oþ*er* hote ap*er*tyue3.[1] ¶ And if it be for aposteme and þe bodye be plettorik, be þer made fleobotomye of basilica; And if þe apostems be hote, be þ*er* made clisterie3 of iuyse of endyue, scariole, coriandre, oile of rose and white of an ey. Aft*er* þat þe sekene3 haþ p*ro*ceded, be þ*er* added to þise henne3 grese fresch, and þe dusty[a] meel of þe milne, and a litel hony. And al þise be giffen leuke in acte.[2] [* leaf 163] *And if þe aposteme be cold fro þe bigynnyng, be þ*er* made ane oyntment of þe iuse of apii and oile of rose, and camamille, and branne, and iuse of caule3. Aft*er* þat þe sekenes haþe p*ro*ceded, be þ*er* added to fenigreke and li*n*nesede, and be þai ministred eu*er*more hote in acte. ¶ Witte þou þat in thenasmon þ*er* is noþing more p*ro*fitable þan 3ettyng in by a clistery of gote3 mylke;

Clysters of goat's milk.

And if þou haue no3t gote3 mylke, tak cow mylk, and put þ*er*-to a subtile whete meel, and boile þam togidre in man*er* of childre*n* pappe; adde þ*er*-to þe raw 3olk of an ey in þe decoccion, and a litel fresch schepe3 grece aft*er* þe liquefaccion, and cole it, and putte in hote bi a clisterie; þis, forsoþ, is mych mitigatyue. ¶ Also þe 3olk of a raw ey temp*er*ed w*it*h bole armoniac to sich þikknes þat it may by a clistery be 3ette into þe lure, ceseþ at þe best thenas-

[1] et similibus calidis aperitivis.

[2] et omnia ista dentur actu tepida.

[a] "flying" *overlined.*

mon ; and þis haue I p*ro*ued oft tymeȝ. ¶ If tenasmon be for ragadias i.[e.] chy*n*nyngȝ[a] wit*h*in þe lure, cure þe ragadias and thenasmon schal be cured. ¶ A remedie agaynȝ thenasmon of what eu*er*y cause it be, aft*er* Bernard of Gordon, *capito* de thenasmoñ ; R*ecipe* fenigrec, se*men* lini, malue bismalue, camamille, mellilote, i.[e.] þe croppeȝ of cauleȝ, an*a* ; be þai brissed and boiled in watre vnto mene þikkeneȝ, and be it coled, and be it warme cast in by a litel clistery. ffor, for certane, outward fomentacions and suffumigacio*n*s p*ro*fiteþ noȝt so mych as medicyneȝ putte in by a clistery, and þat haue I oftyme p*ro*ued.

Bernard de Gordon's clyster for Tenesmus.

¶ Agaynȝ greuo*us* ychyng and vnsuffrable in þe lure take þe iuyse of celydome,[1] of moleyne, an*a*, hony scomyd als mych as of þe iuyseȝ, and boile þam togidre to þe wastyng of þe iuyseȝ ; aft*er* sette it downe fro þe fyre and kepe to vse. When þ*o*u wilt vse þ*er*-of agaynȝ ychyng, tak þ*er*-of als mych as þ*o*u wilt and putte þ*er*-to of pulu*is* of vitriol combuste and alum combuste and orpment, and if nede be boile it agayne vnto it be ane vntement haldyng fast ynoȝ, and putte a litel þ*er*-of into þe lure agaynȝ þe ychyng, and sone it schal cese, and in eu*er*y p*ar*ty of þe body for certay[n]. And þis oyntment is called tapsimel, of tapsibarbasti[b] & melle[c] ; fforsoþe þis is a noble oyntment.

Treatment of Pruritus ani, by tapsimel.

¶ Ragadias may we noȝt cure bot if we bryng in medicyneȝ wit*h*in þe lure, ouþ*er* wit*h* clistery or wit*h* suppository ; ffor medicyneȝ putte wit*h*out-forþe p*ro*fiteþ ouþ*er* litel or noȝt. Wherfor first it byhoueþ for to wirch wit*h* corrosiueȝ to þe mu*n*difiyng, and aft*er*ward wit*h* consolidatyueȝ and desiccatiueȝ, as it is seid afore of þe emoroid*es* hid wit*h*in þe lure. ¶ Agaynȝ ragadias, aft*er* maist*er* Ric*hard* in micrologio suo, R*ecipe* oile made of eiren, or oile of rose, & white of ane ey raw, and iuyse of lyuane,[2] & cimbalarie[d] an*a* ; medle þam togidre & put þam in. ¶ Agaynȝ ragadias wit*h*in þe lure be made sich ane oyntment aft*er* Gilbert*us* ; R*ecipe* oile of rose and of violet*tes* an*a* ℥ij goteȝ or schepeȝ talow ℥iss. be þai al molten togidre at þe fire, and sette þam doune, and moue it continuly wit*h*

Treatment of rhagades, which is chronic ulceration of the rectum.

A ferric ointment recommended by Master Richard the Englishman.

An ointment invented by Gilbert the Englishman.

1 chelidon.

2 et succo lucasiæ

a "cleuyng" *overlined.*

b "moleyn" *overlined.* c "hony" *overlined.*

d "pennyworte" *overlined.*

a spature; and when it is almost cold putte in puluer of R. triasantalorum ℥ss. and medle hem togidre; it heleþ wonderfully. ¶ Also oile of linsede putte in availed agaynȝ þe forseid sekeneȝ; it is forsoþ riȝt desiccatyue.

[leaf 163, back]

Prolapse of the rectum, treated by bleeding and a fomentation of gallic or tannic acid.

17. Agaynȝ goyng out of þe lure: If vertu and age suffre be þer fyrst y-done fleobotomy of þe vtter sophene of þe legge; Afterward be þer done suffumigacion or fomentacion of gall, or of þe rynde of a grene oke or dry; of þe rynde of pome-granate þat is called psidia, and of þe floureȝ of granate þat ar called balaustia; of þe rote of camfery decocte in rayne watre. And if it be in somer þise may be added to, or elleȝ by þam selfe: verueyne, moleyne, plantane, gawel,[1] psillium, iuyse of coriandre, berberiȝ, porcelane, bursa pastoris, rede rose, tanesey, wormode, horsmynt, and sich oþer stiptikeȝ. ¶ Of þise of which þou may haue best make ane hote fomentyng with rayne or rynnyng watre, vinegre added þerto; And after þe fomentyng be sprenkled aboue puluis of bole, of sanguis draconis, of herteȝ horne combuste, bark-duste, psidie, balaustie, mumme and sich like. ¶ Afterward, if it may be done on any maner, be þe longaon putte into his place, and be it fast bondyn with warlyneȝ[2] þat it go noȝt out. Also agaynȝ goyng out of þe lure be it fomented with watre of decoction of cauleȝ, and after anoynt it with aloe and vnguentum vetus broken togidre. ¶ Also agaynȝ þe goyng out of þe lure, chaufe or make hote apostolicon; which chaufed, be longaon touched with it, and alsone it schal entre agayn. ¶ If it be nede do it oftymeȝ when it goþ out; Afterward be it bathed in watre of plantane, of porreȝ, of peritory, or of peritorye[3] alon. With þis medicyne was kyng henry of ynglond cured of þe goyng out of þe lure.

Put back the prolapsed bowel and keep it in place with a dressing.

The remedy which cured K. Henry of this complaint.

[leaf 164]

18. [A treatise on clysters.]

Arderne's improvement on the ordinary clyster pipe;

Be a leche wele puruied þat he haue a couenable instrument for clistryeȝ to be ministred; þat is þat he haue a pipe of tree, namely of box, or of hesel þat aváileþ mych, or of salowe, to þe length of 6 yncheȝ or 7 with on hole alon; ffor old men vsed pipes holed in þe side. Bot witte þou for certayne þat, as I haue lered be experience, a pipe with one hole aváileþ more, and ȝetteþ better in þe

[1] myrrha

[2] ligetur cum cautela.

[3] sed solius parieturiæ

liquore. ¶ Afterward haue he a swyneȝ bledder, or a neteȝ bledder, noȝt blowne to myche, which þ*o*u schalt p*re*parate þus for to be kept. Take þe forseid swyneȝ or neteȝ bladder when it is dry, and putte þ*er*in a sponeful of comon salt, of wat*er* als mych, of hony als mych as of watre; latte þam be dissolued togidre in þe bledder by tuo daies naturale, And eu*er*y day tuyes or þries be þe bledder t*ur*ned or shaken about, þat it may be wette of þe liquore on eu*er*y side. Aft*er*ward be þat putte out þ*a*t is þ*er*-in, and be þe bledder blowne, and be þe mouth bonden þat þe wynde go noȝt out, and hyng it in ane vmbrose[1] place vnto þat þ*er* be had nede þ*er*-of. Þis p*re*par*a*cion, forsoþ, kepeþ þe bledder fro corrupcion long tyme, And fro fretyng of wormeȝ, and makeþ þe bladder stro*n*g and able to þe vse of the forseid werk.

his apparatus for giving enemata.

His method of preparing the bladder.

¶ Be þe clistrye made þ*er* aft*er* my man*er*, for it is liȝt bot noȝt lesse effectuale. Many þings bene p*ro*fitable to þe confeccion of clisteries, if þe lech miȝt haue al redy. Bot oft-tyme þe leche may noȝt fynde in eu*er*y place al þingȝ necessary to hym; þ*er*for it schal noȝt vnworschip[2] a lech for to spede p*ro*fitabily w*ith* fewer þings and liȝter. Old lecheȝ, forsoþ, ordeyned costiuo*us*[3] clystryeȝ, greuo*us* and liȝt, and þai putte in cassia*m* fistula*m*, mirobalan), rerepigre and oþ*er* laxatiueȝ; which clisterieȝ, forsoþ, aft*er* þair receyuyng, made þe pacienteȝ more c*on*stipate, i.[e.] encostyued, þan þai war before; And þ*er*for long tymeȝ and oft tymeȝ I haue p*ro*ued and bene exp*er*te a liȝter man*er* of clystrying and more effectuo*us*, as wele in childre and wy*m*men as in men, als wele in ȝong men as in olde men; And in diu*er*se caseȝ as in wounded men, constipate[4] men, and febro*us* men, and in colica & yliaca. And I spedde effectuo*us*ly w*ith* sich a clistre þat is þ*er* made. ¶ R*ecipe* malueȝ comoñ and grene camamille, or drye if þ*o*u may haue it, and brisse þam a litel, and sethe þam in watre vnto þe watre become grene; þan tak whete branne als myche as sufficeþ, and putte it to þe forseid herbis and boile it a litel; aft*er*ward cole it, and to þe colyng adde to ane handful of salt and clene hony or oile; and be al wele

The simpler the enema the better.

Prescription for a very simple enema.

[1] "schadowye" *overlined.*
[2] "ne schame" *overlined.*
[3] "i. of gret cost" *overlined.*
[4] "costyue" *overlined.*

Salt and water are really enough for an enema.

resolued, mouy*ng* it w*ith* a spature or w*ith* þi hande; þis confection, forsoþ, may be kept by a fourtniȝt if it be nede. ¶ If malueȝ, forsoþ, or camamille may noȝt be hadde, w*ith* water & branne and salt w*ith*out any oþ*er* þing þe forseid nede schall be sped wele ynoȝ for c*er*tayn. ffor whi; for certayne if a lech wanted all oþ*er* þingȝ, w*ith* wat*er* alon & salt boiled togidre and ȝette in by a clistrye b*ri*ngeþ out sq*ui*balleȝ.

[leaf 164, back]

Honey useful in clysters.

Herbs to be used in clysters,

and salt in moderation.

Clysters require skill.

Arderne's methods better than those of the Lombards in London.

Bot witte þou þat þise bene necessary to þe confeccion of clistrieȝ, þat is to sey, Hony, oile, butter, salt, swyneȝ grese, sope white and blak, oile of camamill, oile of rwe, & oile of malueȝ, sanguis ven*er*is, &c. Of which forseid white sope may eu*er* more be necessary to a leche, for it y-putte in þe forseid decoccione and þ*er* schaken wele w*ith* þe hande mych strengtheþ þe clistrye; and þis may eu*er* more be had redy. Also hony when it may be hadde doþe grete help in eu*er*y clistery. ¶ þise bene herbeȝ necessary to þe werk of clistry, s*cilicet* Violette, malueȝ, camamill, m*er*curial*is*, wat*er*cresse, caule lefeȝ, p*er*itorie, &c. Of which som wircheþ mollifying, as malueȝ; some dissoluyng, as camamill, p*er*itorie, and oþ*er*. Bot wytte þou þat in clistrying þe leche owe for to augmente and lessen þe p*ro*porcion of salt aft*er* þat þe vertu of þe pacient may thole, i.[e.] suffre, for þe tendernes of longaon, and aft*er* þat he seþe þe pacient strong, softe or hard for to avoiden. ffor grete qu*an*tite of salt makeþ sone þe clistery for to haste to þe goyng out, And mene quantite bryngeþ noȝt out so sone. þ*er*for be þe lech waker in þis þat he be noȝt negligent ne fole-hardy in his wirchyng. ffor it is werk of a p*er*fite maistrye. ffor þe which I haue geten ane hundreþ tymeȝ grete hono*ur* w*ith* lucre i*n* diu*er*se placeȝ. ffor whi; at london when lumbardeȝ of-tymeȝ ministred clisterieȝ on þair maner to colic men and oþ*er* men constipate,[a] ne myȝt noȝt availe, [1] I, forsoþ, w*ith* þe forseid man*er* of clistriyng, at þe first tyme w*ith*in þe space of a forlong or of tuo, I deliu*er*ed þe pacient for certayne, our lord beyng mene. ¶ When þou wilt forsoþ giffe a clistre, Tak of þe forseid decoccion half a quart at þe moste and putte it in þe bladder, and putte þe gretter ende of þe

[a] "encostiued" *overlined.*

[1] Ego cum predicto modo clisterizandi primo vice infra spatium unius stadii vel duorum patientem, deo mediante, deliveravi pro certo. [Sloane 56, leaf 24.]

pipe into þe bladder, and bynde it faste; and anoynte þe forþ*er* end of þe pipe w*ith* fresch swyneȝ grese, or w*ith* butter, or w*ith* popilion, or w*ith* comon oile, or w*ith* hony. And putte in þi fynger, anoynted first w*ith* some of þe forseid þings, into þe lure; And alsone putte in þe pipe of þe clistre into þe lure. And þan ow þe leche for to presse þe bladder w*ith* þe liquore atuix his hondeȝ and ȝette in þe liquore. And if he fynde as it war ane obstacle in ȝe wombe lettyng þe entryng of þe liquore, as it oftymeȝ falleȝ, þan draw agayne a litel þe pipe, and he schal fele þe liquore entre, and þan ȝette in al þe liquore; which y-ȝette in, make he þe pacient for to lye grouelyng aboue his bedde, and frote & robbe his wombe vpon þe nauyl w*ith* his owne hand or w*ith* anoþ*er* ma*n*neȝ; *And enforce he hymself als long as he may for to w*ith*hold þe clisterye, And when he may no longer hold it, go he to a sege made redy w*ith* a basyne standyng vnd*er*-neþe and þ*er* do his nedeȝ. And se þe lech þe egestions, wheþ*er* it be blode or putride flemme &c, or wormes or sq*u*iballeȝ indurate, or wheþ*er* colre go out or quiter &c. And þus may þe leche be certified what is to do in eu*er*y cure. ¶ Ouer þat þis is namely to be written, þat when þe lech ministreþ clistery to any man, þat in ȝettyng in þe liquore w*ith* þe clistery þe liquor alsone stirt out vpon þe handeȝ of þe leche, so þat þe pacient may noȝt w*ith*hold it ne receyue it; and þat dure 2 daies or 3, for certayne sich a pacient is disposed to þe deþ w*ith*out dout, þat is if þe liquor ȝetted in be noȝt ou*er* scharp of þe salt. Þ*er*for be þe leche circu*m*specte,[1] for ful seldom haue I sene þis reule faile for c*er*tayn, bot neþ*er*lesse it holdeþ noȝt eu*er*, þat is if þe sekeneȝ go agayne to wele-fare.[2] ¶ Also it is to witte þat when þe leche haþe wele clensed, bi þe clistery, þe wombe of feceȝ and oþ*er* sup*er*fluiteȝ seid afore, þan p*ro*-fiteþ it mych for to ȝette in a clistery made of decoccione of malueȝ, if it may be hadde, and of branne and of butter & oile or swyneȝ grece. If malueȝ, forsoþ, may noȝt be had, þan be it made only of decoccion of branne and of þe toþ*er* seid aboue, and be it ȝetted in by þe clistery.

Directions for giving a clyster.

[* leaf 165]

The use of clysters in diagnosis.

The use of clysters in prognosis.

A soothing clyster.

1 "biholdyng aboute hym" *overlined.*

2 "or myȝtynes" *overlined.*

Be þis clistery forsoþe made w*ith*out any salt, And þan owe þe pacient for to w*ith*hold it strongly by al a niȝt and longer. And þis schal conforte þe bowelleȝ and schal mollifien þam, and schal kepe þam fro constreynyng vnto þai be filled w*ith* new feceȝ. Elleȝ, forsoþ, of þe voideneȝ of þe bowelleȝ þe bowelleȝ schuld be constipate, as I haue oft tyme sene.

The use of clysters in colic.

¶ It is to witte þat in curacione of þe colic no medicyne so sone helpeþ as clistery; ffor why; þis bryngeþ out hard sq*ui*balleȝ of what eu*er*y cause þai be w*ith*holden, And it avoideþ sou*er*anly ventoseneȝ, and wonderfully putteþ out viscose flemne & putrified. Wherfor I haue oft-tymeȝ cured many pacienteȝ w*ith* clistery w*ith*out any oþ*er* medicyne, And oft-tymeȝ w*ith*in 3 houreȝ. And þ*er*for it spedeþ for to wirk first w*ith* a clistre in colic & yliaca passions; ffor þe lower bowelleȝ avoided of þair sup*er*fluiteȝ, þe ou*er* bowelleȝ may more liȝtly putte out fro þam þair sup*er*fluiteȝ to þe lawer bowelleȝ.

How clysters act.

¶ As auicen seiþ, al þe bowelleȝ of a ma*n*nes wombe ar continued w*ith* venis miseraicis, out-take longaon, for longaon is noȝt continued to þam. Wherfor þe lyuer may drawe to hym fro ou*er* bowel somwhat, And by þis is it schewed þat if ane hole man bi any case be distitute of appetite of *mete and drynk, þat he may no man*er* ete, þat by þe infusion into þe lure by a clistrye of any norischyng liquore, as of any potage or mylke of almandeȝ or sich oþ*er*, þe lyuer mygth draw þ*er*of to hymself and so norisch þe body.

[* leaf 165, back]

Nutrient enemata recommended.

¶ þerfor witte þou þat clisterieȝ noȝt only availeþ to seke men and constipate, as of þe colic or of sich oþer, bot it availeþ to al men beyng in þe febreȝ, als wele acueȝ as crenic, i.[e.] long tyme lastyng, And to eu*er*y inflacion of þe wombe, and to ventosite of it, and torcions, i.[e.] gryndyng. And som-tyme it availeþ mych in som fluxeȝ of þe wombe. And for certayn it availeþ mich to hole men, constipate and noȝt constipate, if þai be purged twyse at lest or 3 or four tymeȝ in a ȝere w*ith* þe forseid clisterieȝ; þat is tuyse in wynter, and in vere as it war aft*er* lentyn oneȝ, in somer oneȝ, or oft*er* tyme if nede be.

Clysters may be given seasonally and to prevent illness.

¶ ffor why; þe benefite of it may no man nou*m*bre; ffor as it helpeþ fair in necessite, so it p*re*serueþ þam þat vseþ it fro harme & necessite: be it þ*er*for had in reuerence.

[leaf 166]

19. [O]f atramentez, i.[e.] of vitriolez, bene many kyndez; And þat is better þat is more grene and þat is founden in þe yle of Crete [a]; and it is called comonly dragante, bot noȝt dragagante,[1] ffor dragagant is a white gumme and clere like vnto gumme arabic. Also þer is a spice of vitriol þat is called vitriolum romanum, i.[e.] coporose; And it is of ȝalow colour in reward of [2] þe grenner vitriol. And þer is one of white colour bot noȝt schynyng, and þat is seid to availe to þe curez of eiȝen. Vitriol is hote [b] and drye [c] in þe 4 degre after platear,[3] And þer ar 4 maners þerof: Indicum, þat is founden in ynde, and þat is white; Arabicum þat is founden in arabye, and þat is ȝelow; And ciprinum þat is founden in Cipre, and þat is grene; And romanum þat is coprose, þat is more grene is competent to medicyne. It haþe strenght of dissoluyng, consumyng, fretyng.[d] It may be kepte by 10 ȝere effectualy. Also vitriol combuste be itself or with salt combuste vputte vpon a venemyd wonde draweþ þe venym fro byneþ vnto aboue.[4] Also puluer of vitriol combuste streyneþ blode in euery place if it be putte by itself or with iuyse of any herbe streynyng blode, as of rede netle, or bursa pastoris, or moleyne, or walwort. Also it is seid to availe agayns polipe in þe nose if it be putte into þe nose with a tente of coton and melle rosette medled with ȝolk of an ey; it freteþ superflue flesch, and putte into a fistule mortifieþ it. And also it y-medled with diaquilon or apostolicon and y-put vpon fraudulent vlcerez [5] in dry membrez, it cureþ þam meruelously in drawyng, and mortifieþ þam and freteþ þam. Also if vitriol be combust it is lesse mordicatyue, but his drynez is not lessened. fforsoþ al spicez of vitriol bene scharp after lesse and more, and þai haue þair scharpnez in þair superficite; And when þai ar combuste þai bene exsiccatyue without grete mordicacion, and so in exsiccand þai gendre flesch, and most in drye membris and bodiez. ffor why; Vitriol y-put to diuerse membris or diuerse membris [6] it is sene to haue diuerse effecte In dry bodiez, for as coloric

Of Atramentum or vitriol.

The varieties.

The different kinds.

Uses.

A styptic

for nasal polypi

and for proud flesh.

Burnt vitriol less caustic.

Vitriol in the strong and healthy dries wounds and stimulates them to heal;

[1] una species,

[2] in respectu viridioris.

[3] Secundum Platearium

[4] ab inferius ad superius

[5] ulcera fraudu-[lenta].

[6] Nam vitriolum diversis corporibus appositum vel membris.

[a] "or cipre" *overlined.* [b] "calidus" *overlined.*
[c] "siccus" *overlined.* [d] "corrodyng" *overlined.*

and malencoli*ous*; And also putte in dry me*m*bre3 when it fyndeþ strong membre3 agaynstayndyng to his strenght, þan may he no3t bot dry sup*er*fluite3 y-founden in vlcere3 or in wonde3; which forsoþ y-dried, nature gendereþ flesch.

in the weak and feeble it increases the discharge.

In moist bodie3, forsoþe, as in fleumatike men and childre and wy*m*men, and in moiste membre3 of þe bodie, þe membre3 bene feble and may no3t w*ith*stande to þe strength of þe vitriol; and so þai suffre liquefaccion of it, and so putrefaccion is augmented in þe wonde. And as it wirkeþ þus in diu*er*se bodie3, so wirkeþ it in diu*er*se complexions and diuerse membris. And it doþe no3t þus for contrario*us*te of op*er*acion þ*at* it haþe in itself, bot for contrario*us*te of complexions to which it is y-putte; As fire doþ diu*er*sely in dyu*er*se þings. ffor whi; lede or oþ*er* metalle as bras and siluer y-put to þe fire ar molten of þe fire; tyle, stone3, and erþen potte3 y-putte to þe fire ar hardened; and þise be no3t done for þat þe fire haþe contrari*ous* wirkyng in hymself, bot for co*n*trario*us*te of nature of þe forseid þing3. *Wherfor seiþ galiene, if þ*er* be tuo þings euen in helþe, and þe tone be in a dry membre and þe toþer in a moiste, þat þat is in þe dry membre nedeþ more dry medycyne. Emplastre3, forsoþ, þat ar putte to membre3 owen to be of o kynd to þe membrys, aft*er* Iohn Damascene: Tak of vitriol als mych as þ*ou* wilt, i.[e.] 2 vnce3 or 3 or 4, and putte in ane erþen potte whos mouþe be wele stopped w*ith* clay distemp*er*ate w*ith* horse dong, þat is called lutu*m* sapien,[1] and sette it to dry; þe which y-dried, sette[a] þe potte w*ith* þe vitriol among cole3, and make a softe fire by one houre; And aft*er* ane houre make it stronger, and blow strongly w*ith* belowe3 2 houre3, and aft*er* lette in pece vnto þat þe fire defaile by itself. And þe potte y-colded, be it opned, and þou schalt fynde attrament, i.[e.] vitriol, of rede colo*ur* cleuyng to þe side3 of þe potte; whiche remoued fro þe potte, be it poudred subtily vpon a stone, and putte it in a strong leþer bagge and kepe it to þine vse. By sich combustion is his natural hete alt*er*ate and so it is colded, and so his mordicacion is dulled; wherfor it may restreyne blode in nose3 and wounde3 and lure and marice. Also it

Why vitriol acts in such contrary ways.

[* leaf 166, back]

John Damascene's vitriol plaster.

The uses of this ointment;

[1] cujus orificium fortiter obturetur cum luto bene distemperat. cum fimo equino quod vero lutum sapienciæ dicitur.

[a] "birye" *overlined.*

availeþ agayneȝ þe cancre and agaynȝ venemous apostemeȝ and fraudulenteȝ [1]; And to teþe or gomeȝ freten or gnawen medled with symple hony, or better with melle rosate; Or best if þat licium, i.[e.] iuyse of caprifoile with clarefied hony be soþen to þe þikneȝ of hony, and be medled with puluer of vitriol and putte vnto þe gomeȝ; ffor whi; Iuyse of caprifoile þat is called licium availeþ bi itself to al þe viceȝ of þe mouþe. Also vitriol y-medled with hony and licium putte þer-in helpeþ to vlcereȝ of ereȝ, and to þe quitour of þam and fretyng. Also vitriol combuste when it is medled with puluer of hermodactileȝ and putte vnder-neþ þe tung it helpeþ to þe ranule.[a] Ane oyntment þat availeþ to cancrose vlcereȝ, and to wondeȝ, and to apostemeȝ, of which floweþ out blode, and to yuel carbuncleȝ þat ar called pestilencialeȝ, and to apostemeȝ þat ar made of yuel mater, is made þus: Recipe of old swyne grese [2] ℥iii, vitriol ℥iiii. Be þe grese molten ouer þe fire & be it coled, and breke long tyme þe vitriol with oile in a brazen morter, and afterward medled with þe grese ouer þe fire, and make ane oyntement mych fruyteful. If þou wilt make it in maner of one emplastre, putte þer-to wax and blak pich, for pich haþe strenght or vertu of drawyng fro partieȝ bineþ to aboue, and þe same doþe vitriol.

how it may be modified with licium, etc.

An ointment against plague blotches.

20. Alum ȝucaryne is called comonly alumglasse. It is hote[b] and dry[c] in þe 4 degre. It is a veyne of þe erþe y-knowen ynoȝ,[3] bot how mych it is more clere & schynyng so mych is it better. It haþe strenght of consumyng and of gretly desickyng.[d] It availeþ with hote vinegre agaynȝ inflacions of þe gomeȝ; And it availeþ in medicyneȝ agaynȝ þe scabbe. Also poudre of it combuste profiteþ mich bi itself, or y-medled with hony, *in mundifying of liȝt cureȝ. It mundifieth, forsoþ, with a stiptikneȝ,[4] and in þat þat[5] it is stiptik it is confortatyue of membreȝ, for al stiptik þingȝ bene repressiue of humours. þer is, forsoþe, anoþer kynde of alum þat is called alumen scissum, comonly alum plume, and it haþe þredeȝ and it may be diuided and ryuen in sondre. And it is riȝt gode, and it haþe þe same vertueȝ as alum glasse. Alum glasse is

Alum glass,

its uses.

[* leaf 167]

Alum plume.

1 contra apostemata venenosa et fraudulenta

2 adipis porci vetustissimi.

3 satis cognita et commune,

4 cum quadam stipicitate

5 in hoc quod.

a "frog" *overlined.* b "calidus" *overlined.*
c "siccus" *overlined.* d "drying" *overlined.*

The method of preparing alum glass.

brynt þus: Tak a tile stone or a scarþe of a potte,[1] and putte it in þe middeȝ of brynnyng coleȝ so þat þe coleȝ touch it noȝt, and in þat scarþe putte þe hole pece of alum, and alsone it will melt as it war yse, and boile, and afterward it wexeþ hard; and in boilyng it will blow and wex hiȝe in drying and wexing white. And lat it be stille so in þe fire vnto þe blowyng and boilyng vtterly cese, and to it be broȝt into ful white colour; þe which y-sene, sette it fro þe fire and poudre it ful smal vpon a stone, and in a leþer bag kepe it to þine vse.

Alum lotion.

Water of alum is made þus: Tak a quantite of it als mich as þou wilt, and breke it at þe best,[2] to which be added to 8 partieȝ of gode vinegre and strong, and so boile þam in a panne at þe fire vnto þat þe half parte of al-togidre be consumed. Afterward remoue it fro þe fire and cole it; And þis is called watre of alum, which availeþ agaynȝ ychyng of scabbe of salt flemne. And þis watre mundifieþ in coldand, bot watre of sulphur mundifieþ in hetyng or chaufand.[3]

Verdigris and its properties.

21. Viride es i.[e.] vertgreȝ, is hote[a] and drye.[b] It is ful penetratyue and dissolutyue, and it prikkeþ and brynneþ and melteþ, and repressiþ putrefaccion. Wharfor, after galiene, [cap.] 4 de ingenio, of wex and oile and vertgrese may be made anoyntement temperate. ffor whi; vertegrese is ful mich penetratife, dissolutiue, pungityue, vrityue,[4] and liquefactyue. And al þise ar repressed and dulled of wex and oile adde to it; for siþe wax and oile moisteþ riȝt mich and gendreþ putrefaccion, þai dulle þe scharpneȝ of vertgrese, And vertgrese represseþ þeir putrefaccion and humeccacion; wherfor of þise bene made a temperate oyntement.

Arsenic and Auripigmentum.

22. [A]rsenic & auripigment bene boþe one, bot arsenic is noȝt so fair as auripigment; neþerlesse boþe haue a ȝalow colour, but auripigment is gretter and more schynyng, and more disesy for to grynde for his þredineȝ; for in substance he is like vnto plaistre of paris. Bot arsenic is as it war puluer in reward of auripigment, and it is more liȝtly broken; And when it is broken it haþe as it war vermilion within it, of rede colour and of aȝour colour; which vnkunnyng men saiþ to be realgre, &

[a] "calidus" *overlined.* [b] "siccus" *overlined.*

[1] Accipe unam tegulam vel testam unius olle.

[2] et teratur optime.

[3] valet contra pruritum scabei ex salso flemate et ista aqua mundificat infrigidando, sed aqua sulphuris mundificat calefaciendo

[4] uritinum.

þat is false. ffor whi; realgre is ane artificial confection made of alkenemistreȝ[1] bi sublimacion, as arsenic sublimed, And for certayn þai ar noȝt different in op*er*acion in any þing, out-take þat realgre is of rede colo*ur*, and arsenic sublimed is of white colo*ur*; bot neþ*er*leȝ arsenic entreþ in confeccion of realgre, And forþi realgre is called of som men rede auripigment: of þe nameȝ is no stryuyng so þat we vnd*er*stond þe þingȝ. *Auripigment is hote and dry in þe 4 degre, of whiche bene tuo spiceȝ as is seid aboue, ȝelow and rede. Ȝelow is more competent to vse of lecheȝ. It is forsoþ dissolutyue, attractyue, and mu*n*dificatyue, And it haþe in it a vertue putrefactyue by which he putrefieþ strau*n*ge humo*ur*s comyng to a wounde, or ane vlcere, þat þai may noȝt be assimilate, i.[e.] liken to me*m*breȝ, and engendre sup*er*flue flesch or dede flesch. Also it availeþ in medicyneȝ agaynȝ þe scabbe, þe tetre and white morfee y-medled w*ith* blak sope. And for þat we made mencion of arsenic sublimed, þ*er*for it is to witte þat no leche bot if he be more exp*er*te i*n* cirurgie p*re*sume for to wirk w*ith* realgre or arsenic sublimed. ffor of þam ar bredde many diseseȝ for þair distemp*er*ate violence. ffor why; þai boþe wirk w*ith* one man*er* and violence, and þat more violently þan cautery of fire. And if any man ow for to vse þa*m*, þam owe to be putte to in þe lest quantite, for þe vertu of þam aboute fire is þe vttermoste of strenght,[2] and þat is schewed, for þe watre of þam freteþ eu*er*y metall, out-tak gold. Witte þou þat auripigme*nt* is called comonly ortment,[3] whos pulu*er* vseþ falconereȝ agaynȝ pedicleȝ[a] of þaire falconeȝ. Also witte þou þat auripigment is desiccatyue, consumptiue, euaporatyue, eradicatyue, putrefactiue, ruptyue and cauteriatyue. Also witte þou þat of arsenic sublimed or of realgre, þat oneȝ in a tyme in þe bigynnyng of my practiȝing, when I knew noȝt þe violence of þam, I putte of þe pulu*er* of þe tuo forsayd in þe leggeȝ of tuo men; þe which, forsoþe, y-putte in, almost þei wer wode for ake bi tuo daieȝ naturel and more; And þair leggeȝ war bolned out of mesure. Þe þrid daie, forsoþe, þe place wher þe pulu*er* was putte appered of riȝt blak colo*ur*, and þe pacienteȝ war so feble

Realgar is not identical with Arsenic,

but there is nothing in a name.

[* leaf 167, back]

Use arsenic and realgar with the greatest caution;

they are more caustic than fire.

Arderne's first experience with arsenic when he was young;

he thought he had killed two patients;

1 secundum modum alkimistarum id est alkenemyers.

2 Quoniam virtus eorum circa ignem in ultimo fortitudinis et quod patet

3 orpigment

a "lise" *overlined.*

his treatment of them.

þat þai war almost dede. þan I anoynted þair legge3 wit*h* oile of rose or popilion, And I fomented þe leggis in hote water for to euapo*ur* yuel humo*ur*s contened in þe membre3; And aboue þe place I putte rawe larde kytted þinne,[1] wit*h* oile of rose. Aboue þe larde putte I ane emplastre of þe 3olke3 of raw egge3, And stuppe3 of lyne aboue for to hold þe larde. And aboute þe 9 daie þe place combuste beganne to dissolue in þe circu*m*ference and for to putte out quiter. And þe place no3t rep*ar*ate bot fro þe þrid day to þe þrid daye[2] I continued eu*er*-more þis cure in þe forseid man*er*, vnto þat al þe mortified flesch wit*h*in was fully putte out þe which, forsoþ, putte out, þe bone of þe legge[a] appered bare wit*h* a wounde ri3t horrible; þe which y-sene, I filled þe wonde of stupe3 y-kitte smalle, and putte þam aboue þe naked bone; and I putte in of þe 3olk of a raw egg wele temp*er*ate wit*h* sang*u*ine ven*er*is, and I filled al þe wounde þ*er*-with; and so eu*er*y day one3 reparalyng it vnto þe quiter biganne to cese, and þe side3 of þe wounde byganne for to sonde or conglutinate. And witte þou þat when þe side3 of þe wounde come to þe place of þe bone cauteri3ide of þe arsenic, which was blakke, [* leaf 168] *þai mi3t no more grewe, for þe mortified bone mi3t no3t receyue nutriment, þat þ*er* mi3t no flesch grew vpon it, ne be regendred. þe which 3itte sene, I, sewyng þe ignorance of þe comon puple,[3] eu*er*y day I schoue[4] þe bare bone wit*h* instrument p*re*p*ar*ate þ*er*-to, entendyng for to gendre flesch vpon þe bare bone. And I putte to regen*er*atyue3 of flesch, þat is to sey liciu*m* wit*h* mel rosate, and pulu*er* of aloes, & mastike, and mirre, sarcocoll, san. drac*onis*, and þai profited noþing. Neþ*er*le3 þe schauying eu*er*y day continued in þe man*er* of ydiote3, as I seid afore; a daye, as I schoue þe forseid bone, þe bare bone vnder þe instrument moued vp and downe; þat, forsoþ, p*er*ceyued, I meruailed ou*er* mesure, neþ*er*le3 I p*er*ceyued of þat þat þe schauyng of þe bone p*ro*fited noþing: fro þan forþe I lefte þat werk, and I putte noþing elle3 in þe wounde bot liciu*m* wit*h* melle rosate and 3olk of a raw aye ymedled togidre, with carped stupe3 of lyne, and so fro day to day continuyng vnto þe forseid bone,

The tibia died,

and a sequestrum formed,

which Arderne did not notice for some time.

[1] apposui lardum crudum tenue incisum,

[2] de 3° in 3m.

[3] Quo adhuc viso, ignorantiam vulgi prosecutus.

[4] Abrasi.

[a] "schine" *overlined.*

flesch growyng vnder-neþe appered hiȝer þan þe extremiteȝ of þe wounde, and was made more moueable and more; þe which ysene, I putte þe poynt of a knyfe vnder þe side of þe bone and I raised it a litel, and al þe bare bone stirt out, and rede flesch had filled al þe space where þe bone laye, and blode went out. Þat bone, forsoþe, had in length 4 yncheȝ, and 2 in brede; in þikneȝ, forsoþe, it was drawne out almost vnto þe merewgh of þe bone; And þis was in þe schyne bone. Aft*er* þe sep*er*acion, forsoþe, of þe bone, I cured finaly þe wounde w*ith* liciu*m* and mel rosate and raw ȝolk of an ey and pulu*er* sine pari. And þe pacient recouered wonderfully his goyng; he was, forsoþe, a ȝong man. And as it fell on þe tone man, one þe same maner felle it of þe toþer. And witte þou þat I putte noȝt of pulu*er* of arsenic in þe leggeȝ of þe forseid men ou*er* þe qu*an*tite of a corne of senvey,[1] and neþ*er*lesse þe wondeȝ þat come of þe arsenic passed fully þe lengthe and þe brede of a ma*n*neȝ hande. Þerfor vnexp*er*te men be wele war fro þe vse of realgre and arsenic sublimed, and namely in þe face and þe leggeȝ, and synowy placeȝ and bony, and in a ma*n*neȝ ȝerde, and in þe lure; for bot if þai haue grete resistence þai wirke ful cruely.

He removed the dead bone and the wound quickly healed.

The second case was similar,

therefore use arsenic with the greatest care.

23. [L]iciu*m* is þe iuyse of caprifoile, þat is called wode-bynde, and it groweþ in wodeȝ and wyndeþ strongly aboute treeȝ; and it haþ long floureȝ, and it bereþ swete rede berieȝ. Liciu*m* cureþ þe canker in þe marice and in oþ*er* inward me*m*breȝ, for it haþe vertu mu*n*dificatyue, consolidatyue, and confortatyue, and regen*er*atyue of flesch in a bare bone and in schynne boneȝ; and it haþe a vertu mu*n*dificatyue of putrefiyng of þe bone. And gen*er*aly it availeþ in al fretyng sekeneȝ, as in cancre, lupe, fistule, and noli-me-ta*n*ger*e*. And agayne þe cancre in þe mouþe liciu*m* is a p*r*incipal medicyne, boiled w*ith* hony vnto þe þikneȝ of þe hony. And it may be *þus* made: þe iuyse schal be pressed out and sette to þe son for to dry vnto þat it may be pulueriȝed. And þis pulu*er*iȝed availeþ to derke eiȝen, putte i*n* þe eiȝ, and forþi is called oc*ulus* lucid*us*. *Bot it may be made p*ro*fitably oþ*er* wyse, availyng to ful cause of cirurgie, & þat *þus*: þe iuyse of cap*r*ifoile pressed

Licium or juice of woodbine.

Its uses.

Various preparations:

powder is good for the eyes,

[* leaf 168, back]

[1] "a mosterd sede" *overlined.*

the juice with honey for the mouth, and for ulcers everywhere.

out bi itself, be it boiled with alse mich of clarified hony vnto þe wastyng of þe iuyse, and be it kepte vnto vse. And þis availeþ to þe cancre in þe mouþe, and in þe lure, and in þe marice, and al cancrose vlcereȝ and fraudulentȝ of leggeȝ. If þe iuyse, forsoþ, may noȝt liȝtly be pressed out for þe þikneȝ, als it falleþ, oft tyme, þan be þe lefeȝ watred with gode white wyne or rede, and þan may þe iuyse liȝtly be pressed out. ffor whi; witte þou þat caprifoile owe noȝt to be waschen with watre afore þe brissyng, and moste when þer owe to be made licium to cureȝ of þe

It is extracted with wine instead of water,

eiȝen, Bot if it nede alwaieȝ to be wette, be it no maner done with watre bot with wyne, as it is seid. Also lefeȝ of caprifoile brissed by þam-self and with al his substance

and is then used for foul ulcers.

without medlyng of any oþer þing, putte vpon vlcereȝ of leggeȝ desperate & stynkyng, and puttyng out foule blode, and growyng hiȝe to maner of a cancre, and vnobedient to any medicyne, cureþ þam happily and meruelously. And

Arderne used it successfully on a great man.

þis proued I in þe legge of a grete man hauyng a pustle, In curyng of which al medicyneȝ defailed; and with þis was he cured. ffor whi; þe first tyme þat it was putte to it dried þe fistule, and did away þe stynkyng and al þe yuel accidentȝ, and within a moneþ he was plenarely cured.

Pulvis sine pari, its constituents

24. [P]uluis sine pari, or french Poudre sanȝ pere, is made þus: Recipe auripigment. parte 1, þat [is] ʒii; vert-grese ana, or after som men partes ij; Of vitriol combuste, or noȝt combuste, als mich as of boþe þe forseid; Alum ȝucarine combust, or noȝt combuste, als mych as of al þe forseid. Ich on of þise bi þamself be ful subtily grouden on a stone, þe which wele y-growden, be þei eft-sone

and preparation.

grouden al to-gidre vnto þai be riȝt wele medled; and putte þam in leþer bag, and kepe to vse: þis may be kepte bi a ȝere and longer, and þat in gret effecte. þis poudre

The reason for its name;

is seid "without pere" ffor it haþe no pere in wirchyng; ffor why; it mortifieþ and bryngeþ out dede flesch or superflue or putred in al wondeȝ and vlcereȝ. And witte þou þat þis puluis bigileþ neuer þe paciente ne þe cirurgene, for it doþ not wickedly. ffor whi; if þe cirurgene bene vnkunnyng and putte þis puluis in a wonde or in ane vlcere noȝt hauyng dede flesch, it doþ none harme to þe

its uses,

wonde or þe vlcere; bot without any oþer help it schal

at þe best be conglutinatiue, dissiccatyue, and sanatyue of þe wonde; bot neþ*er*lesse no3t w*ith*out mordicacion. ffor, for certayne, if þis pulu*is* war no3t mordicatyue it schuld in prise passe al medicyne3. Þe vse of þis pulu*is* is sich; when þis pulu*is* is putte in a wou*n*de or in ane vlcere, be þ*er* putte to it, w*ith*out any-þing atuix, cotone or stupe3 of lyne cutte smalle with schere3; And þan aboue al þat be put aboue emplastre Nerbone or anoþ*er*, and be it bounden, and so latte it be wiþout remouyng by two nyghte3. *Aft*er* þis tyme, forsoþ, when þou remoue3 þe emplastre and þe coton or þe stupe3 putte aboue þe pulu*is*, If þe pulu*is* putte in go willfully out w*ith* þe dede flesch þi nede3 is wele sped. Þan owe þou for to putte in þe hole of þe vlcere or of þe wonde a drop or tuo of sanguis ven*er*is, w*ith* stuppe3 of lyne or coton, vnto þat þe hole be eftsone3 replete w*ith* flesch. And if, forsoþ, in þe first remouyng þe pulu*is* putte in come no3t wilfully out w*ith* þe mortified flesch, þan ow þe lech for to putte o droppe or tuo of sang*u*is ven*er*is vpon þe pulu*is* in þe wounde or þe vlcere, and aboue coton or stuppe3 of lyne, as it is seid. And aboue al-togidre þe emplastre Nerbone; and so lat it abyde by a naturale day or more aft*er* þe estimacion of þe discrete leche. And when þe dede flesch goþ out of þe vlcere or of þe wounde, be it reparailed as it was seid afore. And to a leche be þis a reule, þat pulu*is* corrosyue be neu*er* remoued in a wonde or ane vlcere byfor þat it wille wilfully go out. Also þ*er* is anoþ*er* reule in which I haue sene erre in my tyme almost al men no3t practi3o*ur*s bot fole3; þat is to say of þe ofte remouyng of wounde3 or vlcere3. Siche op*er*acion, for-soþe, spedeþ no3t, bot letteþ couenable effecte of curyng. And þat by þis reson, for natural hete in þe body, which is p*r*incipal acto*ur* of curyng, expireþ[1] out of ofte remeuyng of a wounde or of ane vlcere, and so is letted digestion of humo*ur*s comyng to þe wounde or to þe vlcere, Wherfor þ*er* may no3t be nade gen*er*acion of quito*ur* and, by sewyng, ne purgyng of þe wounde. Wherfor sup*er*flue humo*urs* rennyng to þe wounde ar gedred togidre and ar holden stil more and more; wherfor þe bolnyng in þe wounde is augmented

and method of application.

[* leaf 169]

The treatment of a wound with dead flesh.

Two good rules for surgeons—(i) Let caustic dressings remain till they are cast out. (ii) Do not dress wounds too often.

The results of neglecting these rules.

[1] "breþeþ" *overlined.*

and, by sewyng, þe ake; for þe tone is occasion of þe to*þer*. Wherfor þe wounde or þe vlcere waxeþ hard and foule, and for þe quit*our* þat it owed of riȝt to putte out, it sendeþ out watry hum*our* & venem*ous*, and so ofte-tymeȝ of liȝt hurtyng ar made incurable yueleȝ. Also þ*er* is ano*þer* err*our* in ofte remeuyng of woundeȝ or of vlcereȝ; ffor as seiþ philosophreȝ, aier chaungeþ þe body and by consequens þe wounde, and þat may be p*ro*ued by ex-

A menstruating woman is noisome to wounds,

p*er*ience. Þe breþ of a me*n*struo*us* woman noyeþ vnto woundeȝ if sche neȝe*n* nere; Or of þe lech if he haue liggen w*ith* his wife or w*ith* ano*þer* woman menstruate, or

and so are garlick and onions.

if he haue eten garleke or onyons. Bot be þis man*er* of wirchyng boldly holden, þat a lech be content only of ane

Dress a wound once a day only.

rep*ar*acione in þe day, þat is if he haue þe medicyneȝ contened in þis boke. ffor when he seþe a wou*n*de or ane vlcere wele cast out quit*our*, and þe bolnyng for to vanysh away, and þe akyng for to be cesed, and þe me*m*bre for to come agayne to þe first habite and colo*ur*, helþe is at þe dore if þe pacient be we[le] gouer*n*ed, i.[e.] if he

The value of sleep to a sick man.

slepe wele in niȝtes. In slepe, forsoþ, nature wirkeþ better aboute digestion of eu*er*y mater beyng in þe body or in þe membris. Bot for þat slepe is oftyme letted of akyng, þ*er*for bifore al þingȝ be it lab*our*ed

[leaf 169, back]*

þat þe akyng be cessed. *ffor akyngȝ afor al o*þer* þings noȝt only presseþ downe vertueȝ of þe body but also of þe

Soothing applications.

medicyneȝ. And þat þing soue*r*anly mitigateþ oile of rose in hote cause, or oile of camamille in cold cause, for it is hote and resolutyue, of which it schal be seid aft*er*-ward. Also ane emplastre of hony and branne and a litil vinegre fried togidre mitigateþ[1] eu*er*y akyng for c*er*tayne. And witte þ*ou* þat þo þingȝ þat ar putte aboue makeþ to þe closyng-in of nat*ur*ale hete and excludyng of þe aier. Be þise þingȝ seid afore of remeuyng of woundeȝ and vlcereȝ comended wele to mynde; And be it done boldly as it is

Arderne used to dress his wounds every third day.

seid, ffor oftymeȝ in many caseȝ I was noȝt wount for to remoue bot fro þe þrid day into þe þrid day, and þat namely in hurtyng of þe schy*n*neȝ; and I sped wele, And I cured many hard þingȝ and forsaken of o*þer* men w*ith* þis pulu*is* sine p*ar*i and o*þer* emplastreȝ y-named. And I

[1] "eseþ" *overlined.*

Pulvis sine pari only once failed Arderne.

saw neu*er* in al my tyme þis forseid pulu*is* defaile, out-take in þe legge of a gret man in which it miȝt noȝt haue no strength of wirchyng as it was wont for to haue i*n* oþ*er*; wherfor I was hugely astoned, bot neþ*er*leȝ I heled hym wele w*ith* grene liciu*m* putte þ*er*-to, our lorde beyng mene, as it is seid aboue.

Pulvis sanguis veneris,

25. [A]nd for þat many men couaiteþ for to here nameȝ of oileȝ and of emplastreȝ and of oyntementȝ, þ*er*for I haue putte þair nameȝ to þam. One for þe rednes and swetneȝ is called sanguis ven*er*is. Of french, forsoþ, for ladieȝ is called sank damo*ur*s or sank de pucelł, ffor why; venus was called goddeȝ of luffe. Sanguis ven*er*is ow þ*us* to be made: ℞*ecipe* pulu*is* of alcannet ℥1. and putte it in a q*ua*rt of comon oile, and þe oile schal become rede to likneȝ of blode, wheþ*er* it be boiled at þe fire or noȝt, for it may be made on boþe man*er*s; and be it kept to vse in ane erþen potte or a pewdre potte. þis man*er* of confeccion of sanguis ven*er*is is riȝt gode for þe alkenet þat is cold and drye in þe first or second gre. ffor þis alkenet co*n*sumeþ humiditeȝ of woundeȝ and of vlcereȝ, for it is subtiliatyue and resolutyue w*ith*out mordicacion, and carminatyue & app*er*tyue, and exsiccatyue w*ith* stiptikneȝ. Wherfor it is gode in hote apostemeȝ w*ith* litel mater in þe bygynnyng, for it is cold and drye and þ*er*for it is rep*er*cussyue and exsiccatyue of hote apostemeȝ. Also it helpeþ to synues and iu*n*ctureȝ, and vlcereȝ of þe mouþe in drying. And it medled w*ith* vinegre & ynoynted helpeþ to þe akyng of þe heued. Sanguis ven*er*is heleþ wele, and purgeþ, and defendeþ fro drede depe woundeȝ made wyth knyfe or arow, and holow vlcereȝ, if it be putte in w*ith* stuppeȝ of lyne, And emplastre Nerbone putte aboue, And it doþe al þingȝ þat p*er*teneþ to cure of a wou*n*de or of aposteme, and þat in a fair maner.

called in french sang d'amour, or sang des pucelles.

Its mode of preparation: (i) for ordinary use,

[leaf 170

(ii) for the better classes.

Bot witte þou þat Sanguis ven*er*is may be made on anoþ*er* man*er*, and þat to noble men, if þe lech may haue in tyme of his confection al þings necessarye vnto his confection, þat is to sey þe blode of a maiden virgyne or of a maiden damisel about 19 or 20 ȝere, which was neu*er* impregned,[1] þof sche be corrupte; for now in þis tymeȝ

[1] "w*ith* child" *overlined.*

A prescription for making a confection of sanguis veneris.

virgineȝ comeþ ful seldome to 20 ȝere. Which blode ow to be drawen out in þe ful of þe mone, þe mone beyng in v*ir*gine and þe sonne beyng in piscibȝ. Also it bihoueþ þe lech haue to þis confection aloes, & mirre, & sang*uis* drac*onis*, and pulu*is* of alkenet. And þus is it made: R*ecipe* blode of a maid, as it is seid afore, to þe which alsone aft*er* þe drawyng out, or it be cold, medle pulu*is* of aloes cicotrine, mirre, sang*uis* drac*onis* an*a* ℥1 or 2 or 3, aft*er* þe qua*n*tite of þe blode; of subtile pulu*is* of alkenet als mich as of al þe toþ*er*. And al þise, forsoþe, be wele medled w*ith* þe blode in man*er* of a paste, and aft*er*ward dry it at þe son: when it is drie kepe it to þine vse.

A method of using the confection sanguis veneris.

When þou wilt, forsoþe, vse þ*er*of, tak a p*ar*ty of it or al, and poudre it wele, and seþe it in grene oile of olyueȝ als mich as sufficeþ; þat is to ane vnce of þe forseid confection þou ow to putte 2 lb. of oile, þat is a quart of a galon, or more if it be nede, and boile þam togidre vnto þat þe oile appere rede; which beyng rede, putt it of þe fire, (sette it of þe fire) and kepe it to þine vse. And when it is boiled cole it noȝt bot lat it abide w*ith* þe oile, for it will satle in þe grounde, and so it will strengþe þe medicyne.

An ointment called Salus Populi.

26. [A]n oyntment þat is called Salus pop*u*li is made þ*us*: R*ecipe* celidon M. ij, ede*re* te*r*restris[1] M. i, and brysse þam togidre; and aft*er*ward take herteȝ talow or schepeȝ talow or boþe, als mych as sufficeþ to þe qu*an*tite of þe herbeȝ; And of oile of olyue als myche als half of þe talow; and boile al w*ith* þe forseid herbeȝ vnto þat þe herbeȝ go to þe grounde of þe vessel and be made blak; aft*er*ward cole þam and lat þam cold, and kepe it to vse. Þis oyntment is hard, and þ*er*fore when it is nede to vse it take of it and putte in ane holow oistre schelle and melt it aboue coleȝ, or aboue a brynnyng candel; And wher þat nede is anoyte þ*er*w*ith*. And witte þou þ*at* it ow noȝt to be putte in woundeȝ or vlcereȝ bot only about þam w*ith*outforþe, þ*at* is if þe skynne about þe wounde be flaien or skalded of hete, or if it haue many puscheȝ[2] & smale, white or rede or blak; þan be þe skyn first wele fomented w*ith* a sponge & hote watre, And aft*er* þ*at* it is

The method of its preparation, how to use it, and in what cases.

Use a fomentation first.

[1] "hayhoue, folefote, horshoue" *overlined.*
[2] "blayneȝ" *overlined.*

dried be it anoynted w*ith* þis anoyntment hote aboue þe place flaien or pusched, And alsone w*ith*out any þing atuix: if it be nede in grete caseȝ þ*o*u may anoynte it aboue w*ith* vnguento arabico or w*ith* comon vnguento albo for to kele it more strongly and dry.

[leaf 170, back]

Its mode of action.

Salus pop*u*li, forsoþ, dryeþ wele and sicatriȝeþ, and it availeþ at þe best to lippeȝ y-brent of þe sone or chynned of þe wynde, and to leggeȝ and fete and handeȝ; and it availeþ agaynȝ brynnyng of fire, and it quencheþ þe wild fire aft*er* þe fallyng of þe puscheȝ. þis oyntment wold I neu*er* wante for many benefeteȝ of it, And witte þ*o*u þat it is best remedi to þam þat haþe þe emoroid*es* or þe fistule or oþ*er* sleiyng.

The Nerbon plaster.

The method of preparation.

To stand so long as it takes one to say a pater noster and an ave.

To be made into pellets.

Whence its name.

27. [A]ne emplastre þat is called Nerbone is made þus: R*ecipe* diaquilon, and w*ith* comon oile or w*ith* oleo siriaco resolue it vp[on] þe coleȝ, and boile it alwaieȝ w*ith* a spatulre vnto it bigynne to wex blak. And if þ*o*u wil haue it riȝt blak boile it langer, and if þ*o*u wilt haue broune boile it lesse. ffor whi; by long boilyng it may be made most blak w*ith*out medlyng of any oþ*er* þing. And aft*er* þat þ*o*u wilt haue it hard or softe be added þ*er*to, or minusched, oile w*ith* which it is resolued. When it haþ boiled ynouȝ sette it fro þe fire and late it stande stille w*ith*out mouyng by þe space of a 'pat*er* nost*er*' & 'aue maria,' þat þe litarge of þe lede þat is in it may descende to þe grounde; and alsone be it ȝette out softly into anoþ*er* panne þat þe litarge be noȝt ȝette out w*ith*alt, and þan moue it w*ith* a spature strongly vnto þat it be colded. When, forsoþ, it is cold þat it may be malaxed, enforme þ*er*of trocist*es* vpon a table in qu*an*tite as it pleseþ þe, and kepe it to þine vse. þis e*m*plastre is called Noirbone, for þof-al it be blak neþ*er*lesse it is gode, for it heleþ wele wondeȝ and vlcereȝ, and it is wele cleuyng to, and it matureþ wele aposteme ȝ and bresteþ þam in any place of þe body.

Siriac oil,

28. [O]leu*m* Siriacu*m* is þ*us* made: R*ecipe* comon malueȝ of gardyneȝ, fatte & fresch, and somewhat brisse hem in a morter, And aft*er* boile hem long in comon oile bot noȝt vnto þe co*n*sumyng of þe herbe, þ*at* þe fatnes of

and plaister.

þe malueȝ be noȝt co*n*sumed. And if þou wilt make it þikke to man*er* of ane emplastre, þan ow þou for to putte w*ith* þe oile as war þrid p*ar*te of schepeȝ talow, and boile hem togidre as it is seid, and kepe it to vse.

Unguentum Arabicum.

29. Vnguentu*m* arabicu*m*, Tapsimel (in þe last end of emoroideȝ), Diaflosmos: seke hem in þe tretyse of þe fistuleȝ.

[leaf 171] Pulvis Grecus.

30. Pulu*is* grec*us* is þus made: R*ecipe* auripigment. citrin. pip*er*. nigri, calc*is* viue, alphice, i.[e.] barlymele an*a*, hony clarified p*artes* iij, vinegre þe ferþe p*ar*te; be þai medled w*ith* þe forseid poudreȝ in man*er* of paste, and be þ*er* made a kake þ*er*of, and be it baken on a hote tyle stone ou*er* þe fire so þ*at* it be noȝt brent bot þat it may be wele poudred vpon a stone. And when it bigy*n*neþ to wex blak on þe tile-stone be it oftyme turned þat it be noȝt brent bot þat [it] be p*er*fitely dried. W*ith* þis pulu*is* haue I cured sich fikeȝ puttyng out blode, & growyng in þe palme of a ma*n*neȝ hand. And if þou haue noȝt pulu*is* grec*us* þou may do þe same in þe forseid þings w*ith* pulu*is* s*ine* p*ar*i. And wytte þou þat I haue oft tyme sene pulu*is* grec*us* for to availe in þe cancre of a manneȝ ȝerde, and in fikeȝ bredyng þ*er*-aboute.

Its preparation, and uses.

Oil of Roses.

31. [O]ile of roseȝ is þ*us* made: R*ecipe* ros*es* þat bene ful spred, and gredre hem erly whileȝ þe dew lasteþ, and clyppe hem w*ith* a paire [of] schereȝ in smale pecys and do hem into a glasen vessel, and do þ*er*to oile of olyue of þe grenest þ*at* þou may fynde, an*a*, & medle hem wele togidre in þi vessel and stoppe it wele; And hete it agaynȝ þe son 20 daieȝ and þan draw it þurȝ a kanuaȝ and cast away þe groundeȝ of þe roseȝ, And putte þat liquo*ur* þat comeþ out into a vessel aȝeyn and stoppe þe vessel þ*at* þ*er* come none aier out. And ich day in þe mornyng when þou schalt hyng out þi potte tak a spature of tre and opne þi potte and stirre it wele, and stoppe it agayne duryng al þe 20 daies.

Its preparation.

Another preparation,

Anoþ*er* man*er* [of] makyng, and more colde. R*ecipe* roseȝ & oile an*a*, and schred þi ros*es* and putte hem into a vessel of glasse w*ith* þine oile, and stoppe it wele. And hang it into a vessel w*ith* watre vp to þe nek duryng tuo moneþeȝ, and eu*er* ich day stirre it oneȝ and stoppe it aȝeyn. And aft*er* þat streyne it and do away þi groundeȝ of þe roseȝ. And þis is more cold þan þe toþer. Also it is made þus aft*er* my man*er* and myne vse. If þou haue noȝt plente of roseȝ take of white ros*es* *with* þe tendrons of þe braucheȝ als mych as þou wilt, and brisse þam in a morter; þe which y-brissed, putte þam in als mych comon oile as þe likeþ, and so latte þam rest 9 daies; aft*er*ward boile þam vpon softe fire vnto þe oile be made grene. Þan if þou may haue fresch roseȝ putte þam in ane erþen potte or leden, als many as þe likest; and be þe forseid oile coled hote ȝette aboue and moued togidre *with* a spature, And alsone stoppe þe mouþe, þat þe vapo*ur* go noȝt out. And biry þe vessel *with* þe oile in moist erþe, and eu*er*y oþ*er* day be þ*er* ȝetted cold watre about þe potte. And be it þus done 40 daies or more, & þis man*er* *con*fection schal be most noble oile roset. And þ*us* ow it to stonde al þe hole ȝere.

when roses are scarce.

32. Oile of violetteȝ may be made in þe same man*er*. Bot witte þou þ*at* oile of violett*es* is laxatiue and oile of rose constrictiue. ffor why; if oile of violettȝ *with* euen porcion of iuyse of M*er*curial[1] be ȝetted in by a clistery in continuel acueȝ or int*er*polate, it remolleþ softely þe boweleȝ and putteþ out þe sup*er*fluiteȝ. Oile of violet haþe aspecte to me*m*breȝ þat bene dried by any infirmitè. It abateþ bolnyngȝ wher þat eu*er* þai be; And it softneþ þe asp*er*itè[2] of þe brest and of þe long, and it ceseþ pleuresy and hote apostemeȝ. And witte þou þat þ*er* is tuo man*er*eȝ of oile roset, complete and rude. Complete is made of ripe oile and of ful roseȝ ripe. Rude is made of vnripe oile and of roseȝ þat haþe [not?] fully opned þair buddeȝ. Oile roset complete is resolutiue, confortatyue, and conueniently cedatyue[3] of akyng. Rude forsoþe is extinctyue of infla*m*macions, confortatyue, aggregatyue, inspissatyue, p*ro*hibityue of curseȝ of humo*ur*s. Oile of ros*es* is special remedy agayns brennyng and hote apostemeȝ, wher þat euer þai be in þe body. ffor whi; in ane or tuo puttyngs to it mitigateþ þe akyng, it dulleþ þe furiositè and þe scharpneȝ of þe mater; It makeþ þe place for to vnbolne,[4]

[leaf 171, back] Oil of Violets.

Its uses.

Oil roset,

how it acts.

1 "smerwort" *overlined.* 2 "scharpneȝ" *overlined.*
3 "cesyng" *overlined.* 4 "swage" *overlined.*

and it remeueþ þe rede colour. ffor-soþe it swageþ and softeneþ þe brennyng & þe prikkyng, þe smertyng and þe akyng, And it comforteþ þe membres boþ in hote causes and in cold; ffor after auctours, Oile roset coldeþ ane hote membre and heteþ a cold membre. And it doþ many oþer profiteȝ in þe body, And þerfor a gode lech puruey hym þat he want neuer oile rosette, syþe þer procedeþ so many helpyngȝ of it to manneȝ body. ffor why; after galien, to euery akyng hote oile rosette is mitigatyue, as it is seid afore.

It should always be kept in stock.

Preparation of Oil of Camomile.

33. [O]ile of camamille is þus made: Recipe camamille grene and fresch, and brisse it somwhat in a morter. After boile it with a softe fire in comon oile als mych as sufficeþ. And putte a litel watre in þe oile þat þe herbe in seþing be noȝt brent; and boile it vnto þe herbeȝ go doune to þe grounde and bigynne to be blak. Which y-done, take flours of camamille, if þou may haue þam, and putte þam in ane erþen potte; And ȝette þe forseid oile coled, als hote as it may, aboue þe floureȝ, and alsone couer þe mouþe of þe potte with parchemyne and sette it in a saue place. fforsoþe if þou may [not?] haue flours of camamille in tyme of þi confeccion, þan in-stede of floureȝ tak M.i of þe tendre braunche ȝ of camamille and putte þam with-out any brissyng in a potte, and putte oile riȝt hote vpon þam, as it is seid afore. *And afterward when þou may haue flours of camamille, take þe forseid oile with þe braunche ȝ of camamille and boile þam eftsoneȝ vpon þe fire; and as it is seid afore, putte to a litel watre or elleȝ a litel vinegre, þat is better, þat þe oile may be more penetratyue, and boile it vnto þe wastyng of þe watre or of þe vinegre; and þat is knowen by boiling of þe oile made with noyse; þan cole it, and ȝette it riȝt hote vpon þe floureȝ as it was seid. Oile of camamille is temperate, and it is a blissyd þing of many helpyngs, and it is a conuenient resolutyue, and of akyng sedatyue, and it is prohibytyue of curseȝ of humours for a litel stiptikneȝ in it. It comforteþ synoweȝ and al synuy membryeȝ; It helpeþ to þe akyng of þe heued, And generaly it availeþ to al akyng, and it is conuenient to al complexions, and it is riȝt subtile. And als mych as it dissolueþ so mych consumeþ it.

Another preparation when the flowers are scarce.

[* leaf 172]

Its uses.

Oil of Mastick. Its preparation.

34. [O]ile of mastic*us* is made þ*us* : R*ecipe* Mastic*us* ℥ 1, thur*is* albi alexandrie ℥ ½ ; be þai poudred & decocte in 1 lb. of oile of rose or of almandeȝ or of noteȝ ; and when it is cocte ynoȝ, cole it and kepe it to vse. Þis oile helpeþ to eu*er*y akyng, of þe stomak, of þe iunctureȝ, of þe schuldreȝ, anoynted agayneȝ þe fire, and to akyngȝ of þe lyuer and of þe splene, putte to hote w*ith* lana succida. It comforteþ vertu assimilatyue in a me*m*bre febled ; wherfor it helpeþ to men in þe ethic, in þe ptisik, and disposed to þe lepre and to þe morfee, and to old men and consumed. And anoynted it moisteþ þe skynne, and reuokeþ and restoreþ þe flesch consumed, and conforteþ þe stomak and makeþ it to diffy in cold cause ; it rep*r*esseþ þe abho*min*aciones of þe stomak, it giffeþ appetite, it scharpeþ þe mynde, It co*n*sumeþ al cold passions, It availeþ to hole men and to seke in al necessiteȝ. When þ*o*u wilt make þis oile agaynȝ þe vices of þe stomak, þan may þ*o*u make it w*ith* oile in which ar soþen som þings p*er*tenyng to co*n*fortyng of þe stomak, as wormode, Mynt, Ma*cis*, galinga, & sich oþer, And so schal it better spede.

Its uses.

Things to be added when it is used as a stomachic.

Oil of Almonds. Its preparation.

35. [O]ile of almandeȝ is made þ*us* : R*ecipe* amigdal. dul*cis*, old & noȝt new, lb. ½, and tak of þe skynneȝ w*ith* hate watre ; aft*er*ward brisse þam lang & wele w*ith*out medlyng of any oþ*er* þing ; which y-brissed, be þai putte in a new strong bagge of lynne cloþe, and hyng þat bag ou*er* þe caldron or ou*er* a potte ful of boilyng wat*er*, so þat þe bagge touch noȝt þe watre bot þat only it receyue þe fume of þe boilyng watre. Aft*er*ward presse þe bag strongly and receyfe þe oile þ*at* comeþ out *and kepe it to þine vse. Bot witte þ*o*u þat þis oile may noȝt long endure. It availeþ mych agayne brynnyng of vryne w*ith*in in þe ȝerd, If it be cast in wyþ a syryng, And agayns oþ*er* brennyngȝ also.

[* leaf 172, back]

Its uses.

Almond water. Its preparation and uses.

36. [W]atre of almandeȝ is made þ*us* : R*ecipe* almand*es* dulc*es* clensed of þair skynneȝ and dryed, and brisse þam in a morter w*ith*out medlyng of any oþ*er* liquo*ur* ; And aft*er* distille þam as þ*o*u distilleþ rose watre. Þis availeþ agaynȝ brenny*n*g of þe

sonne in þe face, And also agaynȝ bry*nn*y*ng* in a manneȝ ȝerd, put i*n* by a siryng.

Oil of Juniper, how distilled.

37. [O]ile of Iunipr*e* is made þ*us*: R*ecipe* a new erþen potte, and putte it into þe erþe euen to þe mouþe; þan tak anoþ*er* erþen potte whos bothme may be receyfed w*ith*in þe mouþe of þe potte þat standeþ in þe erþe; And putte ane holowe canel of yren þurȝ þe bothme of þe ou*er* potte into þe neþ*er* potte þat standeþ w*ith*in þe erþe; þan tak dry stikkeȝ of Iunip*er*i and kutte þam smal and putte þam into þe ou*er* potte, and þan lute þe mouþeȝ of boþe pottes w*ith* clay medled w*ith* horsdong. And make a fire al aboute þe ou*er*more potte, And þan scha[l] oile distille þurȝ þe canel into þe lawer potte, þe which kepe for þin vse, for it is ful noble for akyng. It is gode for al man*er* goute and for þe p*ar*allesy.

Its uses.

Ointment of Juniper.

38. [A]lso ane enoyntment made of it to wondeȝ þ*at* vnneþ bene curable and long tyme haue bene in þe boneȝ: R*ecipe* fruyte of Iunip*er*i & fresch lard of a male swyne and brisse þam togidre; Aft*er*ward take 3 p*artes* of riȝt strong white wyne and seþe þe forseid þingȝ in it, and when it is þikke sette doune fro þe fire. And putte þ*er*of to þe forseid soreȝ & wondeȝ. It p*ur*geþ, it filleþ, it heleþ & it cicatrizeþ.

Its preparation

and uses.

A good plaister for the gout.

39. [A] gode emplastre for þe goute: R*ecipe* blak sope als mich as sufficeþ, to which putte als mych of raw ȝolkeȝ of eyren as is half of þe sope, and medle þam strongly in a dish or in a box vnto þat þe sope lefe his owne colo*ur*; þe which y-done, putte it w*ith* þi fyng*er* or w*ith* a spature vpon subtile stupeȝ of lyne and applie it faste vnto þe akyng place. Aboue þis emplast*re*, forsoþe, putte a strictorie of white of eiren and mele of whete and lynne*n* clouteȝ y-dipped þ*er*in, and putte it fast & applie it aboue þe forseid emplast*er* þat it be noȝt remoued byfore dew tyme, bot if any competent cause aske it. Þis medycyne is liȝt *but noȝt litel effectual, þat haue I p*ro*ued ofttymeȝ, als wele in wymen as in men; þat w*ith* oneȝ puttyng to it ceseþ ful grete akyngȝ als wele in þe kneeȝ as in þe fete and in oþ*er* ioyntureȝ; bot be-war þat it be noȝt p*er*ceyued of þe pacient ne of none oþ*er*; hold it pryuè and chere, and schew it noȝt bot to þi son or ane

Its preparation.

[* leaf 173]

So good that it should only be shown to one's son.

als wele biluffed. I trow, forsoþ, þat it availeþ bifor al oþ*er* medicyneȝ to þe goute, and more sone abateþ þe akyng. And it ow 5 daieȝ or 6 to lye stille w*ith*out remeuyng if it may so bene applied.

Walwort and its virtues.

40. [W]alwort[1] is ane herbe like vnto el[d]re in lefeȝ and fruyte. In odo*ur* it is su*m*what greuo*us* and stynkyng. In tast it is as war bitter, bot in vertu anence old men it is deemed expert and effectuale, and kynde & free to medicyne in many vseȝ; witnesse plini*us*, diascorideȝ, macrobuȝ and many oþ*er*, whos roteȝ, ryndeȝ, and b*ra*ncheȝ and leueȝ and floureȝ bene p*ro*fitable in medicyneȝ. It haþe vertu of dissoluyng, consumyng of gret flemme and viscose w*ith* þe iuyse of it. It availeþ agaynȝ þe gutte of þe ioyntureȝ and contraccion of synueȝ of þe heude & of þe fete. It availeþ also agaynȝ bolnyngȝ and collections inte*r*cutanieȝ wher-so-eu*er* þai bene gedred in þe body. Also it availeþ most agaynȝ brissyngs of me*m*breȝ and falleȝ, if þe membreȝ be fomented in his decoctions. ffor why; it mitigateþ þe akyng, it ceseþ þe bolnyng, it minisi treþ ve*r*tue and strength to synoweȝ and to ioyntureȝ. It availeþ agayneȝ bolnyng of þe womb of cold y-dropisy, if his Iuyse be dronken w*ith* hony and comyne. And witte þou þat þe Iuyse of walwort, or þe poudre of it if it be hadde redy, is namely in eu*er*y medicyne þat is restrictyue of blode. Þe man*er* of makyng and kepyng of it is as þe man*er* of liciu*m* seid afore.

The uses of walwort.

A valence of scabious. Its preparation.

41. Valence of scabio*us* or of Iacee albe is þ*us* made: R*ecipe* Iuyse of scabio*us* in som*er*, and cole it þurȝ a cloþe; and tak swyneȝ grese clensed of þe skynneȝ and stamp it wele in a morter in smytyng it bot noȝt in brekyng vtt*er*ly; and eu*er*more putte in a litel of þe iuyse to þe grese þat it may wele be imbibed and þat þe talow may be made grene; þe which y-done, tak þat grese and cou*er* it w*ith* þe forseid iuyse and so late it stand 9 daieȝ. And aft*er* 9 daieȝ take eftsone þe forseid grese w*ith* þe iuyse and stamp it as afore, and putte out þat þinne watryneȝ and discolored þat goþ out þ*er*of, and so lat it stande 5 daieȝ. *Aft*er* þe 5 day eftsone tak new Iuyse of scabio*us* and stamp it, as it is seid, w*ith* þe forseid grese; þe which

[* leaf 173, back]

[1] "ebulus" *overlined.*

y-done, latte it rest in a vessel *with* þe iuyse al a fourtny3t; which tyme ou*er*passed, eftsone3 bete it as it is seid afore, and purge it of þe wat*r*ine3, and putte it in a clene vessel, and lat it stand stil anoþ*er* fourtni3t, And þan

Its uses.

brisse it wele vnto þat it be al of grene colo*ur*. And whan þe nedeþ for to vse þ*er*of, as vnto þe antrax, putte þ*er*of *with* þi fyng*er* vpon clene stuppe3 of lyne, and strech it and lay it on þe antrax anoynted *with* oile of rose, and remeued it no3t by a naturel day. ffor *with*out dout it schal slee þe antrax and swage þe akyng, and brist it and

Whence its name.

vtterly cure it. And þis medyc[in]e is called Valence of scabio*us* for þe valow of it. It may be kepte many 3ere3, bot it is better if it be eu*er*y 3ere renewed and bette newly *with* oile ros*es*, and putte vp agayne vnto it nede. And witte þou þat scabio*us* y-dronken sleeþ þe antrax, and putteþ away þe venym of it fro þe hert þat it sle no3t þe pacient. Also þe same herbe ydronken t*ur*neþ inward aposteme3 to outward and putteþ þam out insensibily. Also witte þou þat new scabio*us* & fresch y-brissed *with* swynes grese and putte vpon antrax sleeþ it in a day naturel, and takeþ away þe akyng for certayne. Bot for þat scabio*us* may no3t eu*er*more be had redy & fresch, þ*er*for was þis medicyne made þat may long be kept, þ*at* wonderfully sleeþ þe antrax and vtterly cureþ it, as I haue p*ro*ued myself ane hundreþ tyme3. Also witte þou þat Iacea alba is scabio*us*, bot Iacea nigra is matfelon. And witte þ*ou* þat þat scabio*us* þat groweþ among corne3 *with* ane heuenly flo*ur* is bett*er* þan þat þ*at* groweþ in mydowe3 þat haþ no flo*ur*. Aft*er* diascorid*es* trowe þou to þis þat it haþe no pere to þe forseid þing3 wonderfully to be done, and þat softely. I haue p*ro*ued it a hundreþ tyme3 for certayne.

A valence of wormwood.

42. Valence of wormode is þ*us* made: R*ecipe* iuyse of wormode, smalach, plantayn, and *with* swyne3 grese clensed wele of þe skynne3 brisse it wele and long togidre in man*er* as it is seid afore of þe valence of scabio*us*; þe

Its uses.

which y-done, kepe it to þin vse. þis valence of wormode availeþ to brissyngs of legge3 and of schynbone3, and to

[*leaf 174]

wounde3 þat ar made in þe muscle3 *of þe arme3 and of þe legge3 *with* a strey3t wounde, as of a knyfe or of ane arowe,

(1) A resonable gouernance of lawez of lywyng.
(2) Æsculapius helyd menne with ffernices & medicines.
(3) Aschepius taught to geder rotes and herbez, flowriez and frotez.
(4) Aschepius schewed mesures and quantitiez, weghtez and wares.
(5) Aschepius techeth to make puluerez confeccionis & electuariez.
(6) Ypocras & galien schewe certeyne quantitiez in preseruyng.

PLATE IV.—From Sloane MS. 6, Brit. Mus., leaf 176, back.

or of sich oþ*er*. And it aileþ to al woundeȝ for to hold þam opne, and for certayne it mitigateþ wele þe akyng. When þe nedeþ for to vse þ*er*of in woundeȝ, ȝette in first of oile of roseȝ or of violet 2 droppeȝ or þre, and anoynt al þe wounde about of þe same oileȝ, and þe me*m*bre þat is hurt. And aft*er*ward putte aboue of þe forseid valence vpon softe stupeȝ of lyne, and bynde it competently, and lat it so abide a naturel day. Þis medicyne, forsoþ, represseþ wele bolnyng and akyng and holdeþ þe wounde opne, and gendreþ quito*ur*, and draweþ out venym of þe wounde, and quencheþ þe brynnyng of þe me*m*bre. Þis oyntment, forsoþ, luffed I mych; w*ith* þis medicyne cured I a fischer at london, which was hurt in þe lacert of his arme of þe prikkyng of a scharp yren standyng on þe gymeweȝ at þe frere Caromeȝ [1]; Wherfore he was almost dede, what of akyng, bolnyng, and brynnyng, and what of þe vncouenable cure of a barbo*ur* þat putte in þe wounde scharpe tenteȝ of lynne cloþe, and putte aboue diaquilon. His cure, forsoþ, remoued away, I putte to about euensang-tyme of þe forseid valence with anoyntyng of oile of ros*es*, And bifore cokcrow þe pacient was delyu*er*ed of akyng and þe arme biganne for to swage,[a] and in the mornyng he sleped wele, and þe arme was purged of quito*ur* by the wounde. Bot witte þou þat I putte no tent in þe forseid wounde, bot al-only w*ith* ȝettyng in of oile and puttyng aboue of þe valence w*ith*-out any-þing atuix I cured hym finaly; wherfor I gatte mych hono*ur*. At nothyngham, forsoþ, I cured anoþ*er* p*er*fitely w*ith* þe forseid medicyne, þat was smyten in þe arme, bot noȝt þorow, w*ith* a knyfe; of whos life men despaired for akyng and anguysch of þe pacient.

A case cured by this valence in London,

and another at Nottingham.

43. Pulu*is* for to make a man sleep agaynȝ his wille, aft*er* man*er* of Ribaldeȝ and trowans in frau*n*ce, þat felawshypeþ þam by þe waieȝ to pilg*r*imeȝ þat þai may robbe þam of þair siluer when þai ar aslepe. R*ecipe* seme*n* iusq*u*iam*us*, ȝiȝannie, i.[e.] darnel, papau*er*is nigri, i.[e.] chessede, de radice brionie sicc., an*a*; brek al-togidre in a brasen morter into ful smal poudre, of which poudre giffe hym in his potage or in a kake of whete or in drynk, & he

A sleeping powder used by rogues in France.

[1] cum hac medicina curavi quendam pistenarium apud London. qui ex puncturâ ferri acuti stantem super legimeus ad fratres Carmeli in lacerto brachii læsus.

[a] "vnbolne" *overlined.*

schal slepe alsone, wille he wil he noȝt, al-aday or more after þe quantite þat he haþe taken.

[leaf 174, back]

Pills to cause sleep.

Pillules for to prouoke slepe: Recipe amides ʒj, croci ʒiii, opii ʒj; Make þam wyth watre of roses and make pillule [1] and giffe þam; And he þat takeþ þam schal slepe for certayne.

An ointment to prevent pain.

Its preparation.

Ane vntement slepyng, with which if any man be anoynted he schal mow suffre kuttyng in any place of þe body without felyng or akyng. Recipe succus iusquiami,[2] Mandrage, Cicute, lattuce, papaueris albi & nigri, and þe sedeȝ of al þise forseid herbeȝ, if þai may be hadde, ana; opii thebaici, opii Miconis ana, ʒj or ij; fresch swyneȝ grese þat sufficeþ. Breke al þise wele & strongly togidre in a morter, and afterward boile þam strongly and þan cole þam. And if it be noȝt þikke ynoȝ, putte to a litel propoleos, i.[e.] white wex, and kepe it to þine vse.

How used.

And when þou wilt vse þerof, Anoynt his front, his pulseȝ, his templeȝ, his armeholeȝ, and his loneȝ of his heud and his fete, and alsone he schal slepe so þat he schal fele no kuttyng.[3] þis is also if a man may noȝt slepe for oþer cause, as in febreȝ or sich oþer, for þis oyntment ouþer schal giffe hym remedy, or þe pacient schal die. Also one grayne of opii thebaici to þe quantitè of ʒss., distempered with a pynte of wyne[a] or more after þe miȝt of hym þat schal drynk it, schall make hym þat drynkeþ it for to slepe. Also þe sede alon of iusquiami albi giffen in wyne to drynk make þe drynker alsone for to slepe, þat he schal noȝt fele whatso-euer is done to hym. And þis proued I myself for certayne.

Method of treating a patient to bring him round after its use.

And witte þou þat it spedeþ for to draw hym þat slepeþ so by þe nose and by þe chekeȝ and by þe berde, þat þe spiriteȝ be quickened þat he slepe noȝt ouer ristfully. Also be þe lech warre þat he giffe noȝt opium without croce for to drynk, for crocus and cassia lignea bene þe freneȝ, i.[e.] bridelleȝ of opii.[4]

To wake a sleeping man after opium.

44. ffor to wake a man þat slepeþ þus: Putte to his nose gray brede y-tosted & wette in strong vinegre; or put vinegre or mustard in his nose; Or wasch his heued in strong vinegre; Or anoynt his templeȝ with þe iuse of

[1] ℞ Amidi ʒj: croci ʒiii: opii ʒi. Confice cum aquâ rosarum et pillulas deinde forma.

[2] Succus hyoscyami.

[3] Unga frontem pulsus, axillas, volas manuum et plantas pedum et statim dormiet patiens nec incisionem sentiet

[4] Quia crocus et cassia lignea sunt fræna opii.

[a] MS. wynde.

rubarb. And giffe hym som oþer sternutorieȝ, and alsone he schal wake. And witte þou þat it is gode for to giffe hym afterward castoreum, for it is triacle of iusquiamus[1] & opii & sich oþer, wheþer it be giffen in þe mouþe or in drynk, or it be put in þe nose; for castore chaufeþ & most confORteþ þe syneweȝ colded, and solueþ þe paralysye. And also giffe hym þat conforteþ þe brayne, as castore, nucis moschati,[2] roses, nenufare, mirtelleȝ & sumac.

[1] theriaca hyoscyami.

[2] Myristicæ.

Contra spasmum et crampe.

[Sloane MS. 2002, leaf 79]

Contra spasmum et crampe radix brionie in aqua cocta et postea pistata aut per se, vel in agrippa, vel oleo de semine lini, vel in dialthea, vel oleo de lilio aut camomille, collo emplastrata spasmum curat in quocunque membro corporis fuit. Quia in collo [* leaf 79, back] *est origo omnium morborum. Et spasmus est contractio musculorum ad suas origines. Istud carmen sequens contra spasmum expertissimum est a multis inventis eo utentibus, tam in partibus transmarinis quam in istis. Nam apud mediolanis, i.[e.] Melane, in lumbardia tempore quo dominus Leonellus filius regis Anglie nupsit filiam domini Mediolani. Anglici ibidem spasmo vexabantur propter potaciones vinorum fortium et calorum patriæ et nimium repletiones. Unde quidam miles, et filius domini Reginaldi de Gray de Schirlond juxta Chestrefelde, qui fuit apud mediolanum cum domino leonello et habuit secum carmen sequens, et quemdam armigerum a spasmo vexatur ita quod caput suum retro trahebatur fere usque ad collum suum, ad modum balistæ,[a] qui pro dolore et angustia fere exspiravit. Quo viso, dictus Miles accepit carmen, in pergamento scriptum in bursa positum, in collo patientis apposuit [† leaf 80] †dicentibus circumstantibus orationem dominicam ad dominam Maria[m] et, ut mihi juravit fideliter, infra quatuor horas aut quinque sanitati est restitutus. Et postea multos alios a spasmo ibidem liberavit, unde magna fama de illo carmine in illa civitate exercuit:

Item in civitate Lincoln: . . . Item apud London: . . . Item apud villam de Huntingdon:

[a] "crossbow" in the margin.

. . . . *postea claudatur istâ cedulâ admodum unius litera ut non leniter possit aperiri, unde solebam scribere istud literis grecis, ne a laicis perspicietur. [* leaf 80, back]

Quum ut istud carmen scriptum, se honeste in dei omnipotentis nomine gesserit et crediderit, sine dubio a spasmo non erit aggravatus. Istud habeatur in reverentia propter dominum qui virtutem dedit verbis, petris et herbis, et secrete fingitur ne omnes nostant carmen ne forte virtutes datas a deo amittat.

A charm against Spasm and Cramp.

Bryony root boiled in water & afterwards crushed either by itself or in agrippa or in linseed oil or in dialthea or in oil of lily or camomile cures spasm when it is plastered upon the neck in whatever part of the body it may be. Because the source of all diseases is in the neck: And spasm is a contraction of the muscles at their origin. The following charm against spasm has been found most sovran by many who have used it both at home and abroad. For amongst the Mediolani [i.e.] the Milanese, in Lombardy at the time when the Lord Lionel, son of the king of England, married the daughter of the lord of Milan, the English there were troubled with spasm due to their potations of the strong & hot wines of the country & to too many carouses. Whereupon a certain knight, the son of Lord Reginald de Grey de Schirlond near Chesterfield, who was at Milan with the Lord Lionel & had with him the following charm, & saw a certain gentleman so troubled with the spasm that his head was drawn backward nearly to his neck just like a crossbow, & he was almost dead from the pain and starvation. And when the said knight saw this he brought the charm written on parchment & placed it in a purse & put it upon the neck of the patient whilst those who stood by said the Lord's prayer and one to our lady Mary, and, as he swore faithfully to me, within four hours or five he was restored to health. And afterwards he freed many there from spasm, & the great report of that charm spread throughout that state. Again in the

Whence come spasms.

Results of the marriage festivities at Milan when Duke Lionel wedded.

The charm, how used.

city of Lincoln . . . again in London . . . again in the Town of Huntingdon.

The words of the charm

In nomine patris ✠ et filii ✠ et Spiritus sancti ✠ Amen.

⊞ Thebal ⊞ Enthe ⊞ Enthanay ⊞ In nomine Patris ⊞ et Filii ⊞ et Spiritus sancti ⊞ Amen. ⊞ Ihesu Nazarenus ⊞ Maria ⊞ Iohannes ⊞ Michael ⊞ Gabriel ⊞ Raphael ⊞ Verbum caro factum est ⊞.

Why written with Greek letters.

Let it be closed afterwards in the manner of a letter so that it cannot be opened easily, & for this reason I used to write it in greek letters that it might not be understanded of the people. And if any one carries that charm written fairly in the name of God almighty, & believes, without doubt he will not be troubled with cramp. Let it be held in respect on account of the Lord who gave virtue to words, to stones & to herbs, & let it be made secretly that every one should not know the charm lest perchance it should lose the virtues given by God.

APPENDIX

[MS. Rawlinson, B. 102, leaf 30, back.]

Grant to R. de Rupella of land in the Cantred of Tirmany, Connaught, given to him by the Black Prince.

Sciant presentes et futuri quod ego Iohannes de Arderne dedi concessi et hac presenti carta confirmaui Domino Richardo de Rupella pro homagio et servicio suo totam terram meam cum omnibus pertinentijs suis sine aliquo retenemento quam habui in illo Theodo quod vocatur Crohun in Cantredo de Tirmany in Connatia de dono et feoffamento domini Edwardi illustris Regis Angliæ primogeniti in escambium manerij sui de Willinghale et Plesingho cum pertinentijs suis habendam et tenendam de me et heredibus meis eidem domino Richardo et heredibus suis et eorum assignatis adeo libere et quiete sicut idem dominus Richardus tenet terram suam de Clonedach' quam habet de dono et feoffamento predicti domini Edwardi et sicut plenius et liberius et integrius continetur in Carta quam idem dominus Edwardus de dicta terra mihi confecit reddendo inde per Annum mihi et heredibus meis ipse dominus Ricardus et heredes sui et eorum Assignati vnum denarium ad Pascha et faciendo pro me et heredibus meis predicto domino Edwardo et heredibus suis servicium feodi vnius militis pro omnibus servicijs consuetudinibus sectis exactionibus et omnibus demandis secularibus. Et ego Iohannes et heredes mei warrantizabimus acquietabimus et defendemus eidem domino Richardo et heredibus suis et eorum Assignatis totam predictam terram cum omnibus pertinentiis suis sine aliquo retenemento per predictum servicium sicut predictum est contra omnes homines et feminas inperpetuum. Et vt hec mea donatio firma et stabilis permaneat huic Carte Sigillum meum apposui. Hijs testibus, Dominis Iohanne de Ripar', Roberto de Vfforde, Ricardo de Tany, Willelmo de Wokingdon, Rogero de Bello Campo, Richardo de Ispanya, Militibus, Waltero de Essex, Thoma Iocelyn, Iohanne de Rupell', et Alijs.

[This is entered in the Bodleian Catalogue at Oxford under the heading "Arderne Iohannes, chirurgus." Cf. Forewords, p. x.]

NOTES.

1/1. *Ploge* seems to be a variant of the more common form *plage* and is equivalent to 'Plague,' but it is not given in this form in the New English Dictionary.

1/4. An account of John Arderne is given in the Forewords. He calls himself Johannes Arderne Sirurgicus in 1372 and Magister Joh. de Arderne after 1376. I have adopted the simpler form.

1/4. The first pestilence was the Black Death, which entered England at Weymouth about the middle of August 1348, and ravaged the kingdom in 1349. It was pandemic, and yet, in spite of the tremendous mortality which attended its progress, it does not seem to have attracted much attention from the medical men who lived through it. Arderne only uses it in this passage as a means of determining the time when he began to practise in Nottinghamshire, yet he must have seen it in its full fury. Details of the Black Death will be found in Creighton's "History of Epidemics in England," vol. i, and in Father Gasquet's "The Great Pestilence now commonly known as the Black Death." The second pestilence, called the Great Plague, occurred in 1361, and killed amongst others Henry, Earl of Derby and Duke of Lancaster (cf. 1/10). The third pestilence in 1369 killed his daughter Blanche, wife of John of Gaunt.

1/8. *Sir Adam Everyngham.* The Everynghams had long been established at Tuxford. An Adam de Everyngham went bail for several deerstealers, 36 Hen. III (1251), and Thoroton, in the "Antiquities of Nottinghamshire" (ed. 1677, p. 380, col. 2), states that John de Lexington died 41 Hen. III (1256), seized of the manor of Tuxford and hamlet of Warsop, and of the land in Lexington held of Adam de Everyngham. The Records of the Borough of Nottingham (1155–1399, vol. i, p. 389) note on April 27th, 1330, a grant from Richard, son of Richard de Lameleye dwelling in Lampadidnawe in Wales . . . . . to William de Mekisburg of Nottingham of a messuage in Gedeling and all the land formerly held of Sir Adam de Everyngham in Gedelin, Carleton and Stoke Bardolf. The Sir Adam de Everyngham treated by John Arderne died 8th Feb., 2 Ric. II (1378–9), and he was probably operated upon not later than 1358. This treatise on the fistula was written in 1376 (see Forewords, p. xi), so that this passage must have been a later addition to the original manuscript. The armorial bearings of the Everyngham family are Argent, a fess azure, a label of three points gules. Thoroton (ed. 1797, vol. 3, p. 207) gives a pedigree of the family of Everyngham.

1/10. *Sir Henry, that tyme named Erle of Derby.* He was Henry Plantagenet (1299?–1361), son of Henry, Earl of Lancaster, and his Countess Maud. Sir Henry was cousin to Edward III who created him Earl of Derby in 1337, Earl of Lincoln in 1349, and Duke of Lancaster in 1351, being the second person in England to be made a Duke. Sir Henry was one of the original Knights of the Garter, and was looked upon throughout Europe as the very mirror of chivalry, when chivalry was at its height.

Readers of Froissart will recall many of his exploits often in company with that other great Captain, Sir Walter de Manny. Sir Henry sailed for Antwerp with King Edward III in July 1338, and in 1339, after the great sea fight at Sluys, he was left in prison in Flanders as security for the King's debts. It may have been at this time that Arderne was practising at Antwerp, if there is any truth in the tradition (see Forewords, p. xii). In 1343 Sir Henry, then Earl of Derby, was sent to Avignon to Pope Clement VI and Alfonzo XI of Castile. Whilst in Spain he and his fellow ambassador, the Earl of Salisbury, did good service against the Moors at the siege of Algeçiras when cannon are said to have been used for the first time. Arderne treated a Spanish nobleman at Algeçiras (Forewords, p. xi).

1/13. The irregular endings of the technical terms which is noticeable here and in other parts of the MS. (cf. 24/5) is due to the scribe copying them as they stand in the Latin text where the case varies with the construction of the sentence in which it occurs.

1/14. Arderne's knowledge of the Gascony campaign is curiously minute and makes it possible that he had actually taken part in it or that he knew the country intimately. Writing more than thirty years after the event he gives the towns in the order in which they were visited by one of the three divisions into which the Duke of Lancaster, formerly the Earl of Derby, had divided his forces, rather than in the correct geographical order. The army landed at Bordeaux and captured Bergerac on 24th August, 1345. The town was granted to Lancaster as a reward for his services but reverted to the crown upon his death. It came afterwards into the hands of Edward "the Black Prince," and was given by him to John of Gaunt in 1370. The arms of the town "Deux pattes de griffon sur un champ d'or" may still be seen emblazoned in the Great Crowcher Book of the Duchy of Lancaster, says Mr. Armitage-Smith in his "John of Gaunt" (p. 199).

Toulouse. Sir Adam doubtless reached here with the force acting on the Lot and Garonne rivers after the battle of Auberoche on 24th October, 1345, when 300 lances and 600 archers defeated a force estimated at 10,000 strong under the Count of Lille-Jourdain.

Narbonne had some special association for John Arderne, since he named one of his best-beloved ointments Ungt. Noirbon, adding as a pun that though it was black (Noir) it was good (bon).

Poitiers was stormed on 4th October, 1346, with a tremendous slaughter of men, women and children. So much rich booty was taken that raiment was held of no account unless it was cloth of gold or silver, or plumes. The campaign ended here, and the Duke of Lancaster returned to London 13th June, 1347.

1/23. *Mene* is here used in the sense of "an instrument or agency," and is equivalent to "deo favente." It is as favourite a phrase with Arderne as "I dressed him, God cured him," used to be with Ambroise Paré.

1/29. *Balne by Snaith.* Balne is 5¼ miles from Snaith, a small town in the West Riding of Yorkshire. There was a priory at Snaith belonging to the Warwick family.

2/1. *John Schefeld of Briȝtwell a-side Tekyll.* This John was probably a member of the knightly family of Sheffield of Nottingham. The manor of Tickhill was granted to John of Gaunt in 1372 with other rewards for surrendering the Earldom and Honour of Richmond, which was im mediately bestowed upon John de Montford to secure his allegiance then wavering between England and France.

2/2. *Sir Reginald Grey de Wilton*, also known as Grey de Shirlond or De Grey. He was the fourth Lord de Grey and was aged 30 in 1342. He died in 1370, and held the manor of Shirland, co. Derby. His grandfather John, Lord de Grey, was Justice of North Wales and Vice-Justice of Chester 1296–97. Sir Reginald Grey's son, the fifth Lord de Grey, served in Gascony in 1366. The peerage became extinct in 1614 when the fifteenth Lord de Grey died in the Tower after having been found guilty of high treason in connection with the Bye or Priest's Plot. The Calendar of Close Rolls (Ed. III, 1354–1360, No. 1358) gives the names of Sir Reynold de Grey and John Arderne as witnesses to an enrolment of release by Roger de Puttenham, knight of the manor of Wylye, co. Warwick.

2/5. *Sir Henry Blakborne.* A Sir Henry de Blakeburn, son of William, son of Paulinus de Eleston of the County of Lancaster, obtained "a general pardon for his good service in the war of France . . . on condition that he did not withdraw from the King's service so long as he shall stay this time on this side the sea without his special licence." The pardon is granted by K and the testimony of Adam de Swynburn, under-constable of the Army. It is dated "By Calais, September 4th, 1346." There also exists a ratification of the estate of a Henry de Blakeburn as prebendary of Preston, in the church of St. Mary, Salisbury. It bears the date September 22nd, 1351. On May 7th, 1379, "Henry de Blakeburn was presented to the church of Reddcleve-on-Soar by John de Wynewyk, and has since resigned it." ("Cal. of Patent Rolls," Ed. III, viii, 496; ix, 137; and Rich. II (1377–1381), p. 363.)

2/10. The transcriber has left out a line here. The text runs, "Afterward I halid Sir Iohn Masty *par*sone of Stopporte in Chestre-shire."

2/11. Gunnas or Gunnays was a York family in the fourteenth century. Thomas Gunnays was a scrivener in 1363–4; John Gunnays a Tannator in 1389–90, and there was also John, a Marchaunt. ("Register of York Freemen," The Surtees Soc., vol. i, 1896.)

2/13. The scribe has made a mistake in the name. John le Colier was Mayor of Northampton in 1326–7, and again in 1339–40. He seems to have been a most regular attendant at the meetings of the Town Council, because his name appears as a witness to thirty-three documents between the years 1315 and 1340. ("Records of the Borough of Nottingham," vol. i, 1155–1399.) A William Colyar was Mayor of Northampton 1368–9.

2/29. *Towel.* Arderne's translator uses somewhat unusual terms for the parts with which he is dealing. The *towel* is always the Anus. It is, I suppose, a form of "tewel," a pipe or funnell, and the word has survived in the North of England as a "tuyer" in connection with the blast furnaces. *Longanon* or *Longaon* is the ordinary mediæval word for the rectum or lowest segment of the large intestine. The *Lure* is sometimes the ischio-rectal fossa, and sometimes the anus or rectum. The "Promptorium Parvulorum" gives "Mouth of a botel," "Lura," or Leather bagge, adds the Bibliotheca Eliotæ, ed. 1559. The New English Dictionary, s.v. Lure, 2 Her(aldic), says, "A conventional representation of a hawk's 'lure,' consisting of two birds' wings with the points directed downwards and joined above by a ring attached to a cord." Either of these similes suits the anatomy of the ischio-rectal fossa, but it is clearly the simpler one that was in Arderne's mind, as he did not know enough anatomy to visualise the ischio-rectal fossa in accordance with the hawk's lure. Cf. 11/10.

2/40. The opinions of Arderne's immediate contemporaries and predecessors on the subject of Fistula in ano are given in the Forewords (p. xvi).

3/8. The translation quite misses the beauty of this passage, which should read, "It is not opened to them that knock as they pass by, but to those who stand and knock."

3/13. *In diuanudiis.* These words have proved a crux from the earliest times. Some scribes have merely copied the words here printed, others have omitted them entirely. John Arderne clearly wrote a very bad hand, but Miss E. M. Thompson has made the following transcription of Sloane MS. No. 29301 (leaf 22, back, col. 80), which was presumedly a fair copy produced under Arderne's immediate supervision—"Nota de honore dei. Ad honorem ergo dei omnipotentis qui aperuit mihi sensum ut thesaurum in agro studenter absconditum quod longo tempore pectoreque anelo diligencius ac pertinacius diu auidius insuadaverim invenire prout mea suppetat facultas absque scernatis facunditate posteris, domino mediante istoque libello, explicite duxi exarandus. Non ut meipsum laude dignum ex tanto munere ceteris efferam sed, ut ne dominum irretem et pro dragma quam mihi tradidit affatu urgeor delatoris." The badly written words "diu avidius" in this passage were soon corrupted into "in diuanudiis," the "*in*" being an interpolation. "In diuanudiis" easily became "De Dinamidiis," the name of a spurious work ascribed to Galen, and thus Arderne acquired an undeserved reputation as a Grecian.

3/23. The transcriber has omitted the line, "*þat* is leful forsoþ to sey that is knowen & for to witness that is seene."

3/27. This was the Black Prince's campaign in 1355. It lasted eight weeks, and was of a freebooting character.

3/34. Yet John Arderne thought it wise to obtain the Minorite's secret. "Il ne révèle son secret (en 1370) que parce qu'il est vieux et qu'il a tiré des très-beaux bénéfices," says Daremberg (Hist. des. Sci. méd. i, 301, note).

3/36. It is unnecessary to show the debt of the medical profession in the middle ages to Galen, who was born at Pergamos about A.D. 131. Arderne probably quotes Galen through a Latin translation of an Arabic version. He knows him as the author of the Megatechni or De methodo medendi—θεραπευτικῆς μεθόδου—and of the Microtechni, or simply the Techni or Tegni which was the ars medica or τέχνη ἰατρική. The Pantechni or Pantegni used here by Arderne was not one of Galen's writings. It was written in Arabic by Isaac the Jew (d. 932 A.D.), and was translated into Latin by Constantinus Africanus (fl. 1036 A.D.), who issued it as his own. Cf. 55/3. Prof. Ed. Nicaise ("La Grande Chirurgie de Guy de Chauliac," Paris, 1890, p. 52) says that in 1309 the Faculty of Medicine at Montpellier demanded that each bachelor who wished to become a Master must have studied the following books of Galen, "De complexionibus; de malicia complexionis diverse; De simplici medicina; De crisi et criticis diebus; De Ingenio sanitatis." He had also to explain two books which had been lectured upon and one which had not been commented upon, of the Techni and Prognostics, or of the Aphorisms of Hippocrates, or of his Regimen, or the Isagoge of Johannitius, the Febres of Isaac, or the Antidotary of Rhazes. See Dr. Payne on Medical Books in use at Montpellier, Rashdall's "Universities of Europe," Vol. 2, part ii, page 780. The fact that Arderne knew and quotes all these writers lends some support to the theory that he was educated at Montpellier.

4/2. These passages on the Manner or Behaviour of a Leech form the true joy of those who travail amongst the old Masters of Medicine and surgery. They are full of conceits, and give a picture of contemporary manners and customs which it is impossible to obtain in any other way. The parallel passages from Salicet, Mondeville and Lanfrank are given in the Forewords (xix–xxvi), and show that there was a common source for these paragraphs on medical ethics of which the chief was "De adventu medici" of Archimattheus, a master at Salerno.

4/24. The expression "for why" is employed by the translator as the English equivalent for the Latin word "Nam." It does not imply a question therefore, but is used as we should now say "because."

5/8. The greeting of ladies by thrusting the hands into their bosom had a long vogue in England, and it would be interesting to know whether the fashion of wearing low-necked dresses was a cause or an effect of the custom. By the end of the seventeenth century it was only used by near relatives, and Mr. Samuel Pepys records that he availed himself of the privilege.

6/4. Speaking of the cure of scabies by the inunction of a mercurial ointment (MS. Ashmol. 1434, leaf 131 ; cf. 79/1), Arderne says, "I have tried it many times and have made a good deal of money from it, and I got twenty shillings for a single application. And take notice that the inunction must be repeated for forty days, or for a month at least. ("Quod centies probavi et exinde multa lucra adquisivi pro certo et haec xxs. pro uno liserio. Et nota quod tale lisorium per xl dies vel mensem ad minus debet portari.")

6/4. The fees charged by Arderne are very large, if it be remembered that money had at least seventeen times and perhaps twenty times its present value. I have given some account of the fees of our ancestors in Janus (May–June 1909, pp. 287–293), and to the facts there contained I may add an observation obtained by Prof. Ed. Nicaise for his edition of Guy de Chauliac's Surgery (*op. cit.* p. lxii). "A lady was attended in 1348 by three doctors, two Jews and a Christian, and she paid a fee of half a florin to each. The livre tournois at this time was equivalent to one florin and 16 sols of pontifical money—the cash then current at Avignon—and corresponded to 27 francs 34 centimes of modern French money. The general practitioner therefore received 8 francs 17 centimes for each visit, which is equivalent to three visits for a guinea."

6/5. The custom of paying for an operation by an annuity as well as by a fee lingered in England until late in the seventeenth century, for Richard Wiseman (1622?–1676), speaking of a patient, says, "This person retired into the country afterwards and returned to London at the end of two years, and acknowledged to me his cure by settling thirty pounds a year upon me during his life and paid me sixty pounds for the two years passed." Readers of French history, too, will recollect that Louis XIV paid Dr. François Felix the sum of one hundred and fifty pounds and settled a farm upon him in 1686 for curing him of a fistula.

7/29. "The Senator Boetius," says Gibbon, "is the last of the Romans whom Cato or Tully could have acknowledged for their countryman." ("Roman Empire," ed. 1862, v, 27.) He was born at Rome about 475 A.D. and was consul in 510. He was a minister of Theodoric, King of the Ostrogoths, who displaced the Emperor Odoacer. Boethius was afterwards imprisoned at Pavia and was put to death in 525 A.D. He was subsequently canonised as St. Severinus. He wrote the "De consolatione Philosophiæ" (Chaucer's translation of which was published in the Early English Text Soc.'s Extra Series, No. V, 1868), as well as some valuable treatises on

Music and Geometry. The "de disciplina scholarium" mentioned in the text is falsely ascribed to Boetius. It is quoted again 23/27.

7/39. Arderne repeatedly draws attention to the effect of the mind on the body, and makes it appear that what we now call neurasthenia was not unknown in his experience. Cf. 6/23, 8/3, 60/16, 64/32.

8/27. The operation of fistula recommended by Arderne is described in the Forewords (p. xvii) to this volume. Arderne purposely gives fancy names to the instruments and to the remedies he uses as part of a fixed design to keep his methods secret. This secrecy was a common feature of the medical profession until quite recently—indeed it still lingers in parts where medical men dispense "our ointment" or "our linctus." Arderne especially feared the competition of other leeches, cf. 15/9 and 30/3, of the Barbers, cf. 71/16, and of the laity, cf. 103/3, for when he used the charm against tic, tetanus and delirium tremens, he not only disguised the words in Greek characters but he made nonsense of them, "ne a laicis perspicietur."

8/29. The *sequere me* was a flexible probe, and was named appropriately enough because it was the guide to be followed.

9/4. The *acus rostrata*, or "snowted needle," was a grooved director along which the scalpel was passed. The snowted or curved end fitted into a hole in the cochlearia or shield which was introduced later in the operation to protect the opposite side of the rectum at the moment the fistula was divided. This snouted needle was made of silver.

9/12. The *tendiculum*, or dilator, made of boxwood, was used chiefly to keep the ligature taut whilst the fistula was being divided. For this purpose it was provided with a hole into which fitted (9/16) the *wrayste* or "vertile," much in the same way that the peg fits into a violin. The ends of the ligature were passed round the wrayste, which was then twisted until the frænum cæsaris was tight enough.

9/20. The *frænum Cæsaris*, or ligature, constricted the rectal side of the fistula. It seems to be merely a vestigium of an obsolete operation for the cure of fistula. Albucasis used it as an *écraseur*, and Arderne had sufficient reverence for authority not to discard it. But the operation he describes is one of simple division. The tendiculum, the wrayste and the frænum Cæsaris, therefore, are useless because as soon as the division was complete, they all fell out of the wound. Cf. 24/26. They steadied the parts whilst the incision was made, but they complicated the operation by giving the surgeon two instruments to hold in his left hand (the acus rostrata and the tendiculum) whilst he held the scalpel in his right hand. The cochlearia must always have been held by the assistant—the fellow of the leech—as Arderne calls him,—the surgeon's mate—as the Elizabethans knew him.

9/24. The *siringa* is probably only a clyster-pipe. Two forms are given, the one with side-openings, as was then used, the other an improved form recommended by Arderne as the result of his own experience (cf. 74/38) in which there is only a single terminal orifice.

11/1. *Aposteme* is an early form of the word which afterwards became Imposthume. It means a suppurating inflammation or an abscess.

11/6. Arderne's pathology of fistula is excellent and is clearly the result of observation. He has seen and treated cases of ischio-rectal abscess, and has observed how such abscesses have become chronic and ended in a fistula.

11/18. The axillary glands were the emunctories of the heart: the inguinal glands of the liver: the cervical glands of the brain.

11/19. *Chawelleȝ* is quite an unusual word, and except for the Latin version it would be incomprehensible. The Latin gives the English gloss "fauces." It seems, therefore, to be a form derived from the same source as "Chawylbone" which the Promptorium Parvulorum renders Mandibula.

11/20. *Gilbertyn* is Gilbert the Englishman, known to all readers of Chaucer because he is named in the Prologue (l. 429) with Bernard and Gatesden. Gilbertus Anglicus flourished about 1210, and is said to be the first practical English writer on medicine though Master Richard preceded him. Dr. Payne in his Fitzpatrick lectures in 1904 says that Theodoric took his description of leprosy from Gilbertyn, a description evidently at first hand and in many respects very accurate. Gilbert wrote a compendium or Laurea of medicine, printed at Lyons 1510 (cf. 55/10), and a Commentary upon the verses of Gilles de Corbeil "De Urinis" (cf. 59/32). A commentary in English upon these same verses and attributed to John Arderne exists in manuscript in the Hunterian Library at Glasgow (No. 328).

11/21. *Ol. roset.* Oil of roses entered largely into the mediæval pharmacopœia as a soothing application. The ceruse here ordered to be mingled with it is carbonate of lead, and the litharge is protoxide of lead. The lotion thus had the soothing and astringent properties which is still attributed to lead lotion or Goulard extract.

11/24. *Wombe.* Arderne speaks consistently of the belly as the womb both in men and women; when he speaks specifically of the womb in women he employs the term Marice. Cf. pp. 80/39, 85/4 and 86/26.

11/27. Arderne, like his contemporaries, recognises two forms of Mallow. The Althæa rosea—which he calls "tame" mallow (cf. 12/15), because it was grown in the garden, and Malva silvestris—the wild mallow.

11/32. *A Nastar of tree.* Arderne fortunately gives the English equivalent for Nastar in the manuscript No. 112 (T. 5, 14), fol. 77, contained in the Hunterian Library, Glasgow, and says, "Nastare species est clysteris sive enematis 'a glister pipe.'" A Nastar of tree, therefore, is a wooden enema nozzle. The wood may be either boxwood, hazel or willow. His description of the bladder and its method of preparation is given later on; cf. 75/1 *et seqq.*

12/1. *After auctores.* The author is probably Serapion the younger who wrote a large work on pharmacology, which was translated from Arabic into Latin under the title "Liber de medicamentis simplicibus" or "De temperamentis simplicium." He lived about the end of the eleventh century. For Serapion the elder see 55/29, p. 124.

12/9. *Diaquilon.* Three forms of diachylon plaster were used. One called Rhazes' plaster; a second Mesue's, and the third diachylon commune. Arderne here recommends Mesue's diachylon which contained mucilage of Althæa and oil of camomile amongst many other ingredients.

12/15. *M.* The symbol M. is used for Manipulus in dispensing drugs—a handful—and the handful was either large or small. The small handful or pinch was denoted by the letter P. for Pugillus, and it was usually estimated at about the eighth part of the Manipulus.

12/21. *Lana succida* is sufficiently described in the text. It seems to have been a crude method of obtaining what is now called lanolin. An undressed fleece is still used in folk-medicine.

12/21. The persistence of these simple remedies is shown by Miss Edith Durham's interesting account of Higher Albania (Lond. 1909, p. 93). She says, speaking of a comminuted fracture of the leg treated by an old Franciscan at Vukli:—"He then plugged and dressed the wound with a salve of his own making—the ingredients are extract of pine resin, the green bark of elder twigs, white beeswax and olive oil. The pine resin would provide a strong antiseptic. The property of the elder bark I do not know. . . . In gunshot wounds he was very expert. For 'first aid' his prescription was: Take the white of an egg and a lot of salt, pour on to the wound as soon as possible and bandage. This only temporary till the patient could be properly treated with rakia (the local alcoholic drink) and pine salve as above. The wound was to be plugged with sheep's wool, cleaned and soaked in the salve. The dressing to be changed at night and morning and at midday also if the weather be very hot. Should the wound show signs of becoming foul, wash again with rakia as often as necessary. This treatment he had inherited from his grandfather who had it from his. The exact proportions and way of making salve he begged to be excused from telling me as they were a family secret." Every word of this passage would have been approved by Arderne. He would have recognised his Unguentum sambuci (cf. 30/21), the egg medled (cf. 28/4) with salt would have been nothing new to him, the cleaning of the sheep's wool he might have considered an improvement upon his own lana succida (cf. 12/20), as he had an open mind (cf. 35/4), and he would have endorsed thoroughly the old priest's disinclination to give away the secret of a preparation (cf. 15/8).

12/40. *Wormed*, i. e. warmed.

13/20. *Ragadieȝ* was the name given to fissures formed round the anus and vulva. It is used here to denote chronic ulceration. *Frousingeȝ* seems to be a mere repetition of ragadieȝ, as it does not occur in the Latin texts.

13/24. An *ulcus undesiccable* is an ulcer which continues to form pus in spite of treatment. Mediæval surgeons were very skilful in frightening themselves with names.

14/4. There were two Geoffrey Scropes living in the latter half of the fourteenth century. (i) Sir Geoffrey Scrope, knighted before Paris, 1360. He was the eldest son of Sir Henry le Scrope of Masham, Co. York, the first Lord Scrope, who was Governor of Guisnes and Calais in 1360. This Geoffrey Scrope was slain at Piskre, Lithuania, in 1362 (cf. 67/34). (ii) Sir Geoffrey le Scrope, son of Stephen, second Lord Scrope, who was living in 1409, but had died *sine prole* before 1418. The brother of this Geoffrey le Scrope was Stephen le Scrope, Archdeacon of Richmond in Yorkshire, who died September 5, 1418.

14/20. It is clear from this and the following lines that Arderne had seen and noted cases of uræmia following upon long-continued urethral fistulæ. The headache, giddiness, dull pain in the loins and vomiting which occur during the later stages of renal disease are all duly noted.

14/38. Bernard de Gordon was teaching at Montpellier in 1285, and was living in 1318. He wrote the "Lilium medicinæ," but Arderne here shows that he was absolutely ignorant of Anatomy.

15/8. This is another good instance of the secrecy which characterised the practice of surgery at this period. It was still a trade to be taught, and it was many years before it became a profession to be learned. (Cf. 8/25 and 71/15.)

16/4. It would have been impossible for Arderne to have escaped the belief in Astrology which was a feature of his time. He gives the usual table, common to all his contemporaries, for finding the house of the moon on any given day, and he thought that the planets had an influence upon the twelve parts of the body which correspond to the signs of the zodiac.

16/7. *Ptholomeus* was Ptolemy the physician, who lived at Alexandria in the third century B.C., and was perhaps identical with Ptolemy the Geographer. De Mondeville quotes Ptolemy the physician and refers to his "Centilegium"; Guy de Chauliac also speaks of his "Centiloquium." Pictagoras was Pythagoras the Greek philosopher, born about 582 B.C. He was steeped in the mystical lore of Egypt and India; a vegetarian and a social reformer, his name is chiefly associated with the doctrine of Metempsychosis.

Rasis is Abú Becr Mohammed Ibn Zacariyá Ar-Rází, commonly known as Rhazes. He was born in 850 A.D. and died about 932. He was the first great Arabian physician, and his text-book called the "Continent" was only displaced by the work of Haly Abbas. Rhazes is still interesting to us because he first distinguished clearly between Smallpox and Measles.

16/8. *Haly* is Haly the Arabian physician who died in 994 A.D. He wrote the "Royal Book" which displaced Rhazes' text-book, and was in turn displaced by the Canon of Avicenna. Cf. 56/7, p. 124.

21/2. Arderne's account of fistulate or festred gout makes its probable that he is describing the condition which is now known as chronic inflammation of the bone due to infective micro-organisms. Sophocles described Philoctetes as suffering from a similar condition. Cf. 46/25.

21/9. *Ypocras*, i. e. Hippocrates, lived during the golden age in Greece (460–377 B.C.), and was contemporary with Socrates. His writings were known through Galen's commentaries upon the Prognostics, Aphorisms, and on Regimen in Acute Diseases, which had been translated into Latin before the fourteenth century.

21/27. The meaning of this passage may be thus rendered, "Take heed lest thou art so blinded by the desire for money as to operate upon a case thou knowest to be incurable."

22/12. *Lusting* is here equivalent to grudging.

22/17. The details of the operation are admirably given, and it is quite possible to follow each step, a very rare thing in the case of mediæval writers on surgery, but Arderne was a master of this part of his subject. Cf. Forewords, p. xvii.

22/22. The *rig bone* is the vertebral column. Cf. 34/34, 62/8, 70/24.

23/1. Arderne shows his ability by recommending a cutting operation. It proves that he was not afraid of the bleeding which daunted his contemporaries and many of his successors. Cf. 24/32.

23/21. Both John Arderne and Henri de Mondeville were never tired of repeating that surgery was an art to be learnt by practice. It was too much the custom of the time to rely upon authority and to think that everything could be learnt from books.

23/27. *Boece*. Cf. 7/29.

24/5. *Freno cesaris*; 24/9. *frenum cesaris*. Cf. 1/13, p. 108.

24/21. Arderne gives a choice of two cutting instruments, a razor and a lancet. Dr. Stewart Milne ("Surgical Instruments in Greek and Roman Times," Oxford, 1907, p. 31) describes a form of razor in which "a scalpel blade is mounted on a ring and the fore-finger is passed through the ring." Such a razor would have suited Arderne's purpose admirably, but he used some form of scalpel. "Lanceola," says Dr. Freind ("The History of Physic," part 2, p. 177), "in its proper genuine signification is no older than Julius Capitolinus, how long it has been applied to signify a surgical instrument I cannot tell; however, it may be traced as high at least as the time of William of Bretagne, who lived in 1220 and wrote the history of Philip August, whose chaplain he was." He gives some account of the lanceola, and distinguishes it very plainly from the Phlebotomus, both which instruments we see were made use of in that age. "Lanceola dicitur subtile ferrum acutum, cum quo minutores aliqui pungendo venam aperiunt in minutione. Aliqui cum Phlebotomo venam percutiunt." (Lanceola is a name given to a delicate pointed instrument with which some bleeders open a vein by puncturing it in bleeding. Others breathe a vein with a phlebotome.) (Cf. 61/23.)

24/29. Arderne here shows that he knows the last thing a surgeon learns—the knowledge when to stop in operating.

24/32. Surgeons had no satisfactory instruments for stopping bleeding until pressure forceps were invented by Sir Spencer Wells about 1884. Many devices were tried and had their day, but hæmorrhage remained the bugbear of every operating surgeon, and the fear of its occurrence limited the scope of his work. Arderne here recommends the excellent, simple and cleanly method of sponge pressure to arrest the immediate hæmorrhage, and afterwards uses a styptic powder. Arderne gained a great reputation for his prescriptions (cf. Forewords p. xxxi), and it is evident that he was a good physician as well as a practical surgeon; cf. pp. 97 and 98. The styptics here recommended were all in common use. *Boli* is Bolus armeniacus, a yellow earth containing oxide of iron. *Sanguis draconis* was the resin obtained from the fruit of the Calamus draco. *Aloes epaticus:* the mediæval materia medica recognised socotrin aloes and hepatic aloes which was an inferior quality.

25/9. *Walwort* is either the Sambucus or the Pellitory. Arderne probably means the Elder, of which it was said "this tree has not one part but is used in Pharmacy." The juice is still used in the form of Elder wine.

26/11. Directions for making sanguis veneris and oil of camomile are given on pp. 89 and 94.

26/13. *A nastar of tree*, a wooden clyster-pipe; cf. 11/32, p. 113.

26/21. The preparation of Pulv. sine pari is given on p. 86.

27/6. The preparation of Salus populi is given on p. 90. It is characteristic of the time that fancy names are purposely given to all these preparations lest their composition should become known to the barbers or to other leeches.

27/25. *Bolnyng* is equivalent to swelling or swollen.

27/28. *Alum ȝucarin. combust.* is described on p. 81. Three kinds of alum were recognised: alum glass, alum plume, and alum zuccarin. Alum glass was the crude alum crystals; alum plume was the natural aluminium sulphate; alum zuccarin. was the re-crystallised form; but alum zuccarin. was also used as a synonym for sugar candy. The crude alum was sometimes called Alumen roche from the town of Roche in Syria, and as this was often written Alumen Rō it came to be called Alum of Rome.

27/30. *Sarcocolla* is the resin of the Penæa sarcocolla and mucronata. It was thought to make the flesh adhere together, hence its name.

27/31. *Psidie* is pomegranate bark.

27/32. *Terra sigillata*, or Lemnos earth, was imported from Egypt in large pastiles stamped with the Sultan's seal, hence its name. It had astringent properties.

27/38. *Ceruse* is carbonate of lead. *Lithargyrum* or Litharge is the protoxide of lead which forms as a pellicle on the surface of melted lead; lithargyrate of silver and gold are formed similarly when these metals are melted.

28/10. Arderne clearly indicates the calling of an apothecary as distinct from the barbers, surgeons and physicians of the time. As a surgeon he gathered his own simples and made his own preparations, rather to keep their composition a secret than because he was obliged to do so, for the apothecaries would have made them up for him equally well.

30/21. "*Smalach*," says Dr. R. C. A. Prior ("On the Popular Names of British Plants," Lond. 1879, p. 217), "or Smallage, is a former name of the celery, meaning the small ache or parsley compared with the great parsley, olus atrum. *Ach*, Fr. *ache*, is derived from the Latin *apium* by the change of *pi* to *ch*, as in *sapiam* to *sache*."

Wormode is wormwood, the Artemisia absinthium. The word is corrupted from A.S. and O.E. *wermod*. Wormwood was used in the Middle Ages to keep off *mod* or *made*, a maggot; the first syllable, derived from A.S. *werian*, to keep off, has become by similarity of sound *worm*.

30/22. *Molayne* is the Verbascum Thapsus, or Tapsibarbatus ebulus, the hig (hag) taper, or Bullock's lungwort.

Walwort is the dwarf elder, the Sambucus ebulus, sometimes called Danesblood or Danewort.

Sparge or Spurge is the Cataputia minor; *Weybread* is the plantain—Plantago major; *Mugwort* is the Artemisia vulgaris. It is said to have obtained its popular name from its use against *moughte*, *mough* or *moghe*, a moth or maggot. *Auance* is Avens or Herb Benett, *i.e.* Benedicta, the Geum urbanum. "Where the root is in the house the devil can do nothing and flies from it; wherefore it is blessed above all herbs," says Platearius, whose book Arderne had read. Cf. 79/10.

30/23. *Petite Consoude* was the consolida minima or the daisy—Bellis perennis. The name Consoude was given to several different plants in the Middle Ages, *e.g.* the Comfrey, the Bugle and the Wild Larkspur. "And for healing of wounds, so soveraigne it is, that if it bee put into the pot and sodden with pieces of flesh, it will souder and rejoine them, whereupon the Greekes imposed upon it the name of Symphytum-Consound," says Pliny in Philemon Holland's translation (Bk. 27, ch. vi, p. 275).

Wodbynd is the Woodbine or Lonicera Periclymenum.

31/21. *Diaflosmus* is the plaster used as a local application, whilst *tapsimel* is the confection for internal use. Tapsimel here mentioned, and for the first time, had an extraordinary popularity and was officinal as late as 1773. Cf. Forewords, p. xxx.

32/7. The deadly nightshade is called in German Nachtschatten, and it is possible that Arderne may have learnt the Flemish word for it, if he was at Antwerp, as is reported traditionally. Cf. Forewords, p. xii.

33/13. Arderne gives a formula for his unguentum ruptorium (Sloane MS. 29301, leaf 35, col. 1), which is substantially the same as the one mentioned here. It consists of unslaked lime well mingled with black soap and made into a mass, which was afterwards bound with diachylon upon the part to be destroyed. Jamerius (cf. 55/3, Rubrica xxi) also gives a formula for a ruptory, "De unguento quod ruptorium dicitur. Unguentum forte quod ruptorium dicitur. ℞. Saponis saracenici pondus x denariorum; calcis vive pondus viii, capitelli fortissimi pondus v denariorum. Confice sic: calx prius cribellata cum sapone diu conficiatur, deinde addatur capitellum, et cum predictis commisceatur." There were two kinds of lime ointment. The older form was made by "taking of lime that hath been washed at least seven times lb.ss. Wax ℥iii; Oil of Roses lb.i. Let them all be briskly worked together in a leaden mortar, after the wax hath been by a slow fire melted in a sufficient quantity of the same oil." (Alleyne, *op. cit.*, p. 330, col. i, No. 11.) The other ointment was the more active. ℞. Quicklime ℥vj; Auripigment ℥iss.; roots of Florentine Orris ℥i; yellow Sulphur; Nitre ana ℥iss.; a strong lixivium of Bean Stalks lb. ii.; Mix and boil all, in a new pot glazed, to a just thickness, which you may know by anointing a feathered quill therewith, if the feathers easily fall off; then add Oyl of Spike ℥ss.; and make an ointment or liniment." (Salmon's "New London Dispensary," 1678, p. 768, col. 2.) Soap was of two kinds: White soft soap known as French soap, and hard grey soap called Saracenic soap. The latter is meant when the prescription demands black soap.

34/4. Arderne anchored his tents in much the same way as we now anchor drainage tubes in deep wounds by putting a thread through one end. He uses the word "ground" systematically for "bottom," so that where we should say the bottom of the wound he says (34/6) "in the grounde of the fistula."

35/15. *Reparaled* means the same as re-dressing a wound, that is to say, changing the dressings.

36/15. Arderne loved to play upon words. Cf. 37/12 and 91/32. He could not resist the pun with "bubo," which is the technical term for an abscess in the axilla or groin, and also means an owl. Guy makes the same joke (ed. Nicaise, p. 166). Buboes were the characteristic mark of the bubonic plague, and he must have seen many examples. In the later epidemics the Searchers recognised the disease by the botch which is a plague token.

37/6 *et seqq.* Arderne gives a most creditable account of cancer of the rectum, and distinguishes it clearly from dysentery.

37/29. Those who know how many cases of cancer of the rectum are still overlooked and are treated as cases of chronic constipation, will trow with Arderne that there are still many "wele unkunyng leeches" abroad.

38/11 *et seqq.* The treatment and the picture of the later stages of cancer of the rectum are excellent, and are evidently drawn from repeated personal experience.

38/40. Arderne very properly insists on a digital examination in cases of chronic ulceration of the rectum. Such an examination is still too often omitted. Both time and knowledge are then lost, to the great detriment of the patient.

39/8. *Blo* is throughout the scribe's method of spelling blue; "bloness" (cf. 52/27), therefore, is the same as bluish.

39/27. Arderne again warns against the dishonest habit of operating merely for the sake of the fee when no commensurate advantage is gained by the patient.

39/40. *Aysel* is an early form for eissel—vinegar.

40/1. *Virga pastoris* was used by the old writers on materia medica for several varieties of Dipsacus, and more especially for D. pilosus, silvestris and fullonum. It is the Teasel.

40/21. There were several varieties of white ointment. The form attributed to Rhazes contains oil of roses ℥ix; Ceruse carefully washed in rose-water and powdered ℥iii; white wax ℥ii. Avicenna's ointment contained litharge as an ingredient, with the white of eggs beaten into it.

40/27. *Attrament* is here a synonym for Vitriol (cf. 79/1). "Of atramenteȝ, *i. e.* of vitrioleȝ." It also means Ink (cf. 67/28).

40/33. *Celidone* is the Chelidonium majus, the juice of which was greatly esteemed as a collyrium, "because," says Gerarde (p. 911), "some hold opinion that with this herbe the dams restore sight to their young ones, when their eyes be put out." Dr. Prior (*op. cit.* p. 40) says that this notion, quoted by Gerarde from Dodoens and copied by him from Pliny, who had it from Aristotle, was received and repeated by every botanical writer, and is embodied in the Regimen Sanitatis Salerni—

> "Cæcatis pullis ac lumine mater hirundo
> Plinius ut scribit, quamvis sunt eruta reddit."

which was Englished—

> "Young Swallowes that are blind, and lacke their sight,
> The Damme (by Celendine) doth give them light,
> Therefore (by Plinie) wee may boldly say,
> Celendine for the sight is good alway."

41/1. *Few sawage* is erysipelas. Cf. 91/9, p. 133.

41/8. The second pestilence was the epidemic of 1361. Cf. 1/4.

41/33. *The blody fik* is explained in the treatise on hæmorrhoids to be a bleeding pile. Cf. 56/21.

42/38. I cannot identify the powder creoferoboron or (43/2) the emplastre sanguibœtos, nor does Arderne give the formulæ for their preparation.

43/40. *Unguentum viride.* The green ointment in the later pharmacy (1733) consisted of Verdigris; Ung. Ægyptiacum; Oint. of Elder; Colophony and Oil of Spike. The Ung. Ægyptiacum was ascribed to Mesue, and in its simplest form was compounded with verdigris, honey and the sharpest vinegar.

44/38. Women held a well-recognised position as practitioners of medicine in the Middle Ages, and several of the matronæ or mulieres Salernitanæ attained renown at the School of Salernum. The best known is Trotula de Ruggiero, who wrote "de mulierum passionibus." But Arderne seems to allude here to the "ladies bountiful" of his time, for whom he had no great regard. Guy de Chauliac puts them last of his five sects of medical practitioners. The first contained Roger, Roland and the Four Masters who treated wounds with poultices; the second, like Bruno and Theodoric, used dressings of wine and dried up the wounds; the third included William Salicet and Lanfrank, who occupied, he says, a position intermediate between the other two sects. The fourth class embraced those who had been trained on the battlefield, and for whom

Arderne had a sneaking regard; they treated their wounds with charms, oil and wool, and said that God has given virtue to words, herbs and stones (cf. 104/15); whilst the fifth class consisted "of women and many idiots who refer all their sicknesses to the Saints."

45/1. *Drink of Antioch.* Harl. 2378 MS. [B], p. 25, gives a receipt for "*The Drink of Auntioch.*—Take 1 handful of daysye and 1 handful of bugle and 1 handful of red coole and 1 handful of strebery-wyses [stalks] and 1 handful of fenule and half an handful of hempe and as mych of auence, as myche of tansey, as mych of herbe Robert [cf. 54/17], as mych of mader, as mych of comfiry, iiii branche of orpyne, vi croppes of brere, vi croppes of red netle, and thyse herbes ben sothen in 1 galoun of whyt wyn In-to a potell, and afterward put thereto as mych of hony clarifyed and after the mydlyng set it ouer the fyr and thanne steme it a litil, and this drynk schal ben vsed in this manere: ȝif to hym that is wounded or brysed by þe morwen of this drynk iii sponful and vi sponful of water and loke that the seke be wel kept fro gotouse [gouty] metes and drynkys, and from wymmen, and loke also that the maladye be heled with brere-leues or with leues of the rede coole." ("Medical Works of the XIV cent.," by Rev. Prof. G. Henslowe, 1899, p. 77.) There was also an antidote of Antiochus. It was an ancient preparation composed of germander, agaric, colocynth, Arabian stæchas, opoponax, sagapenum, parsley, aristolochia, white pepper, cinnamon, lavender, myrrh and honey. It was used in melancholy, hydrophobia and epilepsy. This was known as Antiochi hiera. There was also a theriacum of Antiochus which was also an antidote to every kind of poison. It contained thyme, opoponax, millet, trefoil, fennel, aniseed, nigella sativa and other herbs.

45/31. A *porret* is a young leek or onion—a scallion—says the New English Dictionary.

46/25. Arderne gives in these passages a tolerably clear account of the condition known to us as tuberculous dactylitis, and to our immediate predecessors as spina ventosa. Cf. 21/2.

47/25. Arderne is perfectly honest in his statements, and does not claim this patient as a cure.

47/28. *The buȝt of the knee* is the bow or bend of the knee.

48/2. The *pede lyon* is the Leontopetalum, Brumaria, Lion's leaf. It was considered to be good against the bites of serpents; the root applied helps the Sciatica and cleanses old filthy ulcers.

48/18. *A spature.* The Spathomele or spatula probe is the commonest of the classical surgical instruments. It consists of a long shaft with an olivary point at one end and a spatula at the other. The olive end was used for stirring medicaments and the spatula for spreading them, when it was employed in pharmacy. But it was so handy that it was often used as a blunt dissector, as Arderne did in this case. It was also used by painters for preparing and mixing their colours. See Dr. Milne, "Surgical Instruments in Greek and Roman Times," p. 58.

48/32. *Ventose.* The cupping instruments were either of horn, copper, or glass, and they were used either with or without scarifications—wet or dry cupping.

48/38. This appears to be Arderne's sole piece of correct anatomical knowledge, except the information he had gained as to the position of the superficial veins of the arms and legs. Cf. 49/12.

49/14. The treatise on Fistulæ ends abruptly with the words "flesshe, etc." The manuscript continues on the opposite page in a different hand, and with an account of isolated cases, inflammation in the arm and leg, with Arderne's treatment.

49/38. The first case seems to be one of thrombosis. The vena epatica is the vena hepatica of the arm and not of the liver. The vein arises on the back of the hand near its ulnar edge, taking origin from the plexus on the back of the hand and fingers. It ascends to the ulnar side of the fore-arm, where it is called the anterior cubital vein. It was known to mediæval anatomists as the Salvatella (cf. 61/22), that on the right side being the salvatella hepatica, and the vein on the left arm the salvatella splenetica. In like manner the external saphenous vein was known as the salvatella pedis aut saphena. William of Salicet (Ed. Pifteau, p. 459) describes them carefully, saying, "Saluatella, hepatica in manu dextra, et splenetica in manu sinistra, quae est inter digitum annularem et auricularem. . . . Salutella pedis aut saphena."

50/1. *Dove's dung* remained in use until after 1733. Alleyne, in his "New English Dispensatory," p. 146, col. 2, says: "The dung is sometimes ordered in cataplasms to be applied to the soles of the feet in malignant fevers and deliriums with an intent to draw the humours downwards; which may not be ill-guessed."

50/7. Arderne gives an account of his early experience of arsenic as a dressing on page 83.

50/24. *Auripigment* is orpiment, or native yellow arsenic.

52/8. The word *garse*, to scarify, seems to have an interesting history if, as the New English Dictionary suggests, it is derived through the Latin from the Greek χαράσσειν, to cut or incise, and has given origin to the English garsh or gash.

52/14. *Epithimation* was identical with the modern fomentation of wounds and inflamed parts. Guy de Chauliac in his seventh treatise, Doct. i, chap. iv (Ed. Nicaise, p. 605): says, "Embrocations and Epithems are simple or compound solutions with which the limbs are bathed and fomented. Sponges or linen being wrung out of them are applied to the part, and are frequently changed."

52/15. *Solsequium* is the chicory or endive; marigold being Calendula officinalis.

52/26. A *felon* was originally any small abscess or boil, but in later times the term was restricted more especially to a whitlow. The gloss *anthrace* written in a contemporary hand seems to imply that Arderne was using the word in its earlier sense and to signify a carbuncle.

52/28. The *canon* seems to have suffered from an attack of gouty eczema, which ended in thrombosis and the formation of a callous ulcer of the leg.

53/15. A *mormale* was an inflamed sore, especially on the leg. Readers of Chaucer will remember of the Cook in the Prologue, line 386, "But great harm was it as it thought me That on his schynne a mormal hadde he." Arderne adopted the treatment still used for callous ulcers: he applied firm pressure, cleansed it, and afterwards applied a stimulating ointment.

54/17. *Herb Robert* is the Geranium Robertianum. It is said to have been called after Robert, Duke of Normandy, to whom the "Regimen Sanitatis Salerni" was inscribed; but it may refer to Knecht Ruprecht, a

German forest spirit. It was thought to be cleansing and binding, stopping blood and helping ulcers.

54/37. The *vena basilica.* Cf. 49/38, p. 121.

55/1. The *sophena vein.* Cf. 49/38, p. 121.

55/3. The introduction to the "Treatise on Piles" is much shortened in this translation. The Latin text runs thus, and I am indebted to Miss E. M. Thompson for the transcription—

"*Extractus pro emoroidis secundum Lanfrancum.*

"Extracta emoroidarum secundum Lanfrancum bononensem discretissimum magistrum Regis francie qui duos libros cirurgie composuit, viz. minorem qui incipit sic 'Attendens, venerabilis amice Bernarde componere librum,' etc. Majorem vero qui incipit sic. 'Protector rite sperancium deus excelsus et gloriosus cuius nomen sit benedictum in secula,' etc. ¶ 'Omne quod investigari potest vno trium modorum investigari potest aut per ejus nomen,' etc. ¶ Item extracta emoroidarum secundum magistrum Bernardum de Gordon' in suo libro, quem librum composuit dictus Bernardus apud Montem Pessulanum i.[e.] Mont Pelers, anno domini millesimo ccc° iii° et anno lecture sue xx° qui sic incipit 'Interrogatus a quodam Socrates quomodo posset optime dicere Respondit si nichil dixeris nisi quod optime sciueris nichil autem optime scimus nisi quod a nobis frequenter dictum est et quod ab omnibus receptum est.' ¶ Item extracta a passionario Magistri Bartholomei qui sic incipit: 'Assiduis peticionibus mi karissime compendiose morborum signa causas et curas inscriptis redigere cogitis,' etc. ¶ Item extracta a micrologio Magistri Ricardi excellentis industrie et a libro Magistri Rolandi et a libro Magistri Gwidonis de gracia pauperum et a practica Rogeri Baron. Et a practica Rogerini et a practica Magistri Johannitii Jamarcii et Gilbertini ac aliorum plurium expertorum quorum doctrinam inspexi et practizando que experciora reperi in hoc libello domino mediante innotescent. ¶ Ricardus qui incipit si quid agam preter solitum veniam date cun[c]ti. ¶ Rolandus Rogerus Braun Rogerinus, Johannitius, Jamarcus, Gwidoñ, Gilbertinus."

Arderne shows here the extent of his reading in connection with hæmorrhoids in the same manner as he does in his commentary on Giles of Corbeuil's treatise de Urinis, where he also quotes his authorities. The first thing perhaps that strikes us is the number of books to which he had access. Books during his lifetime were a luxury of the rich, and those who know the early history of the University of Oxford will remember the gratitude with which the gifts of books from Duke Humphry and the Duke of Bedford were received from 1439 onwards, as "life-giving showers wherewith the vineyard was rendered fruitful, and from which an abundant supply of oil from the olive trees of the University might be expected." Arderne may, of course, have spent his fees in buying MSS. just as some of us do at the present day, but it is probable that he had access to the Libraries of his patrons like John of Gaunt, who were men of letters as well as of affairs, and he was thus able to quote verbatim et literatim, as in the present instance.

Lanfrank of Milan, as has been said (cf. Forewords, p. xxv), was a pupil of William de Salicet. He was one of the great teachers of Surgery at Paris, and died in 1306. The "Chirurgia magna" was issued in 1295–6 as an enlarged edition of the "Chirurgia parva" published in 1270. He taught that Anatomy was the foundation of Surgery.

Bernard of Gordon was Professor at Montpellier, where he began to teach in 1285, and published his "Lilium medicinæ" in 1305. The words quoted by Arderne are printed in the 1542 edition of the "Lilium" as the first words of the Preface. Arderne gives the date as 1303. The Lyons and Paris editions both give it 1305.

Master Bartholomew of Salernum was a pupil of Constantinus Africanus late in the eleventh century. Arderne is mistaken in ascribing the "Passionarius" to him. The book, which is often called the "Passionarius Galeni," was really written by Gariopontus, a teacher at Salernum early in the eleventh century. The edition printed at Basel in 1531 gives the authorship correctly, but the Lyons edition in 1526 calls it Galen's.

Master Richard seems to be Richard the Englishman already mentioned. Cf. 11/20, p. 113. He was also called Ricardus senior, and was a Master at Salerno at the end of the twelfth century. He also lived in France and in England. His book, "Micrologus," is a collection of short treatises written at different times: (1) Practica, (2) De Urinis, (3) Anatomia, (4) Repressiva, (5) Prognostica. Taken alone Micrologus would probably refer to the "Practica." None of Richard's works have been printed.

Master Roland was from Parma, and he edited in 1264 the "Practica Chirurgiæ," which was written by Master Roger in 1180. Roger's book was sometimes called "Rogerina," or "Rogerina major, medius et minor." It was often attributed to Roger Bacon. This was the text-book upon which the Four Masters wrote their celebrated Commentary. "Roger and Roland," says Sir Clifford Allbutt ("The Historical Relations of Medicine and Surgery," Lond. 1905, p. 27), "stand like Twin Brethren in the dawn of modern medicine bearing the very names of romance. Roger's book was no mere cooking of Albucasis. Before Theodoric, Roger refractured badly united bones. For hæmorrhage he used styptics, the suture or the ligature; the ligature he learned no doubt from Paul."

Master Guido is Guy de Chauliac, the contemporary of Arderne, for he flourished in the second half of the fourteenth century. Guy took orders and was physician to Pope Clement VI at Avignon; Arderne with a bias towards religion remained a layman. Both were Master surgeons. Guido held with Lanfrank that Anatomy was the basis of Surgery; Arderne drifted towards drugs, words and charms, and knew no anatomy.

Roger de Barone or de Varone is credited with a treatise "Summa Rogerii," or "Practica parva." The date is disputed, but it was probably written at Montpellier late in the thirteenth century.

Johannice is Johannitius Honein Ben Ishak (809-873), the son of a Christian Apothecary, and one of the great translators of medical works from Greek into Arabic. His introduction to Galen's "Microtechni" was issued in Latin under the title "Isagoge Johannitii."

Jamarcius, in all probability, is Johannes Jamerius, a surgeon of the school of Salernum. Guy de Chauliac quotes him no less than forty times, and says in one passage: "Jamerius followed, who made a sort of rough surgery in which there were many pointless things, but he was chiefly a disciple of Roland" ("Puis est trouvé Jamier qui a fait quelque Chirurgie brutale, en laquelle il a meslé plusieurs fadeizes, toutefois en beaucoup de choses il a suivy Rogier," Cap. i, p. 14, Ed. Nicaise). Dr. Pansier (Janus, 1903) gives an account of the manuscripts of his works at Oxford and Paris, and Prof. Pagel of Berlin has published a manuscript of his surgery (Berlin, 1909), under the title "Chirurgia Jamati."

Master Gilbertyne is Gilbert the Englishman. Cf. 11/20, p. 113.

55/17. *Anence* is clearly a variant of Anent, *i. e.* "according to."

55/24. This passage shows how little the people have learned about medical terms since John Arderne wrote this treatise. "Piles" is still a generic name for all diseases of the rectum in the out-patient room of a hospital, and no one who has had much experience takes a diagnosis of piles as correct until he has verified it by examination.

55/29. John Damascene is the name under which the fourteenth-century writers on surgery concealed the identity of the elder Serapion, who lived in the ninth century. Some of his works were published under the name of Janus Damascenus. The Pandects in seven books were translated into Latin under the name of the Breviarium. Cf. 12/1, p. 113.

56/7. Avicenna, the Prince of Science, was born near Bokhara in 980 A.D. and early showed his precocity, for he knew the Koran and several books of philosophy by heart when he was ten years old. His genius turned first to law, but at the age of 16 he had made such progress in medicine as to warrant his appointment as personal physician to the Sultan Ben Mansur. "Wein, Weib und Gesang" killed him at the age of 57, in June 1037, but not before he had written his "Canon," which was translated into Latin in the twelfth century and remained a text-book until the middle of the seventeenth century.

57/30. *Morphew* was a general name given to skin eruptions which changed their colour. The white morphew appears to have been an early stage of leprosy in some cases; vitiligo in others. Black morphew was a general term which included many different diseases of the skin.

59/32. Ægidius Corboliensis, or Gilles de Corbeil, was descended from the Counts of Corbeil, and devoted himself to the study of medicine at Salerno. He is said to have taught medicine at that school, and afterwards from the end of the twelfth to the beginning of the thirteenth century to have lived at Paris as Major-domo and Physician to Philip Augustus (1180–1223). His two works, "De Urinis, de Pulsibus, de Virtutibus et laudibus compositorum medicamentorum" and "De Signis et symptomatibus ægritudinum" are in metre and expressed in classical Latin far superior to that of contemporary medical authors. Arderne wrote a commentary in English upon the "Tractatus de urinis," and a copy of it exists in the Hunterian Library at Glasgow. It is described in the Catalogue (p. 264) as:—328. Ægidii Corboliensis, Tractatus Metricus de Vrinis. Master John Arderne, Commentary in English on the above Treatise "De Vrinis." (Press Mark U. 7. 22; Q. 7. 16; Q. 7. 130.) Description. Vellum $7\frac{3}{4} \times 5\frac{1}{4}$ ff. 68, originally ff. 69 (or ff. 70), well written in a plain hand in single cols. of about 29 lines, each $5\frac{5}{8} - 5\frac{1}{4} \times 3\frac{1}{2}$, margined with brown crayon, not ruled, signatures, traces only left, practically all gnawed off (by beetles) where not cropped, catchwords, foliation modern (in pencil), rubrics, rubricated initials and ¶ ¶, running titles, initials touched with vermilion, marginalia much cropped, writing retouched in places, *fol. sec.* blank. Early Cent. xv. Binding, thin beech boards, covered quarter calf, coarse dark blue paper sides. Early Cent. xviii.

Collation. Two paper fly-leaves (i^2) both attached || 1^8—3^8, 4^7 (^{8}), 5^8—7^8, 8^7(^{8}), 9(^{6}). Two fly-leaves (ii^2), ii, 2. attached; 4, 6 is cut out (probably to remove a miswritten leaf as the text is continuous); 8, 3 is a half sheet (probably so originally).

Contents:—i. Ægidius (Gilles) of Corbeil's Treatise (in Latin verse) on Urines, with Master John Arderne's Commentary.

Begins (l. i (f. i) r°. lines 1-8); E (rubricated initial with gestures) go Magister Johannes Arderonn hanc (struck out) hoc (above) opusculum composui / de Judicijs / Vrinarum per colores et contenta secundum Indicium / Egidij. et ypocratis. Walterij. Gilis. Gilberti, Gordoni. Johannis de / Sancto Amando. ysaac. Auicenne. theophili, Galyeni. Galterij / et tholomej. in medicinam et medicum domini regis illustrissimi / principis henrici quarti cuius anime propicietur deus. Amen. / de. nigra. vrina. capitulum primum.

Ends (6, 5 (f. 44) v°. line 26); ¶ vryn black and watery in a fat manne mortem significat.

60/6. *Noli-me-tangere.* Guy de Chauliac (ivme traité Doct. i, ch. vi, p. 318, Ed. Nicaise), speaking of chancre ulceré, says that Guillaume de Salicet called it "Noli-me-tangere because the more it was meddled with the worse it became (Finalement, Guillaume de Salicet juge, que chancre est maladie despiteuse et fascheuse, d'autant que plus on la manie, plus il est indigné. Parquoy il conseille que ne soit touché, sinon légèrement, et a cette cause est appellé Noli-me-tangere)." I cannot find the passage in Pifteau's edition of Salicet's Surgery.

60/24. *Millefoile* is the yarrow—Achillæa Millefolium—though Apuleius, according to Dr. Prior, seems to have meant the horse-tail, Equisetum.

60/27. *Bursa pastoris* is the Shepherd's purse, Capsella bursa, which was long considered an excellent styptic.

Parvencis is the Periwinkle, the Vinca major and minor. It seems to have derived its name from the Latin Perivincula because it was used for chaplets.

61/5 and 12. So long as the blood was looked upon as stationary it was a common belief that the vein from which the blood was taken altered the result. Arderne teaches here that letting blood from the external saphenous vein stopped bleeding from a pile, whilst bleeding from the internal saphenous vein increased the hæmorrhage.

61/22. The vena salvatella (cf. 49/38, p. 121) ran along the back of the hand between the third and fourth metacarpal bones. Patients were bled from it when they were chronic invalids owing to "congestion of the liver or spleen," says Prof. Nicaise.

61/23. There is here a clear distinction made between the clumsy phlebotome with its halbert shape and the more delicate and easily manipulated lancet (cf. 24/21).

62/6. It is clear from this passage that Arderne was as unwilling to demean himself by breathing a vein as we should now be to crop a poll. Both were the duties of the barber, who was clearly in an inferior position.

62/14. This mutilated passage runs in another English translation (Sloane MS. No. 76), "Alsoe Gordon saythe that in ouer mich or greate fluxe in reasonable aged persones nothinge avayleth moare then pourginge, for the grosse and slymye matter being pourged awaye the medicyns restrictyue shull worke the better. Mirobalans will worke excellently in that case for they pourge before and stoppe after them, that is, it loseneth by reason of his swiftness in digestion and bringeth forth all grosse humour with yt. yt must be warely prepared, whose preparation is þis. It must be dissolved with warme mylke and whaye and not boyled or sodden with anythinge, for by boylinge the gummy substance vadeth awaye in the smooke and so the strength thereof ys weakened."

62/32. The meaning of this passage seems obscure at first, but Arderne says that *myrobalani* in their different forms were good against the different humours recognised by the ancient physicians—Sanguis, choler, melancholia and phlegma. "Myrobalani are the fruit of several species of Terminalia and of the Phyllanthus emblica," says "Mayne's Expository Lexicon" (Sydenham Soc. edition). They contain a large quantity of tannin and in the M. chebulæ some gallic acid. They were much employed by the Arabian physicians in many diseases; some lauding them as emetics and cathartics which purged away all evil humours; and others as useful in the treatment of diarrhœa and dysentery, acting first as a laxative and then as an astringent—the view taken by Arderne, cf. 62/14. They were formerly much employed in European medicine, but are not now used. The dose was 2 to 8 drachms. Myrobalani *citrina* is the fruit of a variety of Terminalia chebulæ; they were sometimes called White Galls. *Kebuliz* is the fruit of the terminalia chebula which resembles M. bellericæ in figure and ridges, but is larger and darker with a thicker pulp.

Indi, or Myrobalani indicæ, are probably the unripe fruit of Terminalia chebula and T. bellerica. These black myrobalans are oblong shaped and have no stone.

The *belleric* myrobalans are the fruit of Terminalia bellerica. They are yellowish-grey in colour and roundish or oblong in shape. The *Emblici* are the produce of the Emblica officinalis or the Phyllanthus emblica, a plant inhabiting the East Indies and frequently cultivated. The dried fruits are used as a purge and also as a tanning agent.

63/22. *Storax calamita* is the dry resin of the Storax tree.

63/25. *Porcelane* or Porcelayne is the older name of Portulaca communis, purslane. It was recommended at first as a great assuager of choleric heat; afterwards as a cure for scurvy and all skin eruptions; and lastly as an ingredient in salads.

63/29. The Latin text gives lapis hæmatites for *lapis omoptoes.*

Hœmatites. The bloodstone is found in iron mines in Germany and Bohemia of a black, yellowish, or iron colour. The best is brittle, very black and even, free from filth, and of a Cinnabar-like colour. It is to be reduced into a most subtile powder by levigation with plantain water. It is good against the gout, fluxes of the Womb and Belly, spitting blood and bleeding at the nose; mixed with woman's milk it helps blear eyes and suffusions.

Ypoquistid is Hypocistis, the juice of the root of the shrub Cistis or Holly Rose dried in the sun. It was regarded as an astringent, and Acacia was used as a substitute for it. *Sumak* is the rhus obsoniorum of which the fruits were looked upon as cooling and astringent.

Quinque-Nervia is the Plantago lanceolata or Ribwort, of which the distilled water "helps spitting and pissing blood, and the Ptysick, stops the Courses, eases the Cholick and heals a Dysenteria, cools inflammations, dissolves nodes and mundifies Fistulas. The Essence is better," says Salmon in 1678.

64/1. This passage is given in greater detail in the later English translation (Sloane MS. 76), where it runs: "Of the Emmorroydes and Menstrualles. The Emorroydes or menstrualles flowinge strongely, or the pacient sore afflicted with the force of blood, ye must consider of the suerest waye and that which returns blood fastest. First, if the pacient be not very weake, let him bleed somethinge of both Basillic vaynes of the arme and set cuppinge glasses under woman's breistes and so doinge and by bindinge the armes paynedly will provoke the humours to returne, and after that use local remedyes."

64/6. *Muscilage dragaunte.* This should certainly be Muscilage Dragagant. Arderne is careful to explain the difference between *Dragaunte* and *Dragagant.* 79/3–4. *Dragant* is a crude sulphate, acting as an astringent, whilst dragagant is tragacanth.

64/11. *Red coral* was long used as an astringent in diarrhœa and in the form of a compound syrup, and it was employed as a teething powder for children. It is still used as a charm against the evil eye in London, for most babies' rattles mounted in silver are tipped with a piece of red coral.

64/13. *Canell.* Arderne's translator uses canell throughout as the equivalent of Cinnamomum.

64/18. *Coprose* is Green Vitriol. Salmon says in 1678: "This owes its colour to Iron; in London it is well known that most of the old iron which is gathered by many poor people is sold to the Copperas houses at Rotherhith and Deptford, which they boil up with a dissolution of the Pyrites, which is a stone found on the shore of the Isle of Shepey and other such like places, and let the liquor run out into convenient vessels or Cisterns in which it shoots into those forms we meet with amongst druggists. It is chiefly used as an Astringent."

64/25. *Kynnyng* is clearly a variant of the more common form chine, to burst open or split. It is still in familiar use, as in the Chines of the Isle of Wight.

64/32. Arderne shows both in this passage and in previous ones (cf. 7/39, p. 112) that neurasthenia was not unknown in his practice.

64/36. *Clyffyng.* This is an early instance of the confusion between Cliff and clift, the original form of Cleft.

65/27. *Psidie* was pomegranate rind: *Balaustia* being the flowers of the wild pomegranate—Punica sylvestris.

Mummè was divided into five forms. (1) A factitious made of bitumen and Pitch-Pissasphaltum; (2) Flesh of the carcase dried in the Sun, in the country of the Hammonians between Cyrene and Alexandria, being Passengers buried in the Quick-sands; (3) Ægyptian, a liquor sweating from carcases embalmed with Pissasphaltum; (4) Arabian, a liquor which sweats from carcases embalmed with Myrrh, Aloes, and Balsam; (5) Artificial, which is Modern. Of all which the two last are the best, but the Arabian is scarcely to be got; the second and third sorts are sold for it. The artificial or modern mummy is made thus: "Take the carcase of a young man (some say red hair'd) not dying of a disease, but killed; let it lie 24 hours in clear water in the Air; cut the flesh in pieces, to which add powder of myrrh and a little Aloes; imbibe it 24 hours in the spirit of wine and Turpentine, take it out, hang it up twelve hours; imbibe it again 24 hours in fresh spirit, then hang up the pieces in dry air and a shadowy place, so will they dry and not stink." (Salmon, "The New London Dispensatory," 1678, p. 194.) There was a tincture, an essence, an elixir and a balsam of this precious medicine. It dissolved congealed and coagulated blood, provoked the terms, expelled the wind out of both the bowels and the Veins, helped Coughs and was a great Vulnerary. It was also said to purge. The dose was a drachm.

Olibanum is frankincense, the resin obtained from Boswellia Carteri. It was employed as a stimulating expectorant, as an emmenagogue, as an ointment in skin diseases and some diseases of the eyes, and as an ingredient of stimulating plasters.

66/3. *Red Jasper* was considered to be of the nature of the blood stone, for it not only stops bleedings at the nose and other fluxes of blood but also the flux of the terms.

Saphir. "The Saphire is either Oriental or Occidental, and of each there are Male and Female. It is a glorious, clear, transparent, blew, or sky-coloured stone, these are the Males. The females are white and unripe, so they want colour. The stone laid whole to the forehead stays the bleeding at the nose. You may dissolve it in juice of Lemons or Spirit of Vinegar and so use it; drunk in wine it helps against the stinging of scorpions. You may also beat it into a powder and levigate it with rosewater."

"The Ruby or Carbuncle is either white or red; being drunk, it restrains Lust and makes a man lively and cheerful."

66/4. The dung of swine helps the bitings and stinging of serpents, Scorpions, and Mad-dogs. It softens, discusses, and cures hard tumours, Scrophulas, Corns, Warts, Bleeding at the nose, Itch, Small-pox, Scabs, Fractures, Luxations, Wounds, Burns, Scalds, stops Bleeding, etc.

66/7. The belief in the juice of nettle as a blood purifier still lingers among us. As a child I had repeated attacks of urticaria; on several occasions I was ordered a tumblerful of the infusion of nettles to be taken hot and in the morning, fasting, but so far as I remember without effect either in shortening the intervals between the attacks or curing their painfulness.

66/19. *A streit wound:* cf. "streit is the gate and narrow is the way which leadeth unto life" (Matt. vii. 14).

66/25. Arderne here recommends the use of acupressure as a means of arresting hæmorrhage.

67/8. *Comyn.* Dr. Prior derives this word from the Arabic *al qamoun.* It is the Cuminum cyminum. Its seeds have long been in general use as a stomachic.

67/13. *Orpine* is the Sedum Telephium, a well-known inmate of the cottage garden, being esteemed as a vulnerary. The Latin text gives Succus ebulæ, juice of the Danewort or Dwarf elder.

67/28. The Lombards as an enterprising trading community in London are mentioned again in the Treatise on Clysters; cf. 76/32.

67/28. Two kinds of ink seem to have been used by the surgeons in the fourteenth century, Attramentum and Encaustum. The Attramentum seems to have been a sulphate containing powdered galls, whilst the encaustum—literally, purple ink reserved for the royal use—was made with Chalcantum, a generic name for the sulphates of copper, iron and zinc. Salicet (Ed. Pifteau, p. 207) used the purple ink to stain the bone for the purpose of discovering a line or fracture of the skull. Henri de Mondeville (Ed. Nicaise, p. 506) marked out his flaps with it before amputating. Guy de Chauliac (Ed. Nicaise, p. 343) employs attramentum (cf. 40/27, p. 119), as a local astringent in piles, and (p. 521) uses the purple ink for surface marking.

67/31. *Bdellium* is a gum resin somewhat resembling very impure myrrh. It is the product of various species of Balsamodendron.

67/32. *Anteros* was anthera, semen rosarum. Rose threads, viz. the yellow threads in the middle of the flowers. They were used with dentrifrices and to dry up defluxions.

67/34. This Demetrius may have been Demetrius II, King of Georgia, son of David III, who came to the throne in 1126 and died 1158. He was constantly at war with the Mussulmen. It may have been his son Demetrius III who died 1289. Arderne perhaps heard the story from those who had been to Lithuania with Sir Geoffrey Scrope. Cf. 14/4, p. 114.

67/39 and 68/1. The Cuckoo's Bread is the Oxalis Acetosella. It is called also Cuckoo's Meat or Gowk's Meat and Wood Sorrel. It was called Hallelujah because it blossomed between Easter and Whitsuntide, the season at which the 113th to the 117th Psalms were sung. Arderne's translator calls it Alleluia. Cf. 68/1.

68/14. *Galang* is the name given to two kinds of roots obtained from a species of Alpinia, the greater and smaller galanga. The word itself is said to be a corruption of the Chinese liang-kiang, mild ginger.

69/1. Arderne gives the reason for using Crocus or Saffron with opium (cf. 101/35), because it acted as a bridle to that drug.

69/14. This appears to be the original prescription for the Valence which handed Arderne's name down to posterity until after the publication of the "Pharmacopœia Londinensis." (Cf. Forewords, pp. xxx–xxxi.) My copy, said to be the editio quarta, with the frontispiece dated 1632, says (p. 155), "Valentia Scabiosæ Iohannis Ardernii, ex Oppido (vulgo) Newark in Comitatu Nottingham; Chirurgi exerciatissimi; qui floruit anno 1370; tempore Edouardi tertii Regis Angliæ, ipsissimis verbis ex antiquo manuscripto excerpta. . . Tapsivalencia ejusdem authoris. . . Tapsimel ejusdem. . . Hæc ad verbum ex veteri Manuscripto et stylo suo."

69/29. *Populeon* was an ointment made from the buds of the white poplar or Aspen tree. Cf. 77/3.

70/19. *Furfur* is Bran. It entered very largely into the materia medica of the older leeches.

71/21. *A welked grape;* cf. Chaucer, Pardoner's Tale, l. 270, "For which ful pale and welked is my face," in the sense of wrinkled or shrivelled.

71/26. This short treatise on Tenesmus is excellent from a professional point of view, and it does not appear that the use of the term has materially altered in the course of the centuries which have elapsed since Arderne wrote it.

71–74. These are the passages which show Arderne to be a first-rate observer independent of book work. The prognosis holds good to this day. If the enema is returned at once either the bowel is paralysed because the patient is moribund from some obstruction which may be situated high up, or there may be an obstruction near the anus without paralysis, or the bowel is blocked by the impaction of fæces consequent upon obstinate constipation. In the last case the patient may recover, and Arderne says therefore that his rule is not without exceptions.

72/9. *Diagredium* is made from scammony by putting the powder into a hollow quince, covering it with a paste and baking it in an oven or under ashes.

72/12. The iliac passion was a general name for intestinal obstruction at a time when morbid anatomy was unknown. It included a variety of conditions from simple colic to suppurative peritonitis in all its forms. The scene closed with fæcal vomiting, as no attempt was ever made to treat it by surgical means.

72/20. *Scariola* is the endive, Cichorium Endivia.

72/23. *The dusty meel of the milne* is only the finest flour used as a vehicle to make the grease and honey into a mass.

72/27. Cabbage, Brassica sativa or Caulis, was much used by the school of Salernum, and Arderne mentions it previously. Cf. 70/19 and 72/27.

72/28. *Fenigreke* is the fænum græcum, whose seeds were used in emollient clysters, for they are mucilaginous.

73/6. *Mellilote* is here explained by Arderne as the tops of colewort, but the term is usually applied to M. officinalis, the dried flowers of which were used for making poultices. Two varieties were recognised, the white and the yellow.

73/30. The translator has omitted the passage about the ostrich feather and the Prince of Wales which is given in Forewords, p. xxvii. It should come after the word *lure.*

73/32. *Cimbalarie* is the Pennywort—Linaria Cymbalaria—so called from its round leaves. It was good "against all inflammations and hot tumours, St. Antonie's fire and Kibed heels."

74/2. *Triasantalorum.* There were three kinds of Sandal in use, album, rufum, and citrinum. Triasantalorum therefore is a confection of the three Sandals just as Diatritonpipereon is a confection of the three peppers.

74/26. Salicet (Ed. Pifteau) gives two formulas (pp. 171 and 504) for making an unguentum apostolorum. The ointment contained white wax : pine resin : aristolochia : incense : mastic : opoponax : myrrh : galbanum, litharge, etc. Guy de Chauliac (Ed. Nicaise, p. 617) gives a similar formula, and adds that Mesue named it Ceraseos, but Master Anserin de la Porte and Master Pierre de l'Argentiere of Montpellier call it Gratia Dei, because it cures bad ulcers so wonderfully. Henri de Mondeville (Ed. Nicaise, p. 800) calls it the green ointment of the Twelve Apostles on account of its twelve chief ingredients, and states that some writers call it Unguentum Apostolicon, others Unguentum Veneris, or simply the Plaister.

74/30. Pellitory of the wall is the Parietaria officinalis. It grows on old walls and was thought to draw lime from the mortar.

74/31. Allusion to this interpolation in the text is made in Forewords (p. xii). It shows that the translation here printed cannot be earlier than 1413, the year of Henry IV's death.

74/33. The short treatise on Enemata is written to show Arderne's improvements in apparatus as well as in methods. He is, as usual, ahead of his contemporaries in simplifying both.

75/23. *Rerepigre.* This word seems to be a mistake of the copyist for Hiera pigre, Yera pigra, or iera pigra. The sacred bitter, an aloetic purgative which has long been popular. Dr. Payne says it is still sold in the shops of herbalists under the debased name of "Hackry-Packry." The usual formula was that given by Galen.

76/19. *Mercurialis.* The English mercury—chenopodium is sometimes called Good Henry—the all-good, to distinguish it from a poisonous form. The Grimms in their "Wörterbuch" explain this name as having reference to elves and kobolds, which were called "Heinz" or "Heinrich," and as indicating supernatural powers in the plant (Dr. Prior, p. 94). It was thought to be laxative, and was long given by nurses to children with their food.

76/32. Lombards. Cf. 67/28, p. 128.

76/36. This passage may mean either that the patients came to Arderne, or that they were relieved before he got home again.

77/3. *Popilion.* Cf. 69/29, p. 129.

77/12. This is an early use of the treatment of chronic constipation by abdominal massage, which has lately become fashionable again.

78/25. Arderne is here advocating rectal feeding which is now commonly used and with excellent results.

79/1. This last treatise is only a fragment in the present translation. A much fuller text is found in the Bodleian Library, where it exists in three parts. The first MS., Ashmole 1434, leaf 117, begins "Attramentorum, *i. e.* vitriolorum," and ends "facit calcantum." This corresponds, therefore, with p. 79, line 1 to page 81, line 23. The second part is in MS. Digby 161, leaf 16. It begins, "Alumen zucarinum vulgariter alumglas," and ends leaf 23, back, "nobillissimum est ad regem." The translation only contains a small part of this as it ends at page 85, line 22. The third part is in Ashmole MS. 1434, leaf 128, back, to leaf 131. It gives a good account of Arderne's treatment of Scabies by which he made a great deal of money (cf. 6/4, p. 111).

79/1. This passage explains itself. *Dragagant* is Tragacanth, a gummy exudation obtained from incisions made in the stem of Astragalus gemmifer. It is a demulcent and is still used in medicine as a vehicle to suspend heavy and insoluble powders like the subnitrate of bismuth.

79/4. *Dragant* is a modification of Chalcanthum from chalcis or vitriol romanum. Cf. 64/6. *Calcothar* is the red oxide of iron obtained by calcining sulphate of iron or green coperose.

79/10. Platearius was the name of a distinguished medical family living in the twelfth century. John, the elder, wrote "Practica brevis" and "Regulæ urinarum." John, the son, wrote "Tractatus de ægritudinum curatione" and "De conferentibus et nocentibus corporis humani." Matthew, brother of John the son, made a name for himself, but his writings are unknown. Matthew (floruit 1130–1150), grandson of John the elder and son of John the younger, wrote "De simplici medicina liber," quoted from the first words of the text as "circa instans." John, the third son of Matthew the elder and therefore cousin of Matthew "circa instans," was also known to fame.

79/18. *Venemyd wound.* The expression is still in common use, only we say a "poisoned wound," and bacteriology has given us an explanation of its occurrence.

79/27. *Fraudulent ulcers.* Guy de Chauliac divides ulcers into corrosive, sordid, cavernous, fistulous and chancre. The fraudulent ulcer is sordid, the characters are a sore or stinking scab. Henri de Mondeville also describes (Ed. Nicaise, p. 421, note) a fraudulent corrosive ulcer.

80/27. *Lutum sapienciæ,* also called lutum sapientum, was used by the alchemists for sealing their vessels. It was made with flour, white of egg, chalk and clay.

80/39. Arderne uses *marice* as the special term for the uterus, and employs the word *womb* where we should say "belly." Cf. 11/24, p. 113.

81/11. *Pulv: hermodactileȝ.* Hermodactylus is a name given to many plants with tuberous roots, notably to hermodactylus tuberosus. One form was used as a cure for gout, and may have been colchicum.

81/30. The *scab* is here scabies or the itch, a contagious disease which the habits of the time made prevalent through every class of society.

82/31. Arsenic was known at this time in the forms of the yellow sulphide, orpiment or Auripigmentum, and the red sulphide or Realgar. Arderne gives an interesting and evidently truthful account of his early experiences with the drug as a local application. Henri de Mondeville held a similar respect for it, perhaps based also on the grounds of experience, for he says "Realgar is strongly corrosive, dangerous and poisonous" (Ed. Nicaise, p. 850).

85/22. The translator has left out a most interesting case which reads as if the patient had Actinomycosis. Digby MS. 161, leaf 18, gives these details, the translation is mine. "A certain man, however, at Bridgeford-on-Trent, in the county of Nottingham, had a bad ulcer upon the back of his hand, and there were grains in it like barleycorns full of blood, and if the hand was compressed by the fingers a sanious and stinking discharge was driven out with itching and sometimes with pain." The patient was completely cured after realgar and soap had been applied.

The text runs:—"Quidam homo tamen in Briggeforde super Trent in Comitatu Notyngham', habuit serpiginem granosam super tergum manus et grana erant similia granis ordei plena sanguine et si manus cum digitis compressa sanies sub granis erumpebat cum fetore pruritu et aliquando cum dolore.

"Quando vero post multa medicamina recepta cum pulvere realgar' et sapone nigro commixtum totum herpetem predictum bene liniui et firmiter applicaui. Paciens vero ingentem dolorem per diem naturalem perpessus est, et manus nimis erat inflatus pre dolore et calore. Quo viso, superposui vitellum oui crudum cum oleo rosarum, et manum bene cum dicto oleo permixi tandem incepit fieri diuisio circa extremitates ulceris et medicina predicta nihil nocuerat sano corio sed tantummodo quod infectum fuerat mortificauit. Continuato vero medicamine de vitello et oleo rosarum tota illa pellis dicte manus infecta, bene est emulsa et omnino separata sine neruorum aut venarum lesione. Qua vero reparata vulnus cum vitello oui crudo et cum melle rosarum mixto et alfita subtilicia cum stupis lini delicatis inter ossa et emplastrum apposit'.

"Emplastrum jamdictum super stupas lini mundas extensum supraposui et cum hac sola cura peroptime pacientem curaui sine mutilacione neruorum aut venarum. Post consolidacionem vulneris supraposui emplastrum de diaquilo resoluto cum unguento maluarum et lilii et supposui longo tempore donec pellis noua fuerat bene digesta et ne reciperet alteracionem a aëre vel alio casu contingente."

87/25. These rules show the excellence of Arderne's practice. The simplest dressings were only renewed when it was necessary. He was in every way an opponent of meddlesome surgery, and thus takes a very high place, not only amongst his contemporaries, but amongst all surgeons.

88/9. And yet almost immediately he shows the lack of critical faculty which characterizes so many mediæval writers. The superstition about the harmfulness of a menstruating woman is well known to all students of folk-medicine. The question is still raised in all seriousness from time to time both in lay and medical papers.

89/7. *Pulv: sanguinis veneris.* The use of human blood was no new thing. Dr. J. F. Payne has an interesting article on the subject, "Arnold de Villa Nova on the therapeutic use of human blood" (Janus, 1903, pp. 432 and 477). Jamerius (cf. 55/3, p. 123) used a powder which he called "human powder," many years before Arderne, "against all wounds." The formula ran, "℞. Symphyti; balaustie, rosarum, squinanti, masticis olibani ana ℥ij: aluminis, arilli uvarum ana ℥j, atramenti, sanguinis draconis ana ʒss : galbani ʒij : galle asiane ʒj : colofonie, boli armenici ana ʒij : sanguinis humani ʒvi. Effunde super pellem arietis et siccati et ejusdem pellis arietine combuste et pulveriȝate ʒiij" [rubric xxxvii].

89/14. *Alkanet* is the root of Anchusa tinctoria. It was formerly used as an astringent, but is now only used as a colouring material.

89/30. *A hollow ulcer* or ulcus concavum is the same thing, says Henri de Mondeville (Ed. Nicaise, p. 425), as a deep or hidden ulcer. It is any ulcer whose whole extent is not visible. It is often called by "les ydiotes cirurgiens," or "cyrurgici rurales," a fistula, but it differs from a true fistula both in treatment and results.

90/23. The gloss on *edere terrestris* is useful to identify the plant as the ground-ivy, Hedera helix, because the term hedera terrestris was also applied to the Yew, Taxus baccata—called in Mid. Latin *ivius*. Dr. Prior (*op. cit.*, p. 261) gives a most interesting account of the chain of blunders which led to the confusion between a creeping form of Hedera and a full-grown evergreen shrub.

91/9. *Wild fire* is a synonym for erysipelas. Cf. 41/1. The Persian fire was sometimes shingles (or herpes zoster) : sometimes a carbuncle. St. Anthony's fire meant erysipelas in some cases, ergotinism or endemic gangrene in others.

91/24. *Pater noster and Ave maria.* On this method of estimating small portions of time *see* Forewords, p. xxix.

94/35. *Curseȝ of humours* is the flowing of a discharge, just as we still speak of menstruation in a woman as "the courses."

95/14. *Abhominaciones of the stomach.* This is a good example of the early spelling of abomination, due, says The New English Dictionary, "To an assumed derivation from *ab homine*, away from man, inhuman, beastly." It really comes from *ab* and *omen*. The word is genuinely expressive of the conditions in gastric catarrh.

97/5. *Walwort* is the dwarf-elder, Sambucus ebulus.

97/9. *Plinius* is Pliny the Younger whose "Natural History" is still good reading whether in the original or in Philemon Holland's translation.

Dioscorides is Dioscorides Pedacius who lived in the time of Nero and Vespasian, and was celebrated as the great classical botanist and pharmacologist. His great work, "περὶ ὕλης ἰατρικῆς," appeared in five books.

Macrobius is quoted also by Guy de Chauliac (Ed. Nicaise, p. 12), and by Gilbertus Anglicus. Macrobius died 415 A.D. He wrote "Saturnalia," containing miscellaneous remarks on physics, antiquities, literary criticism, etc.

98/6. *Anthrax* is considered both by Salicet and by de Chauliac. Salicet (Ed. Pifteau, p. 176) says that anthrax and carbuncle are the same, except that anthrax is the more malignant and acute. It was called "Bonne Bube," says Guy (Ed. Nicaise, p. 100), "in the opposite sense because it is very wicked and very dangerous," just as we call the fairies "good folk" or say of a baby "how ugly he is."

100/15. The *gymeweȝ*. The New English Dictionary gives this word as a variant of gemew or gemow, the plural of gemel, twins ; and of a door double. It gives as a quotation 1523, in Kirkpatrick, "Relig. Ord. Norwich" (1848) 170, "Within the White Freris, in Norwich, at the Jemowe door." It would be interesting to know whether the gymeweȝ or Jemowe door was peculiar to the Carmelites.

Frere Caromeȝ. It is clear from the Latin text that the Frere Caromeȝ were the Carmelites or White Friars who had their convent and church east of the Temple in London. The Carmelite Convent was founded by Sir Richard Gray in 1241, upon ground given by Edward I. In 1350 Courtenay, Earl of Devon, rebuilt the Whitefriars church, and in 1420 Robert Marshall, Bishop of Hereford, added a steeple. At the Dissolution Dr. Butts was given the Chapter house as a residence. The church was pulled down in the reign of Edward VI, but the refectory of the convent remained as the Whitefriars theatre. The right of sanctuary remained for many years, as is known to every reader of Scott's novels. The Library at Lambeth Palace contains a will (Staff. 2, p. 548, Will 91) dated Feb. 1, 1446, and proved May 12, 1449. The will is made by John Arderne, armiger, who desires to be buried by Margaret his wife, if dying in London, or by Elizabeth his wife, if dying at Leygh. "His body," the document states, "is actually buried in the Carmelite church under the marble tomb with Margaret." The will is dated at St. Margaret's, Westminster, and leaves his effects to John, his son, and Bridget, his daughter.

100/33. In 1376, about the time Arderne was writing this treatise, the Commons petitioned the king "that Ribalds . . . and sturdy Beggars may be banished out of every town" (Ribton Turner, "Vagrants and Vagrancy," p. 52).

A truant was any vagabond, beggar or rogue.

100/35. *Jusquiamus* is henbane, Hyoscyamus niger or alba.

100/36. *ȝiȝannie* is the cockle or tares which the wicked man sowed (Matt. xiii. 25). Darnel was a general name for all kinds of cornfield weeds, says Dr. Prior (*op. cit.* 64).

Chessede is chess-seed, chesses being a name applied to the poppy-chasses and chese boules, from the shape of its capsule.

Briony root was looked upon as a powerful hydrogogue purging agent, whilst the juice of the plant was a remedy for gout.

The ribald's potion would not have done much harm even in considerable doses.

101/10. *Cicuta* is water hemlock, the Cicuta virosa.

101/12. *Opium* is a tear which flows from the wounded heads or leaves of the black poppy, being ripe. Some promiscuously use it with Meconium, but they do ill ; for opium is a drop or tear, Meconium the gross expressed juice from the whole plant. However, they are both of one quality : opium is the finer gum and the stronger, Meconium is the coarser and weaker, yet the more malign.

"Opium is three-fold. 1. Black and hard, from Syria and Aden. 2. Yellower and softer, from Cambaia. 3. White, from Cairo or Thebes, which last, commonly called Thebian opium, is the best, being heavy, thick, strong-scented like Poppy, bitter and sharp, inflammable, almost of the colour of Aloes, and easie to dissolve in water. The counterfeit when washed colours the water like saffron." (Salmon's "New London Dispensatory," 1678, p. 167, col. 2.)

101/16. *Propoleos* is bee bread. Henri de Mondeville in his "Antidotaire" (Ed. Nicaise, p. 831) says : "85. Cera, en grec Propolis, en Arabe Scham'a (Schamha) : elle tient le milieu entre les quatre qualités."

102/3. *Castor* was long looked upon as "a most noble Drug of great use in all distempers of the head." It is the secretion from the cloacal glands of the *castor fiber* obtained from the Hudson Bay territory. Its properties have hardly yet been adequately tested, and it is possible that it may regain some of its former prestige.

102/8. The *nux moschata* or myristica is the nutmeg, which was looked upon as a comforter of the head and stomach. Mace, which is the arillus of the fruit dried in the sun, has similar properties.

102/8. *Nenufare* is the water-lily used in medicine as an oil, syrup and water. The lily with yellow flowers stoppeth the lask and bloody flux, but the white-flowered lily is the strongest, and is powerful in stopping the Whites, drunk in red wine.

Mirtelleȝ is the Rubus hortensis, the garden bramble or dwarf myrtle bush. The leaves astringe and stop fluxes; the fruit and berries bind, cool in fevers, quench thirst, stop vomitings.

102/8. The Manuscript stops here abruptly, but I have copied the charm from another source, partly on account of its intrinsic interest, partly because of the sidelight it sheds on the Duke of Clarence's wedding festivities and of Arderne's desire for secrecy.

104/5. In some of the later manuscripts the words Enthe and Enthanay have become Gnthe and Gnthenay.

104/8. *Verbum caro factum est* were words of power in the middle ages. Friar Odoric of Pordenone, who was in Northern China about 1320 when the Yang-tsi floods caused the devastation which some think started the Black Death, says ("Yule, Cathay and the way thither," Hakluyt Soc. I, 156, quoted in Creighton's "History of Epidemics," I, 155): "I saw such numbers of corpses as no one without seeing it could deem credible. And at one side of the valley, in the very rock, I beheld as it were the face of a man very great and terrible, so very terrible indeed that for my exceeding great fear my spirit seemed to die in me. Wherefore I made the sign of the Cross, and began continually to repeat *verbum caro factum*, but I dared not at all come nigh that face, but kept seven or eight paces from it."

INDEX.

EARLY ENGLISH TEXT SOCIETY

THE Subscription to the Society, which constitutes full membership for private members and libraries, is £3. 3*s*. (U.S. and Canadian members $9.00) a year for the annual publications, due in advance on the 1st of JANUARY, and should be paid by Cheque, Postal Order, or Money Order made out to 'The Early English Text Society', to Mr. R. W. Burchfield, Hon. Secretary, Early English Text Society, 40 Walton Crescent, Oxford. Individual members of the Society are allowed, after consultation with the Secretary, to select other volumes of the Society's publications instead of those for the current year. The Society's Texts can also be purchased separately from the Publisher, Oxford University Press, through a bookseller, at the prices put after them in the List, or through the Secretary, by members only, for their own use, at a discount of 2*d*. in the shilling.

The Early English Text Society was founded in 1864 by Frederick James Furnivall, with the help of Richard Morris, Walter Skeat, and others, to bring the mass of unprinted Early English literature within the reach of students and provide sound texts from which the New English Dictionary could quote. In 1867 an Extra Series was started of texts already printed but not in satisfactory or readily obtainable editions.

In 1921 the Extra Series was discontinued and all the publications of 1921 and subsequent years have since been listed and numbered as part of the Original Series. Since 1921 nearly a hundred new volumes have been issued; and since 1957 alone more than a hundred volumes have been reprinted at a cost of £40,000.

In this prospectus the Original Series and Extra Series for the years 1867–1920 are amalgamated, so as to show all the publications of the Society in a single list. In 1963 the prices of all volumes down to O.S. 222, and still available, were increased by one half, and the prices of some texts after O.S. 222 were also increased, in order to obtain additional revenue for reprinting.

LIST OF PUBLICATIONS

Original Series, 1864–1968. Extra Series, 1867–1920

O.S. 1. **Early English Alliterative Poems**, ed. R. Morris. (*Reprinted* 1965.) 42*s.* 1864
2. **Arthur**, ed. F. J. Furnivall. (*Reprinted* 1965.) 7*s.* 6*d.* ,,
3. **Lauder on the Dewtie of Kyngis, &c.**, 1556, ed. F. Hall. (*Reprinted* 1965.) 12*s.* 6*d.* ,,
4. **Sir Gawayne and the Green Knight**, ed. R. Morris. (*Out of print, see* O.S. 210.)
5. **Hume's Orthographie and Congruitie of the Britan Tongue**, ed. H. B. Wheatley. (*Reprinted* 1965. 12*s.* 6*d.* 1865
6. **Lancelot of the Laik**, ed. W. W. Skeat. (*Reprinted* 1965.) 42*s.* ,,
7. **Genesis & Exodus**, ed. R. Morris. (*Out of print.*) ,,
8. **Morte Arthure**, ed. E. Brock. (*Reprinted* 1967.) 25*s.* ,,
9. **Thynne on Speght's ed. of Chaucer**, A.D. 1599, ed. G. Kingsley and F. J. Furnivall. (*Reprinted* 1965.) 55*s.* ,,
10. **Merlin**, Part I, ed. H. B. Wheatley. (*Out of print.*) ,,
11. **Lyndesay's Monarche, &c.**, ed. J. Small. Part I. (*Out of print.*) ,,
12. **The Wright's Chaste Wife**, ed. F. J. Furnivall. (*Reprinted* 1965.) 7*s.* 6*d.* ,,
13. **Seinte Marherete**, ed. O. Cockayne. (*Out of print, see* O.S. 193.) 1866
14. **King Horn, Floriz and Blauncheflur, &c.**, ed. J. R. Lumby, re-ed. G. H. McKnight. (*Reprinted* 1962.) 40*s.* ,,
15. **Political, Religious, and Love Poems**, ed. F. J. Furnivall. (*Reprinted* 1965.) 55*s.* ,,
16. **The Book of Quinte Essence**, ed. F. J. Furnivall. (*Reprinted* 1965.) 10*s.* ,,
17. **Parallel Extracts from 45 MSS. of Piers the Plowman**, ed. W. W. Skeat. (*Out of print.*) ,,
18. **Hali Meidenhad**, ed. O. Cockayne, re-ed. F. J. Furnivall. (*Out of print.*) ,,
19. **Lyndesay's Monarche, &c.**, ed. J. Small. Part II. (*Out of print.*) ,,
20. **Richard Rolle de Hampole, English Prose Treatises of**, ed. G. G. Perry. (*Reprinted* 1920.) 10*s.* ,,
21. **Merlin**, ed. H. B. Wheatley. Part II. (*Out of print.*) ,,
22. **Partenay or Lusignen**, ed. W. W. Skeat. (*Out of print.*) ,,
23. **Dan Michel's Ayenbite of Inwyt**, ed. R. Morris and P. Gradon. Vol. I, Text. (*Reissued* 1965.) 50*s.* ,,
24. **Hymns to the Virgin and Christ; The Parliament of Devils, &c.**, ed. F. J. Furnivall. (*Out of print.*) 1867
25. **The Stacions of Rome, the Pilgrims' Sea-voyage, with Clene Maydenhod**, ed. F. J. Furnivall. (*Out of print.*) ,,
26. **Religious Pieces in Prose and Verse**, from R. Thornton's MS., ed. G. G. Perry. (*See under* 1913.) (*Out of print.*) ,,
27. **Levins' Manipulus Vocabulorum, a rhyming Dictionary**, ed. H. B. Wheatley. (*Out of print.*) ,,
28. **William's Vision of Piers the Plowman**, ed. W. W. Skeat. A–Text. (*Reprinted* 1968.) 30*s.* ,,
29. **Old English Homilies** (1220–30), ed. R. Morris. Series I, Part I. (*Out of print.*) ,,
30. **Pierce the Ploughmans Crede**, ed. W. W. Skeat. (*Out of print.*) ,,

E.S. 1. **William of Palerne or William and the Werwolf**, re-ed. W. W. Skeat. (*Out of print.*) ,,
2. **Early English Pronunciation**, by A. J. Ellis. Part I. (*Out of print.*) ,,

O.S. 31. **Myrc's Duties of a Parish Priest**, in Verse, ed. E. Peacock. (*Out of print.*) 1868
32. **Early English Meals and Manners: the Boke of Norture of John Russell, the Bokes of Keruynge, Curtasye, and Demeanor, the Babees Book, Urbanitatis, &c.**, ed. F. J. Furnivall. (*Out of print.*) ,,
33. **The Book of the Knight of La Tour-Landry**, ed. T. Wright. (*Out of print.*) ,,
34. **Old English Homilies** (before 1300), ed. R. Morris. Series I, Part II. (*Out of print.*) ,,
35. **Lyndesay's Works, Part III**: The Historie and Testament of Squyer Meldrum, ed. F. Hall. (*Reprinted* 1965.) 12*s.* 6*d.* ,,

E.S. 3. **Caxton's Book of Curtesye**, in Three Versions, ed. F. J. Furnivall. (*Out of print.*) ,,
4. **Havelok the Dane**, re-ed. W. W. Skeat. (*Out of print.*) ,,
5. **Chaucer's Boethius**, ed. R. Morris. (*Out of print.*) ,,
6. **Chevelere Assigne**, re-ed. Lord Aldenham. (*Out of print.*) ,,

O.S. 36. **Merlin**, ed. H. B. Wheatley. Part III. On Arthurian Localities, by J. S. Stuart Glennie. (*Out of print.*) 1869
37. **Sir David Lyndesay's Works, Part IV**, Ane Satyre of the thrie Estaits, ed. F. Hall. (*Out of print.*) ,,
38. **William's Vision of Piers the Plowman**, ed. W. W. Skeat. Part II. Text B. (*Reprinted* 1964.) 40*s.* ,,
39, 56. **The Gest Hystoriale of the Destruction of Troy**, ed. D. Donaldson and G. A. Panton. Parts I and II. (*Reprinted as one volume* 1968.) 84*s.* ,,

E.S. 7. **Early English Pronunciation**, by A. J. Ellis. Part II. (*Out of print.*)
8. **Queene Elizabethes Achademy, &c.**, ed. F. J. Furnivall. Essays on early Italian and German Books of Courtesy, by W. M. Rossetti and E. Oswald. (*Out of print.*) ,,
9. **Awdeley's Fraternitye of Vacabondes, Harman's Caveat, &c.**, ed. E. Viles and F. J. Furnivall. (*Out of print.*) ,,

O.S. 40. **English Gilds**, their Statutes and Customs, A.D. 1389, ed. Toulmin Smith and Lucy T. Smith, with an Essay on Gilds and Trades-Unions, by L. Brentano. (*Reprinted* 1963.) 70*s.* 1870
41. **William Lauder's Minor Poems**, ed. F. J. Furnivall. (*Out of print.*) ,,
42. **Bernardus De Cura Rei Famuliaris**, Early Scottish Prophecies, &c., ed. J. R. Lumby. (*Reprinted* 1965.) 12*s.* 6*d.* ,,
43. **Ratis Raving**, and other Moral and Religious Pieces, ed. J. R. Lumby. (*Out of print.*) ,,

E.S. 10. **Andrew Boorde's Introduction of Knowledge, 1547, Dyetary of Helth, 1542, Barnes in Defence of the Berde, 1542–3**, ed. F. J. Furnivall. (*Out of print.*) ,,
11, 55. **Barbour's Bruce**, ed. W. W. Skeat. Parts I and IV. (*Reprinted as Volume I* 1968.) 60*s.* ,,

O.S. 44. **The Alliterative Romance of Joseph of Arimathie, or The Holy Grail**: from the Vernon MS.; with W. de Worde's and Pynson's Lives of Joseph: ed. W. W. Skeat. (*Out of print.*) 1871

O.S. 45. **King Alfred's West-Saxon Version of Gregory's Pastoral Care, ed., with an English translation,** by Henry Sweet. Part I. (*Reprinted* 1958.) 45*s.* 1871

46. **Legends of the Holy Rood, Symbols of the Passion and Cross Poems, ed. R. Morris.** (*Out of print.*) „

47. **Sir David Lyndesay's Works,** ed. J. A. H. Murray. Part V. (*Out of print.*) „

48. **The Times' Whistle,** and other Poems, by R. C., 1616; ed. J. M. Cowper. (*Out of print.*) „

E.S. 12. **England in Henry VIII's Time:** a Dialogue between Cardinal Pole and Lupset, by Thom. Starkey, Chaplain to Henry VIII, ed. J. M. Cowper. Part II. (*Out of print*, Part I is E.S. 32, 1878.)

13. **A Supplicacyon of the Beggers,** by Simon Fish, A.D. 1528–9, ed. F. J. Furnivall, with **A Supplication to our Moste Soueraigne Lorde, A Supplication of the Poore Commons,** and **The Decaye of England by the Great Multitude of Sheep,** ed. J. M. Cowper. (*Out of print.*) „

14. **Early English Pronunciation,** by A. J. Ellis. Part III. (*Out of print.*) „

O.S. 49. **An Old English Miscellany,** containing a Bestiary, Kentish Sermons, Proverbs of Alfred, and Religious Poems of the 13th cent., ed. R. Morris. (*Out of print.*) 1872

50. **King Alfred's West-Saxon Version of Gregory's Pastoral Care,** ed. H. Sweet. Part II. (*Reprinted* 1958.) 45*s.* „

51. **Þe Liflade of St. Juliana,** 2 versions, with translations, ed. O. Cockayne and E. Brock. (*Reprinted* 1957.) 37*s.* 6*d.* „

52. **Palladius on Husbondrie,** englisht, ed. Barton Lodge. Part I. (*Out of print.*)

E.S. 15. **Robert Crowley's Thirty-One Epigrams, Voyce of the Last Trumpet, Way to Wealth, &c.,** ed. J. M. Cowper. (*Out of print.*) „

16. **Chaucer's Treatise on the Astrolabe,** ed. W. W. Skeat. (*Out of print.*) „

17. **The Complaynt of Scotlande,** with 4 Tracts, ed. J. A. H. Murray. Part I. (*Out of print.*) „

O.S. 53. **Old-English Homilies,** Series II, and three Hymns to the Virgin and God, 13th-century, with the music to two of them, in old and modern notation, ed. R. Morris. (*Out of print.*) 1873

54. **The Vision of Piers Plowman,** ed. W. W. Skeat. Part III. Text C. (*Reprinted* 1959.) 52*s.* 6*d.* „

55. **Generydes,** a Romance, ed. W. Aldis Wright. Part I. (*Out of print.*) „

E.S. 18. **The Complaynt of Scotlande,** ed. J. A. H. Murray. Part II. (*Out of print.*) „

19. **The Myroure of oure Ladye,** ed. J. H. Blunt. (*Out of print.*) „

O.S. 56. **The Gest Hystoriale of the Destruction of Troy,** in alliterative verse, ed. D. Donaldson and G. A. Panton. Part II. (*See* O.S. 39.) 1874

57. **Cursor Mundi,** in four Texts, ed. R. Morris. Part I. (*Reprinted* 1961.) 25*s.* „

58, 63, 73. **The Blickling Homilies,** ed. R. Morris. Parts I, II, and III. (*Reprinted as one volume* 1967.) 63*s.* „

E.S. 20. **Lovelich's History of the Holy Grail,** ed. F. J. Furnivall. Part I. (*Out of print.*) „

21, 29. **Barbour's Bruce,** ed. W. W. Skeat. Parts II and III. (*Reprinted as Volume II* 1968.) 84*s.* „

22. **Henry Brinklow's Complaynt of Roderyck Mors** and **The Lamentacyon of a Christen Agaynst the Cytye of London,** made by Roderigo Mors, ed. J. M. Cowper. (*Out of print.*) „

23. **Early English Pronunciation,** by A. J. Ellis. Part IV. (*Out of print.*) „

O.S. 59. **Cursor Mundi,** in four Texts, ed. R. Morris. Part II. (*Reprinted* 1966.) 42*s.* 1875

60. **Meditacyuns on the Soper of our Lorde,** by Robert of Brunne, ed. J. M. Cowper. (*Out of print.*) „

61. **The Romance and Prophecies of Thomas of Erceldoune,** ed. J. A. H. Murray. (*Out of print.*)

E.S. 24. **Lovelich's History of the Holy Grail,** ed. F. J. Furnivall. Part II. (*Out of print.*)

25, 26. **Guy of Warwick,** 15th-century Version, ed. J. Zupitza. Pts. I and II. (*Reprinted as one volume* 1966.) 55*s.* „

O.S. 62. **Cursor Mundi,** in four Texts, ed. R. Morris. Part III. (*Reprinted* 1966.) 37*s.* 6*d.* 1876

63. **The Blickling Homilies,** ed. R. Morris. Part II. (*See* O.S. 58.) „

64. **Francis Thynne's Embleames and Epigrams,** ed. F. J. Furnivall. (*Out of print.*) „

65. **Be Domes Dæge** (Bede's *De Die Judicii*), &c., ed. J. R. Lumby. (*Reprinted* 1964.) 30*s.* „

E.S. 26. **Guy of Warwick,** 15th-century Version, ed. J. Zupitza. Part II. (*See* E.S. 25) „

27. **The English Works of John Fisher,** ed. J. E. B. Mayor. Part I. (*Out of print.*) „

O.S. 66. **Cursor Mundi,** in four Texts, ed. R. Morris. Part IV. (*Reprinted* 1966.) 25*s.* 1877

67. **Notes on Piers Plowman,** by W. W. Skeat. Part I. (*Out of print.*) „

E.S. 28. **Lovelich's Holy Grail,** ed. F. J. Furnivall. Part III. (*Out of print.*) „

29. **Barbour's Bruce,** ed. W. W. Skeat. Part III. (*See* E.S. 21.) „

O.S. 68. **Cursor Mundi,** in 4 Texts, ed. R. Morris. Part V. (*Reprinted* 1966.) 30*s.* 1878

69. **Adam Davie's 5 Dreams about Edward II, &c.,** ed. F. J. Furnivall. 9*s.* „

70. **Generydes,** a Romance, ed. W. Aldis Wright. Part II. 7*s.* 6*d.* „

E.S. 30. **Lovelich's Holy Grail,** ed. F. J. Furnivall. Part IV. (*Out of print.*) „

31. **The Alliterative Romance of Alexander and Dindimus,** ed. W. W. Skeat. (*Out of print.*) „

32. **Starkey's England in Henry VIII's Time.** Part I. **Starkey's Life and Letters,** ed. S. J. Herrtage. (*Out of print.*) „

O.S. 71. **The Lay Folks Mass-Book,** four texts, ed. T. F. Simmons. (*Out of print.*) 1879

72. **Palladius on Husbondrie,** englisht, ed. S. J. Herrtage. Part II. 9*s.* „

E.S. 33. **Gesta Romanorum,** ed. S. J. Herrtage. (*Reprinted* 1962.) 80*s.* „

34. **The Charlemagne Romances: 1. Sir Ferumbras,** from Ashm. MS. 33, ed. S. J. Herrtage. (*Reprinted* 1966.) 50*s.* „

O.S. 73. **The Blickling Homilies,** ed. R. Morris. Part III. (*See* O.S. 58.) 1880

74. **English Works of Wyclif,** hitherto unprinted, ed. F. D. Matthew. (*Out of print.*) „

E.S. 35. **Charlemagne Romances: 2. The Sege of Melayne, Sir Otuell, &c.,** ed. S. J. Herrtage. (*Out of print.*) „

36, 37. **Charlemagne Romances: 3 and 4. Lyf of Charles the Grete,** ed. S. J. Herrtage. Parts I and II. (*Reprinted as one volume* 1967.) 50*s.* „

O.S. 75. **Catholicon Anglicum,** an English-Latin Wordbook, from Lord Monson's MS., A.D. 1483, ed., with Introduction and Notes, by S. J. Herrtage and Preface by H. B. Wheatley. (*Out of print.*) 1881

76, 82. **Ælfric's Lives of Saints,** in MS. Cott. Jul. E VII, ed. W. W. Skeat. Parts I and II. (*Reprinted as Volume I* 1966.) 60*s.* „

E.S. 37. **Charlemagne Romances: 4. Lyf of Charles the Grete**, ed. S. J. Herrtage. Part II. (*See* E.S. 36.) 1881

38. **Charlemagne Romances: 5. The Sowdone of Babylone**, ed. E. Hausknecht. (*Out of print.*) „

O.S. 77. **Beowulf**, the unique MS. autotyped and transliterated, ed. J. Zupitza. (*Re-issued as* No. 245. *See under* 1958.) 1882

78. **The Fifty Earliest English Wills**, in the Court of Probate, 1387–1439, ed. F. J. Furnivall. (*Reprinted* 1964.) 42*s*. „

E.S. 39. **Charlemagne Romances: 6. Rauf Coilyear, Roland, Otuel, &c.**, ed. S. J. Herrtage. (*Out of print.*) „

40. **Charlemagne Romances: 7. Huon of Burdeux**, by Lord Berners, ed. S. L. Lee. Part I. (*Out of print.*) „

O.S. 79. **King Alfred's Orosius**, from Lord Tollemache's 9th-century MS., ed. H. Sweet. Part I. (*Reprinted* 1959.) 45*s*. 1883

79 *b*. *Extra Volume*. **Facsimile of the Epinal Glossary**, ed. H. Sweet. (*Out of print.*) „

E.S. 41. **Charlemagne Romances: 8. Huon of Burdeux**, by Lord Berners, ed. S. L. Lee. Part II. (*Out of print.*) „

42, 49, 59. **Guy of Warwick**: 2 texts (Auchinleck MS. and Caius MS.), ed. J. Zupitza. **Parts I, II, and III.** (*Reprinted as one volume* 1966). 84*s*. „

O.S. 80. **The Life of St. Katherine**, B.M. Royal MS. 17 A. xxvii, &c., and its Latin Original, ed. E. Einenkel. (*Out of print.*) 1884

81. **Piers Plowman**: Glossary, &c., ed. W. W. Skeat. Part IV, completing the work. (*Out of print.*) „

E.S. 43. **Charlemagne Romances: 9. Huon of Burdeux**, by Lord Berners, ed. S. L. Lee. Part III. (*Out of print.*) „

44. **Charlemagne Romances: 10. The Foure Sonnes of Aymon, ed. Octavia Richardson. Part I.** (*Out of print.*) „

O.S. 82. **Ælfric's Lives of Saints**, MS. Cott. Jul. E vii, ed. W. W. Skeat. Part II. (*See* O.S. 76.) 1885

83. **The Oldest English Texts**, Charters, &c., ed. H. Sweet. (*Reprinted* 1966.) 63*s*. „

E.S. 45. **Charlemagne Romances: 11. The Foure Sonnes of Aymon**, ed. O. Richardson. Part II. (*Out of print.*) „

46. **Sir Beves of Hamtoun**, ed. E. Kölbing. Part I. (*Out of print.*) „

O.S. 84. **Additional Analogs to 'The Wright's Chaste Wife'**, O.S. 12, by W. A. Clouston. (*Out of print.*) 1886

85. **The Three Kings of Cologne**, ed. C. Horstmann. (*Out of print.*) „

86. **Prose Lives of Women Saints**, ed. C. Horstmann. (*Out of print.*) „

E.S. 47. **The Wars of Alexander**, ed. W. W. Skeat. (*Out of print.*) „

48. **Sir Beves of Hamtoun**, ed. E. Kölbing. Part II. (*Out of print.*) „

O.S. 87. **The Early South-English Legendary**, Laud MS. 108, ed. C. Hortsmann. (*Out of print.*) 1887

88. **Hy. Bradshaw's Life of St. Werburghe** (Pynson, 1521), ed. C. Horstmann. (*Out of print.*) „

E.S. 49. **Guy of Warwick**, 2 texts (Auchinleck and Caius MSS.), ed. J. Zupitza. Part II. (*See* E.S. 42.) „

50. **Charlemagne Romances: 12. Huon of Burdeux**, by Lord Berners, ed. S. L. Lee. Part IV. (*Out of print.*) „

51. **Torrent of Portyngale**, ed. E. Adam. (*Out of print.*) „

O.S. 89. **Vices and Virtues**, ed. F. Holthausen. Part I. (*Reprinted* 1967.) 30*s*. 1888

90. **Anglo-Saxon and Latin Rule of St. Benet**, interlinear Glosses, ed. H. Logeman. (*Out of print.*) „

91. **Two Fifteenth-Century Cookery-Books**, ed. T. Austin. (*Reprinted* 1964.) 42*s*. „

E.S. 52. **Bullein's Dialogue against the Feuer Pestilence, 1578**, ed. M. and A. H. Bullen. (*Out of print.*) „

53. **Vicary's Anatomie of the Body of Man, 1548**, ed. 1577, ed. F. J. and Percy Furnivall. **Part I.** (*Out of print.*) „

54. **The Curial made by maystere Alain Charretier, translated by William Caxton, 1484, ed. F. J.** Furnivall and P. Meyer. (*Reprinted* 1965.) 10*s*. „

O.S. 92. **Eadwine's Canterbury Psalter**, from the Trin. Cambr. MS., ed. F. Harsley, **Part II.** (*Out of print.*) 1889

93. **Defensor's Liber Scintillarum**, ed. E. Rhodes. (*Out of print.*) „

E.S. 55. **Barbour's Bruce**, ed. W. W. Skeat. Part IV. (*See* E.S. 11.) „

56. **Early English Pronunciation**, by A. J. Ellis. Part V, the present English Dialects. (*Out of print.*) „

O.S. 94, 114. **Ælfric's Lives of Saints**, MS. Cott. Jul. E vii, ed. W. W. Skeat. **Parts III and IV.** (*Reprinted as Volume II* 1966.) 60*s*. 1890

95. **The Old-English Version of Bede's Ecclesiastical History, re-ed. T. Miller. Part I, 1.** (*Reprinted* 1959.) 45*s*. „

E.S. 57. **Caxton's Eneydos**, ed. W. T. Culley and F. J. Furnivall. (*Reprinted* 1962.) 40*s*. „

58. **Caxton's Blanchardyn and Eglantine**, c. 1489, ed. L. Kellner. (*Reprinted* 1962.) 50*s*. „

O.S. 96. **The Old-English Version of Bede's Ecclesiastical History, re-ed. T. Miller. Part I, 2.** (*Reprinted* 1959.) 45*s*. 1891

97. **The Earliest English Prose Psalter**, ed. K. D. Buelbring. Part I. (*Out of print.*) „

E.S. 59. **Guy of Warwick**, 2 texts (Auchinleck and Caius MSS.), ed. J. Zupitza. **Part III.** (*See* E.S. 42.) „

60. **Lydgate's Temple of Glas**, re-ed. J. Schick. (*Out of print.*) „

O.S. 98. **Minor Poems of the Vernon MS.**, ed. C. Horstmann. Part I. (*Out of print.*) 1892

99. **Cursor Mundi.** Preface, Notes, and Glossary, Part VI, ed. R. Morris. (*Reprinted* 1962.) 25*s*. „

E.S. 61. **Hoccleve's Minor Poems**, I, from the Phillipps and Durham MSS., ed. F. J. Furnivall. (*Out of print.*) „

62. **The Chester Plays**, re-ed. H. Deimling. Part I. (*Reprinted* 1967.) 37*s*. 6*d*. „

O.S. 100. **Capgrave's Life of St. Katharine**, ed. C. Horstmann, with Forewords by F. J. Furnivall. (*Out of print.*) 1893

O.S. 101. **Cursor Mundi.** Essay on the MSS., their Dialects, &c., by H. Hupe. Part VII. (*Reprinted* 1962.) 25*s*. „

E.S. 63. **Thomas à Kempis's De Imitatione Christi**, ed. J. K. Ingram. (*Out of print.*) „

64. **Caxton's Godeffroy of Boloyne, or The Siege and Conqueste of Jerusalem, 1481**, ed. Mary N. Colvin. (*Out of print.*) „

O.S. 102. **Lanfranc's Science of Cirurgie**, ed. R. von Fleischhacker. Part I. (*Out of print.*) 1894

O.S. 103. **The Legend of the Cross, &c.**, ed. A. S. Napier. (*Out of print.*) 1894

E.S. 65. **Sir Beves of Hamtoun**, ed. E. Kölbing. Part III. (*Out of print.*) "

66. **Lydgate's and Burgh's Secrees of Philisoffres** ('Governance of Kings and Princes'), ed. R. Steele. (*Out of print.*) "

O.S. 104. **The Exeter Book** (Anglo-Saxon Poems), re-ed. I. Gollancz. Part I. (*Reprinted* 1958.) 45*s.* 1895

105. **The Prymer or Lay Folks' Prayer Book**, Camb. Univ. MS., ed. H. Littlehales. Part I. (*Out of print.*) "

E.S. 67. **The Three Kings' Sons**, a Romance, ed. F. J. Furnivall. Part I, the Text. (*Out of print.*) "

68. **Melusine**, the prose Romance, ed. A. K. Donald. Part I, the Text. (*Out of print.*) "

O.S. 106. **R. Misyn's Fire of Love and Mending of Life** (Hampole), ed. R. Harvey. (*Out of print.*) 1896

107. **The English Conquest of Ireland**, A.D. 1166–1185, 2 Texts, ed. F. J. Furnivall. Part I. (*Out of print.*) "

E.S. 69. **Lydgate's Assembly of the Gods**, ed. O. L. Triggs. (*Reprinted* 1957.) 37*s.* 6*d.* "

70. **The Digby Plays**, ed. F. J. Furnivall. (*Reprinted* 1967.) 30*s.* "

O.S. 108. **Child-Marriages and -Divorces, Trothplights, &c.** Chester Depositions, 1561–6, ed. F. J. Furnivall. (*Out of print.*) 1897

109. **The Prymer or Lay Folks' Prayer Book**, ed. H. Littlehales. Part II. (*Out of print.*) "

E.S. 71. **The Towneley Plays**, ed. G. England and A. W. Pollard. (*Reprinted* 1966.) 45*s.* "

72. **Hoccleve's Regement of Princes, and 14 Poems**, ed. F. J. Furnivall. (*Out of print.*) "

73. **Hoccleve's Minor Poems, II**, from the Ashburnham MS., ed. I. Gollancz. (*Out of print.*) "

O.S. 110. **The Old-English Version of Bede's Ecclesiastical History**, ed. T. Miller. Part II, 1. (*Reprinted* 1963.) 45*s.* 1898

111. **The Old-English Version of Bede's Ecclesiastical History**, ed. T. Miller. Part II, 2. (*Reprinted* 1963.) 45*s.* "

E.S. 74. **Secreta Secretorum**, 3 prose Englishings, one by Jas. Yonge, 1428, ed. R. Steele. Part I. 36*s.* "

75. **Speculum Guidonis de Warwyk**, ed. G. L. Morrill. (*Out of print.*) "

O.S. 112. **Merlin.** Part IV. Outlines of the Legend of Merlin, by W. E. Mead. (*Out of print.*) 1899

113. **Queen Elizabeth's Englishings of Boethius, Plutarch, &c.**, ed. C. Pemberton. (*Out of print.*) "

E.S. 76. **George Ashby's Poems, &c.**, ed. Mary Bateson. (*Reprinted* 1965.) 30*s.* "

77. **Lydgate's DeGuilleville's Pilgrimage of the Life of Man**, ed. F. J. Furnivall. Part I. (*Out of print.*) "

78. **The Life and Death of Mary Magdalene**, by T. Robinson, *c.* 1620, ed. H. O. Sommer. 9*s.* "

O.S. 114. **Ælfric's Lives of Saints**, ed. W. W. Skeat. Part IV and last. (*See* O.S. 94.) 1900

115. **Jacob's Well**, ed. A. Brandeis. Part I. (*Out of print.*) "

116. **An Old-English Martyrology**, re-ed. G. Herzfeld. (*Out of print.*) "

E.S. 79. **Caxton's Dialogues, English and French**, ed. H. Bradley. (*Out of print.*) "

80. **Lydgate's Two Nightingale Poems**, ed. O. Glauning. (*Out of print.*) "

80A. **Selections from Barbour's Bruce (Books I–X)**, ed. W. W. Skeat. 20*s.* "

81. **The English Works of John Gower**, ed. G. C. Macaulay. Part I. (*Reprinted* 1957.) 60*s.* "

O.S. 117. **Minor Poems of the Vernon MS.**, ed. F. J. Furnivall. Part II. (*Out of print.*) 1901

118. **The Lay Folks' Catechism**, ed. T. F. Simmons and H. E. Nolloth. (*Out of print.*) "

119. **Robert of Brunne's Handlyng Synne**, and its French original, re-ed. F. J. Furnivall. Part I. (*Out of print.*) "

E.S. 82. **The English Works of John Gower**, ed. G. C. Macaulay. Part II. (*Reprinted* 1957.) 60*s.* "

83. **Lydgate's DeGuilleville's Pilgrimage of the Life of Man**, ed. F. J. Furnivall. Part II. (*Out of print.*) "

84. **Lydgate's Reson and Sensuallyte**, ed. E. Sieper. Vol. I. (*Reprinted* 1965.) 42*s.* "

O.S. 120. **The Rule of St. Benet** in Northern Prose and Verse, and Caxton's Summary, ed. E. A. Kock. (*Out of print.*) 1902

121. **The Laud MS. Troy-Book**, ed. J. E. Wülfing. Part I. (*Out of print.*) "

E.S. 85. **Alexander Scott's Poems**, 1568, ed. A. K. Donald. (*Out of print.*) "

86. **William of Shoreham's Poems**, re-ed. M. Konrath. Part I. (*Out of print.*) "

87. **Two Coventry Corpus Christi Plays**, re-ed. H. Craig. (*See under* 1952.) "

O.S. 122. **The Laud MS. Troy-Book**, ed. J. E. Wülfing. Part II. (*Out of print.*) 1903

123. **Robert of Brunne's Handlyng Synne**, and its French original, re-ed. F. J. Furnivall. Part II. (*Out of print.*) "

E.S. 88. **Le Morte Arthur**, re-ed. J. D. Bruce. (*Reprinted* 1959.) 45*s.* "

89. **Lydgate's Reson and Sensuallyte**, ed. E. Sieper. Vol. II. (*Reprinted* 1965.) 35*s.* "

90. **English Fragments from Latin Medieval Service-Books**, ed. H. Littlehales. (*Out of print.*) "

O.S. 124. **Twenty-six Political and other Poems** from Digby MS. 102, &c., ed. J. Kail. Part I. 18*s.* 1904

125. **Medieval Records of a London City Church**, ed. H. Littlehales. Part I. (*Out of print.*) "

126. **An Alphabet of Tales**, in Northern English, from the Latin ed. M. M. Banks. Part I. (*Out of print.*) "

E.S. 91. **The Macro Plays**, ed. F. J. Furnivall and A. W. Pollard. (*Out of print*; *see* 262.) "

92. **Lydgate's DeGuilleville's Pilgrimage of the Life of Man**, ed. Katherine B. Locock. Part III. (*Out of print.*) "

93. **Lovelich's Romance of Merlin**, from the unique MS., ed. E. A. Kock. Part I. (*Out of print.*) "

O.S. 127. **An Alphabet of Tales**, in Northern English, from the Latin, ed. M. M. Banks. Part II. (*Out of print.*) 1905

128. **Medieval Records of a London City Church**, ed. H. Littlehales. Part II. (*Out of print.*) "

129. **The English Register of Godstow Nunnery**, ed. A. Clark. Part I. 18*s.* "

E.S. 94. **Respublica**, a Play on a Social England, ed. L. A. Magnus. (*Out of print. See under* 1946.) "

95. **Lovelich's History of the Holy Grail.** Part V. **The Legend of the Holy Grail**, ed. Dorothy Kempe. (*Out of print.*) "

96. **Mirk's Festial**, ed. T. Erbe. Part I. (*Out of print.*) "

O.S. 130. **The English Register of Godstow Nunnery**, ed. A. Clark. Part II. 27*s.* 1906

131. **The Brut, or The Chronicle of England**, ed. F. Brie. Part I. (*Reprinted* 1960.) 45*s.* "

132. **John Metham's Works**, ed. H. Craig. 27*s.* "

E.S. 97. **Lydgate's Troy Book**, ed. H. Bergen. Part I, Books I and II. (*Out of print.*) "

E.S. 98. **Skelton's Magnyfycence**, ed. R. L. Ramsay. (*Reprinted* 1958.) 45*s*. 1906

99. **The Romance of Emaré**, re-ed. Edith Rickert. (*Reprinted* 1958.) 22*s*. 6*d*. ,,

O.S. 133. **The English Register of Oseney Abbey, by Oxford**, ed. A. Clark. Part I. 27*s*. 1907

134. **The Coventry Leet Book**, ed. M. Dormer Harris. Part I. (*Out of print*.) ,,

E.S. 100. **The Harrowing of Hell, and The Gospel of Nicodemus**, re-ed. W. H. Hulme. (*Reprinted* 1961.) 40*s*. ,,

101. **Songs, Carols, &c.**, from Richard Hill's Balliol MS., ed. R. Dyboski. (*Out of print*.) ,,

O.S. 135. **The Coventry Leet Book**, ed. M. Dormer Harris. Part II. (*Out of print*.) 1908

135 *b*. *Extra Issue*. Prof. Manly's **Piers Plowman and its Sequence**, urging the fivefold authorship of the *Vision*. (*Out of print*.) ,,

136. **The Brut, or The Chronicle of England**, ed. F. Brie. Part II. (*Out of print*.) ,,

E.S. 102. **Promptorium Parvulorum**, the 1st English-Latin Dictionary, ed. A. L. Mayhew. (*Out of print*.) ,,

103. **Lydgate's Troy Book**, ed. H. Bergen. Part II, Book III. (*Out of print*.) ,,

O.S. 137. **Twelfth-Century Homilies in MS. Bodley 343**, ed. A. O. Belfour. Part I, the Text. (*Reprinted* 1962.) 25*s*. 1909

138. **The Coventry Leet Book**, ed. M. Dormer Harris. Part III. (*Out of print*.) ,,

E.S. 104. **The Non-Cycle Mystery Plays**, re-ed. O. Waterhouse. (*See end-note*, p. 8.) ,,

105. **The Tale of Beryn, with the Pardoner and Tapster**, ed. F. J. Furnivall and W. G. Stone. (*Out of print*.) ,,

O.S. 139. **John Arderne's Treatises on Fistula in Ano, &c.**, ed. D'Arcy Power. (*Out of print*.) 1910

139 *b, c, d, e, f, Extra Issue*. **The Piers Plowman Controversy: *b*. Dr. Jusserand's 1st Reply to Prof. Manly; *c*. Prof. Manly's Answer to Dr. Jusserand; *d*. Dr. Jusserand's 2nd Reply to Prof. Manly; *e*. Mr. R. W. Chambers's Article; *f*. Dr. Henry Bradley's Rejoinder to Mr. R. W. Chambers.** (*Out of print*.) ,,

140. **Capgrave's Lives of St. Augustine and St. Gilbert of Sempringham**, ed. J. Munro. (*Out of print*.) ,,

E.S. 106. **Lydgate's Troy Book**, ed. H. Bergen. Part III. (*Out of print*.) ,,

107. **Lydgate's Minor Poems**, ed. H. N. MacCracken. Part I. **Religious Poems.** (*Reprinted* 1961.) 55*s*. ,,

O.S. 141. **Erthe upon Erthe**, all the known texts, ed. Hilda Murray. (*Reprinted* 1964.) 30*s*. 1911

142. **The English Register of Godstow Nunnery**, ed. A. Clark. Part III. 18*s*. ,,

143. **The Prose Life of Alexander**, Thornton MS., ed. J. S. Westlake. (*Out of print*.) ,,

E.S. 108. **Lydgate's Siege of Thebes**, re-ed. A. Erdmann. Part I, the Text. (*Reprinted* 1960.) 24*s*. ,,

109. **Partonope**, re-ed. A. T. Bödtker. The Texts. (*Out of print*.) ,,

O.S. 144. **The English Register of Oseney Abbey, by Oxford**, ed. A. Clark. Part II. 18*s*. 1912

145. **The Northern Passion**, ed. F. A. Foster. Part I, the four parallel texts. (*Out of print*.) ,,

E.S. 110. **Caxton's Mirrour of the World**, with all the woodcuts, ed. O. H. Prior. (*Reprinted* 1966.) 42*s*. ,,

111. **Caxton's History of Jason**, the Text, Part I, ed. J. Munro. 27*s*. ,,

O.S. 146. **The Coventry Leet Book**, ed. M. Dormer Harris. Introduction, Indexes, &c. Part IV. (*Out of print*.) 1913

147. **The Northern Passion**, ed. F. A. Foster, Introduction, French Text, Variants and Fragments, Glossary. Part II. (*Out of print*.) ,,

[An enlarged reprint of O.S. 26, **Religious Pieces in Prose and Verse**, from the Thornton MS., ed. G. G. Perry. (*Out of print*.) ,,

E.S. 112. **Lovelich's Romance of Merlin**, ed. E. A. Kock. Part II. (*Reprinted* 1961.) 30*s*. ,,

113. **Poems by Sir John Salusbury, Robert Chester, and others, from Christ Church MS. 184, &c.**, ed. Carleton Brown. 27*s*. ,,

O.S. 148. **A Fifteenth-Century Courtesy Book and Two Franciscan Rules**, ed. R. W. Chambers and W. W. Seton. (*Reprinted* 1963.) 25*s*. 1914

149. **Lincoln Diocese Documents, 1450–1544**, ed. Andrew Clark. (*Out of print*.) ,,

150. **The Old-English Rule of Bp. Chrodegang, and the Capitula of Bp. Theodulf**, ed. A. S. Napier. (*Out of print*.) ,,

E.S. 114. **The Gild of St. Mary, Lichfield**, ed. F. J. Furnivall. 27*s*. ,,

115. **The Chester Plays**, re-ed. J. Matthews. Part II. (*Reprinted* 1967.) 37*s*. 6*d*. ,,

O.S. 151. **The Lanterne of Light**, ed. Lilian M. Swinburn. (*Out of print*.) 1915

152. **Early English Homilies**, from Cott. Vesp. D. XIV, ed. Rubie Warner. Part I, Text. (*Out of print*.) ,,

E.S. 116. **The Pauline Epistles**, ed. M. J. Powell. (*Out of print*.) ,,

117. **Bp. Fisher's English Works**, ed. R. Bayne. Part II. (*Out of print*.) ,,

O.S. 153. **Mandeville's Travels**, ed. P. Hamelius. Part I, Text. (*Reprinted* 1960.) 25*s*. 1916

154. **Mandeville's Travels**, ed. P. Hamelius. Part II, Notes and Introduction. (*Reprinted* 1961.) 25*s*. ,,

E.S. 118. **The Earliest Arithmetics in English**, ed. R. Steele. (*Out of print*.) ,,

119. **The Owl and the Nightingale**, 2 Texts parallel, ed. G. F. H. Sykes and J. H. G. Grattan. (*Out of print*.) ,,

O.S. 155. **The Wheatley MS.**, ed. Mabel Day. 54*s*. 1917

E.S. 120. **Ludus Coventriae**, ed. K. S. Block. (*Reprinted* 1961.) 60*s*. ,,

O.S. 156. **Reginald Pecock's Donet**, from Bodl. MS. 916, ed. Elsie V. Hitchcock. 63*s*. 1918

E.S. 121. **Lydgate's Fall of Princes**, ed. H. Bergen. Part I. (*Reprinted* 1967). 50*s*. ,,

122. **Lydgate's Fall of Princes**, ed. H. Bergen. Part II. (*Reprinted* 1967.) 50*s*. ,,

O.S. 157. **Harmony of the Life of Christ**, from MS. Pepys 2498, ed. Margery Goates. (*Out of print*.) 1919

158. **Meditations on the Life and Passion of Christ**, from MS. Add., 11307, ed. Charlotte D'Evelyn. (*Out of print*.) ,,

E.S. 123. **Lydgate's Fall of Princes**, ed. H. Bergen. Part III. (*Reprinted* 1967.) 50*s*. ,,

124. **Lydgate's Fall of Princes**, ed. H. Bergen. Part IV. (*Reprinted* 1967.) 60*s*. ,,

O.S. 159. **Vices and Virtues**, ed. F. Holthausen. Part II. (*Reprinted* 1967.) 25*s*. 1920

[A re-edition of O.S. 18, **Hali Meidenhad**, ed. O. Cockayne, with a variant MS., Bodl. 34, hitherto unprinted, ed. F. J. Furnivall. (*Out of print*.) ,,

E.S. 125. **Lydgate's Siege of Thebes**, ed. A. Erdmann and E. Ekwall. Part II. (*Out of print*.) ,,

E.S. 126. **Lydgate's Troy Book**, ed. H. Bergen. Part IV. (*Out of print.*) 1920
O.S. 160. **The Old English Heptateuch**, MS. Cott. Claud. B. iv, ed. S. J. Crawford. (*Reprinting* 1968.) 60*s*. 1921
161. **Three O.E. Prose Texts**, MS. Cott. Vit. A. xv, ed. S. Rypins. (*Out of print.*) ,,
162. **Facsimile of MS. Cotton Nero A. x (Pearl, Cleanness, Patience and Sir Gawain)**, Introduction by I. Gollancz. (*Reprinted* 1955.) 150*s*. 1922
163. **Book of the Foundation of St. Bartholomew's Church in London**, ed. N. Moore. (*Out of print.*) 1923
164. **Pecock's Folewer to the Donet**, ed. Elsie V. Hitchcock. (*Out of print.*) ,,
165. **Middleton's Chinon of England, with Leland's Assertio Arturii and Robinson's translation**, ed. W. E. Mead. (*Out of print.*) ,,
166. **Stanzaic Life of Christ**, ed. Frances A. Foster. (*Out of print.*) 1924
167. **Trevisa's Dialogus inter Militem et Clericum, Sermon by FitzRalph, and Bygynnyng of the World**, ed. A. J. Perry. (*Out of print.*) ,,
168. **Caxton's Ordre of Chyualry**, ed. A. T. P. Byles. (*Out of print.*) 1925
169. **The Southern Passion**, ed. Beatrice Brown. (*Out of print.*) ,,
170. **Walton's Boethius**, ed. M. Science. (*Out of print.*) ,,
171. **Pecock's Reule of Cristen Religioun**, ed. W. C. Greet. (*Out of print.*) 1926
172. **The Seege or Batayle of Troye**, ed. M. E. Barnicle. (*Out of print.*) ,,
173. **Hawes' Pastime of Pleasure**, ed. W. E. Mead. (*Out of print.*) 1927
174. **The Life of St. Anne**, ed. R. E. Parker. (*Out of print.*) ,,
175. **Barclay's Eclogues**, ed. Beatrice White. (*Reprinted* 1961.) 45*s*. ,,
176. **Caxton's Prologues and Epilogues**, ed. W. J. B. Crotch. (*Reprinted* 1956.) 45*s*. ,,
177. **Byrhtferth's Manual**, ed. S. J. Crawford. (*Reprinted* 1966.) 63*s*. 1928
178. **The Revelations of St. Birgitta**, ed. W. P. Cumming. (*Out of print.*) ,,
179. **The Castell of Pleasure**, ed. B. Cornelius. (*Out of print.*) ,,
180. **The Apologye of Syr Thomas More**, ed. A. I. Taft. (*Out of print.*) 1929
181. **The Dance of Death**, ed. F. Warren. (*Out of print.*) ,,
182. **Speculum Christiani**, ed. G. Holmstedt. (*Out of print.*) ,,
183. **The Northern Passion (Supplement)**, ed. W. Heuser and Frances Foster. (*Out of print.*) 1930
184. **The Poems of John Audelay**, ed. Ella K. Whiting. (*Out of print.*) ,,
185. **Lovelich's Merlin**, ed. E. A. Kock. Part III. (*Out of print.*) ,,
186. **Harpsfield's Life of More**, ed. Elsie V. Hitchcock and R. W. Chambers. (*Reprinted* 1963.) 84*s*. 1931
187. **Whittinton and Stanbridge's Vulgaria**, ed. B. White. (*Out of print.*) ,,
188. **The Siege of Jerusalem**, ed. E. Kölbing and Mabel Day. (*Out of print.*) ,,
189. **Caxton's Fayttes of Armes and of Chyualrye**, ed. A. T. Byles. 37*s*. 6*d*. 1932
190. **English Mediæval Lapidaries**, ed. Joan Evans and Mary Serjeantson. (*Reprinted* 1960.) 40*s*. ,,
191. **The Seven Sages**, ed. K. Brunner. (*Out of print.*) ,,
191A. **On the Continuity of English Prose**, by R. W. Chambers. (*Reprinted* 1966.) 21*s*. ,,
192. **Lydgate's Minor Poems**, ed. H. N. MacCracken. Part II, **Secular Poems**. (*Reprinted* 1961.) 60*s*. 1933
193. **Seinte Marherete**, re-ed. Frances Mack. (*Reprinted* 1958.) 45*s*. ,,
194. **The Exeter Book**, Part II, ed. W. S. Mackie. (*Reprinted* 1958.) 37*s*. 6*d*. ,,
195. **The Quatrefoil of Love**, ed. I. Gollancz and M. Weale. (*Out of print.*) 1934
196. **A Short English Metrical Chronicle**, ed. E. Zettl. (*Out of print.*) ,,
197. **Roper's Life of More**, ed. Elsie V. Hitchcock. (*Reprinted* 1958.) 30*s*. ,,
198. **Firumbras and Otuel and Roland**, ed. Mary O'Sullivan. (*Out of print.*) ,,
199. **Mum and the Sothsegger**, ed. Mabel Day and R. Steele. (*Out of print.*) ,,
200. **Speculum Sacerdotale**, ed. E. H. Weatherly. (*Out of print.*) 1935
201. **Knyghthode and Bataile**, ed. R. Dyboski and Z. M. Arend. (*Out of print.*) ,,
202. **Palsgrave's Acolastus**, ed. P. L. Carver. (*Out of print.*) ,,
203. **Amis and Amiloun**, ed. McEdward Leach. (*Reprinted* 1960.) 40*s*. ,,
204. **Valentine and Orson**, ed. Arthur Dickson. (*Out of print.*) 1936
205. **Tales from the Decameron**, ed. H. G. Wright. (*Out of print.*) ,,
206. **Bokenham's Lives of Holy Women (Lives of the Saints)**, ed. Mary S. Serjeantson. (*Out of print.*) ,,
207. **Liber de Diversis Medicinis**, ed. Margaret S. Ogden. (*Out of print.*) ,,
208. **The Parker Chronicle and Laws (facsimile)**, ed. R. Flower and A. H. Smith. 126*s*. 1937
209. **Middle English Sermons from MS. Roy. 18 B. xxiii**, ed. W. O. Ross. (*Reprinted* 1960.) 60*s*. 1938
210. **Sir Gawain and the Green Knight**, ed. I. Gollancz. With Introductory essays by Mabel Day and M. S. Serjeantson. (*Reprinted* 1966.) 25*s*. ,,
211. **Dictes and Sayings of the Philosophers**, ed. C. F. Bühler. (*Reprinted* 1961.) 60*s*. 1939
212. **The Book of Margery Kempe**, Part I, ed. S. B. Meech and Hope Emily Allen. (*Reprinted* 1961.) 70*s*. ,,
213. **Ælfric's De Temporibus Anni**, ed. H. Henel. (*Out of print.*) 1940
214. **Morley's Translation of Boccaccio's De Claris Mulieribus**, ed. H. G. Wright. (*Out of print.*) ,,
215. **English Poems of Charles of Orleans**, Part I, ed. R. Steele. (*Out of print.*) 1941
216. **The Latin Text of the Ancrene Riwle**, ed. Charlotte D'Evelyn. (*Reprinted* 1957.) 45*s*. ,,
217. **Book of Vices and Virtues**, ed. W. Nelson Francis. (*Out of print.*) 1942
218. **The Cloud of Unknowing and the Book of Privy Counselling**, ed. Phyllis Hodgson. (*Reprinted* 1958.) 40*s*. 1943
219. **The French Text of the Ancrene Riwle**, B.M. Cotton MS. Vitellius. F. vii, ed. J. A. Herbert. (*Reprinted* 1967.) 50*s*. ,,
220. **English Poems of Charles of Orleans**, Part II, ed. R. Steele and Mabel Day. (*Out of print.*) 1944
221. **Sir Degrevant**, ed. L. F. Casson. (*Out of print.*) ,,
222. **Ro. Ba.'s Life of Syr Thomas More**, ed. Elsie V. Hitchcock and Mgr. P. E. Hallett. (*Reprinted* 1957.) 52*s*. 6*d*. 1945
223. **Tretyse of Loue**, ed. J. H. Fisher. (*Out of print.*) ,,
224. **Athelston**, ed. A. McI. Trounce. (*Reprinted* 1957.) 30*s*. 1946
225. **The English Text of the Ancrene Riwle**, B.M. Cotton MS. Nero A. xiv, ed. Mabel Day. (*Reprinted* 1957.) 35*s*. ,,

226. **Respublica**, re-ed. W. W. Greg. (*Out of print.*) 1946
227. **Kyng Alisaunder**, ed. G. V. Smithers. Vol. I, Text. (*Reprinted* 1961.) 45*s.* 1947
228. **The Metrical Life of St. Robert of Knaresborough**, ed. J. Bazire. (*Out of print.*) „
229. **The English Text of the Ancrene Riwle**, Gonville and Caius College MS. 234/120, ed. R. M. Wilson. With Introduction by N. R. Ker. (*Reprinted* 1957.) 35*s.* 1948
230. **The Life of St. George by Alexander Barclay**, ed. W. Nelson. (*Reprinted* 1960.) 40*s.* „
231. **Deonise Hid Diuinite**, and other treatises related to *The Cloud of Unknowing*, ed. Phyllis Hodgson. (*Reprinted* 1958.) 42*s.* 1949
232. **The English Text of the Ancrene Riwle**, B.M. Royal MS. 8 C. 1, ed. A. C. Baugh. (*Reprinted* 1958.) 30*s.* „
233. **The Bibliotheca Historica of Diodorus Siculus translated by John Skelton**, ed. F. M. Salter and H. L. R. Edwards. Vol. I, Text. (*Reprinted* 1968.) 80*s.* 1950
234. **Caxton: Paris and Vienne**, ed. MacEdward Leach. (*Out of print.*) 1951
235. **The South English Legendary**, Corpus Christi College Cambridge MS. 145 and B.M. M.S. Harley 2277, &c., ed. Charlotte D'Evelyn and Anna J. Mill. Text, Vol. I. (*Reprinted* 1967.) 50*s.* „
236. **The South English Legendary**. Text, Vol. II. (*Reprinted* 1967.) 50*s.* 1952
    [E.S. 87. **Two Coventry Corpus Christi Plays**, re-ed. H. Craig. Second Edition. (*Reprinted* 1967.) 25*s.*] „
237. **Kyng Alisaunder**, ed. G. V. Smithers. Vol. II, Introduction, Commentary, and Glossary. 50*s.* 1953
238. **The Phonetic Writings of Robert Robinson**, ed. E. J. Dobson. (*Reprinted* 1968.) 30*s.* „
239. **The Bibliotheca Historica of Diodorus Siculus translated by John Skelton**, ed. F. M. Salter and H. L. R. Edwards. Vol. II. Introduction, Notes, and Glossary. 25*s.* 1954
240. **The French Text of the Ancrene Riwle**, Trinity College, Cambridge, MS. R. 14, 7, ed. W. H. Trethewey. 55*s.* „
241. **Þe Wohunge of ure Lauerd**, and other pieces, ed. W. Meredith Thompson. 45*s.* 1955
242. **The Salisbury Psalter**, ed. Celia Sisam and Kenneth Sisam. 90*s.* 1955–56
243. **George Cavendish: The Life and Death of Cardinal Wolsey**, ed. Richard S. Sylvester. (*Reprinted* 1961.) 45*s.* 1957
244. **The South English Legendary**. Vol. III, Introduction and Glossary, ed. C. D'Evelyn. 30*s.* „
245. **Beowulf** (facsimile). With Transliteration by J. Zupitza, new collotype plates, and Introduction by N. Davis. (*Reprinted* 1967.) 84*s.* 1958
246. **The Parlement of the Thre Ages**, ed. M. Y. Offord. (*Reprinted* 1967.) 40*s.* 1959
247. **Facsimile of MS. Bodley 34** (Katherine Group). With Introduction by N. R. Ker. 50*s.* „
248. **Þe Liflade ant te Passiun of Seinte Iuliene**, ed. S. R. T. O. d'Ardenne. 40*s.* 1960
249. **Ancrene Wisse**, Corpus Christi College, Cambridge, MS. 402, ed. J. R. R. Tolkien. With an Introduction by N. R. Ker. 40*s.* „
250. **Laȝamon's Brut**, ed. G. L. Brook and R. F. Leslie. Vol. I, Text (first part). 80*s.* 1961
251. **Facsimile of the Cotton and Jesus Manuscripts of the Owl and the Nightingale**. With Introduction by N. R. Ker. 42*s.* 1962
252. **The English Text of the Ancrene Riwle**, B.M. Cotton MS. Titus D. xviii, ed. Frances M. Mack, and Lanhydrock Fragment, ed. A. Zettersten. 40*s.* „
253. **The Bodley Version of Mandeville's Travels**, ed. M. C. Seymour. 40*s.* 1963
254. **Ywain and Gawain**, ed. Albert B. Friedman and Norman T. Harrington. 40*s.* „
255. **Facsimile of B.M. MS. Harley 2253** (The Harley Lyrics). With Introduction by N. R. Ker. 84*s.* 1964
256. **Sir Eglamour of Artois**, ed. Frances E. Richardson. 40*s.* 1965
257. **Sir Thomas Chaloner: The Praise of Folie**, ed. Clarence H. Miller. 42*s.* „
258. **The Orcherd of Syon**, ed. Phyllis Hodgson and Gabriel M. Liegey. Vol. I, Text. 84*s.* 1966
259. **Homilies of Ælfric: A Supplementary Collection**, ed. J. C. Pope. Vol. I. 84*s.* 1967
260. **Homilies of Ælfric: A Supplementary Collection**, ed. J. C. Pope. Vol. II. 84*s.* 1968

Forthcoming volumes

261. **Lybeaus Desconus**, ed. M. Mills. (*At press.*) 1969
262. **The Macro Plays**, re-ed. Mark Eccles. (*At press.*) „
263. **Caxton's History of Reynard the Fox**, ed. N. F. Blake. (*At press.*) 1970
264. **Scrope's Epistle of Othea**, ed. C. F. Bühler. (*At press.*) „
265. **The Cyrurgie of Guy de Chauliac**, ed. Margaret S. Ogden. Vol. I, Text. 1971

The Paston Letters, ed. N. Davis.
Wulfstan's Canons of Edgar, ed. R. G. Fowler.
Caxton's Knight of La Tour Landry, ed. M. Y. Offord.
The Towneley Plays, ed. A. C. Cawley and M. Stevens.
Lydgate's St. Alban and St. Amphibalus, ed. G. F. Reinecke.

Other texts are in preparation including three further English versions of the Ancrene Riwle.

Supplementary Texts

The Society proposes to issue some Supplementary Texts from time to time as funds allow. These will be sent to members as part of the normal issue and will also be available to non-members at listed prices. The first of these, Supplementary Text 1, expected to appear early in 1970, will be *Non-Cycle Plays and Fragments*, ed. Norman Davis (about 42*s.*). This is a completely revised and re-set edition of the texts in Extra Series 104 with some additional pieces.

May 1968

Publisher: LONDON · THE OXFORD UNIVERSITY PRESS, ELY HOUSE, 37 DOVER ST., W. 1